DIPLOMAT,
DISSIDENT,
SPOOK

A CANADIAN DIPLOMAT'S CHRONICLES
THROUGH THE COLD WAR AND BEYOND

by Bill Warden

edited by Lisa Warden

Foreword by Mikhail Gorbachev

Tellwell Talent

www.tellwell.ca

ISBN

978-1-77302-911-5 (Paperback)

978-1-77302-910-8 (eBook)

This book is dedicated to the memory of its author, Bill Warden (1934-2011), and to Bill's late sister, Mary, and brother, David.

Here we are seeking out the reds
Trying to keep the communists in order
Just remember when you're sleeping in your beds
They're only two days drive from the Texas border

How can a country large as ours
Be scared of such a threat
Well if they won't work for us
They're against us you can bet
They may be sovereign countries
But you folks at home forget
That they all want what we've got
But they don't know it yet

Tra-la-la-la, tra-la-la-la, tra-la-la-la
We're making the world safe for capitalism

Billy Bragg
The Marching Song of the Covert Batallions

TABLE OF CONTENTS

Foreword

I first met William Warden — a prominent diplomat and public figure — in March 1992. He came to Moscow in his capacity as the Director of the International Centre at the University of Calgary in order to explore the possibility of cooperation between the University and the Foundation for Socio-Economic and Political Studies (The Gorbachev Foundation), which I and my associates had recently established. From the moment we first shook hands I felt a deep empathy with him. Tall, slender, with an open expression and a kind smile, he exuded a gentle intelligence and decency.

My initial impressions of him were reinforced when it emerged in the course of our discussions that Bill (as he was called by those close to him), who had served in the Canadian Embassy in Moscow in the 1960s and who knew Russian well, understood the problems we faced and, most importantly, genuinely sympathized with the democratic ideas of Russia's reformers. Little did we know then that for more than a decade Bill Warden's public activity would be intimately associated with the activities of the Gorbachev Foundation. And, I am glad that that is how it turned out. To judge by the last chapter of his memoirs, I am certain that this stage of his biography was also very significant for Bill.

On that occasion Bill conveyed to me an invitation from the administration of the University of Calgary to come to Canada and give lectures to the Canadian public on the process of democratic reform in Russia. I thanked him for the invitation, but, I admit, I was secretly doubtful about the chances of a lengthy overseas visit: the situation in Russia was complicated, and the Foundation needed to define and consolidate itself. It needed to find its place in the socio-political life of the country, and a large number of commitments had accumulated for me, overloading my calendar of important meetings and trips. Bill, however, manifested an enviable persistence. He went energetically into action, initiating the creation of a National Committee to prepare the Gorbachev visit to Canada, headed by public figures known throughout Canada. He guaranteed the support of government bodies and the media and constantly "flitted" between Moscow, Ottawa and Calgary, coordinating the program for the visit, firming up details of the impending meetings and discussions.

In short, my visit to Canada did take place, in the spring of 1993. It was enormously successful, leading to an increased interest in Russia, and helped the Canadian public to understand our "*perestroika*" and appreciate its influence on the change in the entire global situation, and its influence on the end of the Cold War that threatened the world with nuclear disaster. It would not be wrong to say that to a very great extent we owe the success of the visit to Bill Warden, who accompanied our delegation through the entire trip, everywhere performing sheer marvels of dependability and anticipation.

One of the concrete results of our visit was the creation of the University of Calgary-Gorbachev Foundation Joint Trust Fund (UCGF). During the discussions about the possibilities for future collaborations between us, the idea was raised of creating a fund to support Russo-Canadian research projects that would help advance democracy in Russia. Bill assured us that such an idea would meet with approval in university circles and that the Government of Canada would support its implementation. And he was not mistaken; after my meeting with Prime Minister Brian Mulroney the joint program came into being.

Bill Warden was the first chair of the UCGF Joint Trust Fund. Thanks to his energy, experience and wisdom this program of collaboration between academics from the two countries researching real problems of public policy in Russia functioned fruitfully for more than a decade. Under the auspices of the UCGF program more than 40 research and training projects were undertaken in Moscow and many regions of Russia. Their conclusions and recommendations found practical application in the activities of government and civil organizations at federal and/or regional levels. The main results of this theoretical and practical partnership between academics in Russia and Canada at the interface of social sciences and social practice are described in a major monograph for which I provided a preface.[1]

It is difficult to imagine that this significant undertaking could have been accomplished without Bill Warden. He was the driving force behind the Russo-Canadian program of the UCGF, putting into it his intellect and his tireless energy. It was in those years of our close partnership that his talent as a brilliant administrator, true professional, convinced democrat and wonderful human being were revealed in full to me and my colleagues at the Gorbachev Foundation.

I am convinced that in our present complex and contradictory world the memoirs of a multifaceted and talented person such as Bill Warden are essential for readers of various generations. This book provides food for thought, teaches goodness and gives hope.

Mikhail Gorbachev

Translated from Russian by Nicholas Zekulin

---

1   Publichnaia politika v Rossii: po itogam proekta "Universitet Kalgari — Gorbachev Fond." Moscow: Al'pina Biznes Buks, 2005. 358 pp.

Предисловие

Я впервые встретился с ВильямомВорденом – видным дипломатом и общественным деятелем – в марте 1992 года. В качестве руководителя Международного центра Университета Калгари он приехал в Москву, чтобы выяснить возможности сотрудничества Университета с только что созданным мною и моими соратниками Фондом социально-экономических и политологических исследований (Горбачев-Фондом). С первого же рукопожатия я почувствовал к нему глубокую симпатию. Высокий, стройный, с открытым взглядом и доброй улыбкой он излучал мягкую интеллигентность и порядочность.

Когда в беседе выяснилось, что Билл (так его называли в кругу близких людей), в 60-е годы работавший в Москве в канадском посольстве и хорошо знавший русский язык, понимал наши проблемы, а главное, искренне сочувствовал демократическим идеям российских реформаторов, мои первые впечатления о нем окрепли. Мы тогда не знали, что более чем на десятилетие, общественная деятельность Билла Вордена будет тесно связана с деятельностью Горбачев-Фонда. И я рад тому, что так получилось. Уверен, что и Биллу, судя по заключительной главе его мемуаров, этот период его биографии представлялся весьма значимым.

Тогда же Билл передал мне приглашение администрации Университета Калгари посетить Канаду и выступить пред канадской общественностью с лекциями о демократическом процессе в России. Я поблагодарил за приглашение, но, признаюсь, внутренне сомневался в возможности длительного визита за океан: в России была сложная ситуация, Фонд должен был определиться и окрепнуть, найти свое место в общественно-политической жизни страны; у меня накопилось множество неотложных обязательств, календарь важных встреч и поездок был заполнен до отказа. Однако Билл проявил завидную настойчивость. Он развернул бурную деятельность, инициировал создание Национального комитета по подготовке визита Горбачева в Канаду, который возглавили известные всей стране, авторитетные общественные деятели. Билл заручился поддержкой правительственных организаций и средств массовой информации и постоянно «мотался» между Москвой, Оттавой и Калгари, согласовывая программу визита, уточняя детали предстоящих встреч и бесед.

Словом, мой визит в Канаду состоялся весной 1993 года. Он прошел с большим успехом, способствовал росту интереса к России, помог канадской общественности понять нашу «перестройку», оценить ее влияние на изменение всей мировой ситуации, на прекращение «холодной войны», угрожавшей миру ядерной катастрофой. Не ошибусь, если скажу, что в огромной степени успехом визита мы обязаны Биллу Вордену, сопровождавшему нашу делегацию по всему маршруту и повсюду проявлявшему чудеса ответственности и предусмотрительности.

Одним из ощутимых результатов нашего визита стало создание общественного траст фонда «Университет Калгари – Горбачев-Фонд (УКГФ)». В процессе обсуждения перспектив нашего дальнейшего сотрудничества была высказана мысль о создании фонда для поддержки российско-канадских исследовательских проектов, способствующих демократическому развитию России. Билл уверил нас, что эта идея получит одобрение в университетских кругах, а правительство Канады окажет поддержку в ее реализации. И он не ошибся: после моей встречи с премьер-министром Брайаном Малруни совместная программа заработала.

Билл Ворден был первым председателем траст фонда УКГФ. Благодаря его энергии, опыту и мудрости эта программа сотрудничества ученых двух стран в исследовании актуальных для России проблем публичной политики плодотворно действовала на протяжении более десяти лет. В рамках программы УКГФ в Москве и многих регионах России было выполнено более 40 исследовательских и тренинговых проектов. Их выводы и рекомендации нашли практическое применение в деятельности государственных и гражданских организаций на федеральном и/или региональном уровне. Основные итоги этого научно-практического партнерства ученых России и Канады на стыке общественной науки и социальной практики изложены в фундаментальной монографии с моим предисловием.[1]

Трудно себе представить, чтобы это большое дело можно было осуществить без Билла Вордена. Он был мотором российско-канадской программы УКГФ, вкладывал в нее свой интеллект и свою кипучую энергию. В эти годы нашего тесного партнерства для меня и моих коллег по Фонду во всей полноте раскрылся его талант блестящего администратора, истинного профессионала, убежденного демократа, замечательного человека.

Уверен, что в нынешнем сложном и противоречивом мире мемуары такого многогранного, одаренного человека, каким был Вильям Ворден, нужны читателям разных поколений. Эта книга дает пищу для размышлений, учит добру и вселяет надежду.

---

[1] Публичная политика в России: по итогам проекта «Университет Калгари – Горбачев-Фонд. – М.: Альпина Бизнес Букс, 2005. 358 с.

Bill Warden, 1981.

Bill and Laine Warden with Mikhail Gorbachev, 1993.

Bill with sons Scott (left) and Tom, Christmas 2010.

Introduction

Christmas 2010. My brothers, Scott and Tom, and my dad, Bill, the author of these memoirs, were horsing around in their new Ho Chi Minh attire while I filmed them with the video camera. I was living in Vietnam at the time and had brought home a plethora of communist kitsch for Christmas.

"Comrades, salute!" I ordered. The ragtag troupe raised their hands in mock militarism, followed by an outburst from Tom in something that sounded vaguely like Vietnamese. It was actually complete gibberish. His burlesque "down with America" retro Cold War diatribe was for the benefit of the camera, and for Uncle David, my dad's brother, who had joined us in the living room via Skype. My dad shifted from a proper military salute to the middle finger variety. "For George Bush," he quipped, still in character. Josefina, my parents' vintage 1968 Cuban parrot, cackled animatedly in the next room.

The role my dad was playing in the impromptu skit wasn't far off the mark. At first glance, his life's ideological evolution appears to have proceeded in a sweeping trajectory from right to left – from young, idealistic, starry-eyed student in 1950s Berlin, open-minded enough to be curious about what made his communist counterparts on the other side of the Iron Curtain tick, yet unwavering in his belief in the fundamental superiority of the capitalist West, to, decades later, staunch supporter of the emancipatory socialist impulses of a Daniel Ortega or an Archbishop Oscar Romero, stinging critic of what he viewed as the insidious, ill-advised policies of the Harper and Bush administrations. Did the cold warrior take a sharp turn to the left at some point? Was it case of ideological schizophrenia, or did something else lie beneath?

I remember my frustration as a university student, arguing with my father, then at the top of the diplomatic food chain, about what I saw as Canada's stingy immigration and foreign aid policies, the plight of dissenters and the disappeared under nefarious, Western supported, right-wing regimes in Latin America, the fundamental injustices faced by the Palestinians and other causes about which I felt strongly. To a fiery, impassioned youth, the career diplomat's constant level-headedness, his explanations of why things were the way they were, his refusal to share in my outrage – all these only served to exacerbate my disaffection. I viewed him as an apologist for, and a participant, if a reluctant one, in a world gone wrong.

If you're not a socialist at 21, I was told, you have no heart. If you're still one at 51, you have no brain. It wasn't long before the pure, crystalline convictions of youth started to cloud over, in my case. After graduate school, I moved to Los Angeles, got a job in the squalid world of public relations and in that setting was soon disabused of my utopian notions regarding welfare liberalism. While I drifted to the right politically, if only temporarily, my father sashayed left. He would express concern that the depraved likes of Rush Limbaugh made me chuckle. I would egg him on by surreptitiously signing him up to volunteer for George Bush's re-election campaign, or Republican Party email updates. If Christopher Hitchens could veer right, I argued, then so could I. I would decry what I saw as my father's hypocrisy for refusing to travel to the US, in pompous protest of George W's policies, while he quite happily gallivanted around the likes of Mugabe's Zimbabwe or the backwater caliphates of other tin pot dictators on election-observation missions.

"Dad, how is it that a former CIA spy goes all peacenik?" I would ask during one of our sporadic sparring matches. I'd felt particularly betrayed when he finally divulged his CIA role. He'd kept it secret for donkey's years. Eventually, the cat was let out of the bag by academics researching Canada's intelligence role in the 1960s in Cuba.[2] My dad, thus absolved of the fetters of secrecy on that point, quite enjoyed comparing notes with others who'd preceded him in

---

2   See University of Northern British Columbia Professor Don Munton's "Our Men in Havana: Canadian foreign intelligence operations in Castro's Cuba", in *International Journal*, vol. 70, no. 1. The first public discussion of the work of Canada's "diplomat-spies" in Cuba took place in 2002 at the Annual Meeting of the Canadian Association for Security and Intelligence Studies in Ottawa.

the same post in Cuba, most notably fellow Canadian diplomat John Graham, who later in life had become one of his closest friends.[3]

I wondered if my brothers and I, or other Foreign Service kids, had ever functioned inadvertently as CIA informants during our childhood years in Cuba. We spoke Spanish like locals, and developed connections to which the adults never would have otherwise been privy. I, for one, would regularly toddle on my three-year-old legs to the house across the street. Snagged by Castro from embittered Cuban émigrés, the sprawling bungalow, and indeed most of the neighborhood, was now held by something akin to the Comrade Friendship Society and sported a steady roster of Viet Cong exchange students. These were hard-core commies, the up and coming Party vanguard of the besieged Indo-Chinese nation. Their house soon became one of my favourite hangouts. The *becados* would welcome me with open arms, shower me with attention and kindness, and teach me various Spanish communist songs they were learning in their "cultural" program, completely unaware that on my mother's side I was descended from a long line of American imperialist aggressors. Afterwards I would toddle back across the street, unruly blond hair freshly coiffed à la Hanoi peoples' chic, and proceed to perform my proletarian repertoire at home, much to my parents' amusement. Did these songs, or my descriptions of the goings-on across the street, or Tom and Scott's accounts of their forays into enemy lair chez Juanito Carillo, their Cuban playmate

---

3   John Graham also published a memoir of his years in the diplomatic corps. See *Whose Man in Havana?* University of Calgary Press, 2015.

whose dad was a senior official in the Cuban government, ever make it into my father's reports to Langley?

Severing ties with the Canadian diplomatic corps when he left the Foreign Service in 1988 enabled my father to give rein, finally, to the inner maverick he'd kept well bridled for years. An initial stint as diplomat-in-residence at the University of Calgary morphed into a second career as irritant-at-large. The shackles of diplomacy shed, his position heading up the university's International Centre permitted him to focus on pursuits about which he was far more passionate, such as human rights in Latin America, and poking a stick at power gone awry through his column in the once liberal *Calgary Herald*. Timing-wise, the Cold War was fizzling, and in Canadian foreign policy, commercial concerns had long since trumped the lofty realm of ideology and international relations. Hardly motivated by the Department's onerous bureaucratic requirements for hoop jumping and its banal preoccupation with selling Canadian widgets, conditions were ripe for the cold warrior to change course. The question remains whether he jumped ideological ship at a certain point, or if the political position my father assumed after leaving the Foreign Service simply reflected a consistent and fuller manifestation of impulses and sensibilities he had harboured all along.

Although I took occasional wicked pleasure in goading my dad about his radical metamorphosis from cold warrior and erstwhile CIA spy to pinko peacenik, to be fair, from start to finish he remained firmly rooted in liberal principles. His allegiance was never to a particular ideology as such, but to the debunking of policies, regardless of the party promulgating them, he perceived as disingenuous, unjust or oppressive – especially to the more vulnerable in society – and to the safeguarding of free and open debate. He was not so naïve as to accept wholesale the liberal illusion that a stable political system with diverse and robust institutions could, in and of itself, secure justice and freedom for its subjects, but he certainly subscribed to the liberal principle that open debate and free expression were crucial for keeping a check on power. If he had socialist sympathies – which a glance at some of his newspaper columns, reprinted in the last chapter of this book, make evident – it was in the complex liberal tradition of George Orwell, in whose writings the ever-present tension between resistance to totalitarianism and support for policies sympathetic to society's underdogs has been well documented. As Orwell wrote in his preface to the Ukrainian edition of *Animal Farm*, "I became pro-Socialist more out of disgust with the way the poorer section of the industrial workers were oppressed and neglected than out of any theoretical admiration for a planned society."

In my father's case, the impulses were similar. Class struggle and proletarian rule would never produce Utopia. "The revolution devours its children," he told me repeatedly, expounding on the fate of the architects of past revolutionary upheavals in settings as diverse as Russia, France and Iran. His battle was to be waged with a pen, the preferred beneficiaries of which were those to whom the spoils of power did not reach, or on whose backs or at whose cost it was maintained. His post-diplomatic role was to knock public orthodoxies he deemed duplicitous or insidious. If he repeatedly voiced concern about the Right's bête noire of inequitable wealth distribution, it was not simply because he was an overly sentimental, liberal Canadian excessively concerned with the sufferings of his fellow man. Nor was it out of any rigid allegiance to trite socialist dogma. He came by his interest in disparities in wealth distribution honestly, having witnessed firsthand the sort of diabolical regimes that emerge in reaction to widespread poverty and glaring inequity. "Communism was not a historical accident," he maintained. Keenly aware that the conditions under which the communist regimes of the 20th century emerged were still very much present in various parts of the world, he insisted on continuing to sound the warning bell, arguing that the circumstances which gave rise to its perverse mutations had not been addressed, and adamant that in the era of globalization, the free market was not an ideologically neutral instrument.

Likewise, the dangers to liberty from the Right, in his view, were looming ever larger in the wake of the dissolution of the Soviet Union. With no "Evil Empire" to ballast the will to power of an ascendant Right on the world stage, he feared what would emerge to fill the ideological vacuum left in its place. I can only imagine his horror at the prospect of our truculent southern neighbour blossoming into full-blown Trumpistan. Some political actors in the West, he wrote, seemed to feel they had been presented with a blank cheque to push for global domination, "with the peculiar sense that what is good for America is good for the world." He wondered with trepidation what more radical ideologies, such as militant Islamism, would emerge that would "make socialism seem benevolent by comparison," and expressed apprehension about the implications for individual liberty of the measures that would most certainly be employed to combat these new threats to Western power. If he drifted further left in later years, it was surely exacerbated by what he saw as the toxic trajectory taken by the Canadian political Right in the post-Mulroney era, and its degeneration into a "branch plant" of the U.S. And what better place for a contrarian to re-enter the Canadian political troposphere following a diplomatic career than the University of Calgary — ground zero for the neocon puppeteers who were busy engineering the reinvention and take-over of what remained of Canadian conservatism.

My father is no longer here to poke a stick at the political establishment. If he'd had his druthers, he would have lived another couple of decades. It was with bitter regret that he marched into hospital on a cold Victoria morning in January 2011. The quadruple by-pass he'd undergone some fifteen years earlier was still holding, if barely, but one of the valves in his heart was leaking badly and needed to be replaced. If he didn't have the surgery, the doctors told him his chances of surviving another year or two were only fifty percent. If he did have it, there was a ten percent chance he'd die on the table, and an even higher chance of stroke. Not great odds. All he could think about was his sister Mary's demise at age 50. It was 1985 when she bid a tearful farewell to her children in the hospital corridor as they wheeled her into the operating room for heart surgery. She never made it out. Sadly, that was to be my father's fate as well.

Knowing my dad, I understand why he took the risk. He was not the sort to make peace with death. He loved life with a hungry passion and did all he could to extend it, including radically modifying his diet and taking up a zealous exercise program years earlier. Had he opted out of the surgery, he would have been forever moping about, second-guessing himself, wondering if he could have squeezed just another year or two or five out of his allotted span by going under the knife. By the same token, he was in no denial about the risks of proceeding. The air was heavy – unbearably so – as they rolled him down the hall away from us and into the surgery suite. I wanted to run after him, stop him and tell him he didn't have to do this. "Dad, don't do it. Just come home and carry on as you are. It's not worth it," I longed to say. But he'd made his decision and wasn't turning back. I called after him in a voice quivering with emotion and said the only thing I could think of to encourage him without breaking down in sobs myself: "See you this afternoon, Dad." He, too, could not speak without falling apart. He just held up his hand in a soft wave of acknowledgement before he disappeared behind the sliding doors.

My father put up a valiant fight in the cardiac intensive care unit, but it was not to be. The condition of his heart was a lot worse than they'd realized, resulting in an inordinately long and desperate surgery. One by one his organs revolted in the wake of the surgical assault. Three days later, he was no longer able to command his body through sheer force of his will, as he'd always done. His spirit slipped its bodily cloak and was finally reassigned abroad for good.

Nothing prepares you for the shock of such a loss, or the ensuing avatars of that trauma as it contorts into panic, then dread, then fury and finally grief. My father had been clear with us about the risks, but he'd always done risky things and come out on top. Not this time.

The week before he went into hospital, my dad gave me a draft of his memoirs. He'd been working on a chapter here and there earlier on, and had sent me previous incarnations of several of the chapters in years past, but hadn't yet gotten around to pursuing publication. He said that if for some reason he didn't make it out of the hospital, I should publish them if I saw fit, or even simply post them on the blog we'd set up for him to start work on once he'd recovered from the surgery. I received the chapters with due solemnity, but didn't seriously think I'd be dadless a week later; that I was lent a whole new significance to the task.

As if to spur me on, his voice came through from beyond the grave the week after his death via the *Letters* page of Maclean's magazine dated January 17, 2011, in which he maintained that it was only thanks to Wikileaks, in contrast to what we'd been fed all along by government and media, that Canadians had learned the truth about what was really going on in Afghanistan — that we had been sacrificing lives and money in what amounted to a hopeless cause. It served as a potent reminder that power cannot be left to police itself, that its totalitarian impulses can always be found breathing down our necks and that free expression is crucial for keeping its excesses in check.

In spite of his qualified endorsement of Wikileaks, those looking in these pages for a whistle-blowing tell-all à la Julian Assange, or a Snowden-style data dump will be disappointed. Ever the faithful public servant, my father was of the view that a certain degree of secrecy was necessary and appropriate for honest and effective government. In response to my interminable curiosity about his covert activities over the years, he did divulge some tales but, to my chagrin, he also told me there were secrets he would take with him to the grave.

What these memoirs provide is threefold. First, they afford a personal account of my father's journey through the Cold War and across the globe through the lens of his career as a Western diplomat. The tale traces not only his professional growth in Canada's Foreign Service, but his ideological evolution as well. What he initially takes for black and white while young and naïve morphs into an increasingly complex moral landscape. Secondly, the narrative offers an insider's view of the evolution of the Foreign Service arm of Canada's government over the crucial period of the past half-century, and the implications of that evolution for Canadian foreign policy and Canada's stature internationally today. Finally, the chronicle leaves us with some profound and disturbing questions about the ideological vacuum left by the demise of the Soviet Union, the radical ideologies of disaffection vying to take its place and the risks to democracy posed by Western power itself in its quest for self-assertion. For those of us who knew and loved my father, this book serves as a delightful memento and a life-affirming reminder of his warm and mischievous spirit.

P.S. All footnotes in the text are mine.

Lisa Warden

Chapter One

AN INNOCENT ABROAD

Berlin 1961

As I rounded the corner onto Unter den Linden and headed for the café, the black Wartburg sedan slid to a halt and four men in the black uniforms of the East German Security Service emerged looking as if they meant business. My back was drenched in instant perspiration and I could feel the panic threshold rising. So Vasily had decided I was not the innocent I claimed to be and was playing his trump.

For a student in search of adventure and excitement, Berlin in those spring days of the late 1950s was paradise. Premier Khrushchev's threat to renew the Blockade hung heavy in the air. President John F. Kennedy was a novice in the White House and there was no telling how he would measure up to the bully in the Kremlin. In the student hostel on Rudeloffweg across from the four-power governing body of Berlin, the Allied Kommandatura, we devoured the news each morning and debated furiously every nuance in every official statement. The tension generated an emotional high, a sense of exhilaration heightened by our frequent forays into the enemy's lair, East Berlin.

I had come to Berlin first in the autumn of 1958 to study at the Free University. My source of support lay in undertaking to work as an assistant, teaching several hours of English each week at a high school in Berlin-Charlottenburg. I never took this venture into pedagogy very seriously except as a source of Deutsche Marks, although I began to look forward to the students' daily skirmishes for their amusement value. The students were models of Teutonic discipline as long as Herr Professor was present and ruling with an iron rod. No sooner would he turn the class over to me and disappear for a cigarette, however, than – gentle soul and inexperienced as I was in matters of keeping order – an utter transformation would take place. The stiffness and stuffiness dissolved into instant and total chaos and uproar as students mounted their desks, boxed with one another, launched paper missiles in all directions and generally let everything that had earlier been repressed hang out. For therapeutic value, students rated my classes very highly and they were popular among the participants. I enjoyed them as much as the students did and was often invited to share a Saturday night brew with one group or another.

My main purpose in coming to Berlin was to study Russian history and the Soviet system. And what a rich treasure trove in terms of practical wisdom the enclave deep inside the Soviet-dominated territory offered. The Free University itself boasted several thousand students who either had fled to West Berlin as refugees from East Germany, or who commuted each day from the Eastern sector of the city. Movement in those days before the construction of the infamous Wall was still possible within the greater Berlin city limits. My own roommate in the hostel, a native of Karl-Marx Stadt by the name of Manfred Korn, had crossed the line only a few months previously. I found it curious that even though the comrade-mentality had been drilled into him for years under the Communist system, he still insisted on leaping out of bed each morning as I emerged from beneath my thick quilt, extending his hand and ceremoniously greeting me: "Guten Morgen, Herr Warden!" "Manfred," I would ask, "Why don't you just call me Bill?" Despite my protests, the same formal routine continued not only in the morning, but preceded lights-out each night.

It seemed that scarcely a week passed during our two years in the former German capital that we did not have cause for excitement. Occasionally the Communist Party would stage a rally in West Berlin in the same Sporthalle where Goebbels, Hitler's propaganda minister, had held forth, and we would all troop down to jeer, hurl abuse and hope for confrontation between the Communists and the ranks of helmeted police. On other occasions, militant cadres from the Humboldt University in East Berlin would appear in the precincts of the Free University, where they debated the issues of the day. Generally, they acquitted themselves not badly because they made a point of having at their fingertips facts and figures, even if utterly tendentious, and of maintaining discipline. All the while, their Western counterparts jostled and argued amongst themselves and worked themselves up into an inarticulate lather.

Life in Berlin was not a game, though. This was brought home to us when on occasion individual students, particularly from among those who had originally come from the East, would venture to the other Berlin to meet friends or relatives – and never reappear. We came to regard this as a tragic but not abnormal part of life in the divided city.

I was utterly fascinated by the politics of Berlin. Access to the Soviet sector was a simple matter, in those days before the Wall, of simply walking across the street or riding the subway. Together with my wife-to-be and other student friends we explored East Berlin. Grey it may have been, and still extensively marked by bomb damage, but it was enemy territory, a dark shadowy world of espionage, and this endowed the city with a permanent ability to get one's adrenaline flowing.

We walked the border, fascinated by the arbitrary line – here following an old tramline, there running straight through the middle of a house on a sedate, tree-lined avenue. We went to the Three-Penny Opera and thrilled to the majestic sounds of the Red Army Choir. We attended political meetings and, always alert to the consequences of missing our stop and ending up in the forbidden territory of East Germany proper, travelled the elevated railway – known as the

S-Bahn — to the eastern fringes of the city to meet friends, partake of their humble fare and endlessly discuss matters of the day. We knew that "our" system in the West was better: one had only to compare "our" opulence with "their" penury. But an incongruous and rather discordant note was struck by the fact that most of the East Germans we met impressed us as being rich on soul and high on friendship, in contrast to the crass materialism of "our" own Germans in the West. The idea of getting inside Communist East Germany itself, normally closed tight to Western visitors, to see what made it tick, became something of an obsession.

In my enthusiasm for exploiting every opportunity afforded by Cold-War Berlin, shortly after my arrival in 1958 I one day boarded the S-Bahn and made my way to the historic but now Communist Humboldt University in East Berlin. There I submitted my application for admission to courses in Marxism and dialectical materialism. This seemed straightforward enough. Surely the Communists could be expected to welcome the opportunity to expose a young capitalist to Marxist doctrine. But not so! Instead I was greeted with deep distrust. Why on earth would I want to study Marxism? The stern, unsmiling comrades in the admission office, it appeared, had never before had anyone voluntarily seek entrance to their dismal courses, and anyone who did was automatically deemed suspect.

After an interval of several weeks and much to my surprise, I received a notice advising me that I should report to the Philosophical Institute of Humboldt University at the beginning of the January term to begin my two courses. I remember absolutely nothing of the course content. It was the most deadly drivel, consisting mainly of dogmatic commentaries on incomprehensible readings from Marx, Engels and Lenin. I was happy to join my fellow students in snoozing and agonizing my way through these excruciatingly boring sessions.

Not all passed me by, however. What attracted my continuing participation, and in fact the reason I was there, was the opportunity to rub shoulders with the comrades of the Institute. I wanted to see what made them tick. These were, from the perspective of a fresh-faced student from Canada, an extraordinary bunch. They were all dedicated young Communists with minds about as open as a sprung bear-trap. Their destiny in life was to become the next generation of East German philosophers, and the image they cut was that of a caricature from a cartoon featuring the Hitler Youth. The Third Reich was less than a decade and a half behind us at that point, and I was totally intrigued by these young men and women who, despite their different ideology, did not seem much removed from their look-alikes of a few years earlier in terms of their blind allegiance and readiness to mouth slogans.

What really struck me as humorous – and indeed ironic – was the fact that among the young Communist group, most with birth dates between 1930 and 1940, was a generous sprinkling of young people bearing names such as Herman (after Goering), Josef (after Goebbels) and Eva (after Braun, Hitler's mistress). The comrade assigned to keep an eye on me bore the unlikely proletarian label of Adolph Bismarck. Adolph was in fact not an unfriendly type;

indeed we spent many hours strolling and chatting, and drinking black coffee while comparing life in the East with that in the West. "Adolph," I would say, "let's walk a few blocks over to the other side and have coffee there for a change." But Adolph's vigorous defence of the socialist paradise always foundered on one undeniable reality: the system did not trust him enough to allow him to meet me anywhere other than on his side of the Brandenburg Gate. "Bill," he would say in frustration, "you just don't understand!"

Lured by the appeal of the forbidden, I set as a major goal the securing of permission from the East German authorities to travel beyond Berlin and into the heartland of the country. In those days, other than attending the annual Leipzig Trade Fair, getting into the rigidly controlled German Democratic Republic as a Westerner was only a bit less difficult than contemplating passage to a far planet. The unvarnished truth, of course, was that life there, in contrast to that in West Germany or West Berlin, was totally drab and repressive. The authorities could not seriously believe that anyone would really want to visit the place, except with ulterior motives.

The Communists had good reason for their paranoia. If ever there was a spy capital, Berlin was it in those days. The city was the stuff of which good espionage novels were made. Like Hong Kong in the Orient, Berlin served as the turbulent meeting point between two hostile political systems. Russian troops faced American, British and French forces eyeball to eyeball. Even we penniless students, who should have been concentrating on our studies, felt caught up in the web of conspiracy, plot and counterplot.

Perhaps it was the penury in which most of us lived that got some of us into trouble. We were always looking for a way to make a little extra cash on the side. In the East Europe Institute of the Free University, which was my principal place of study, I was befriended by an American some years my senior who was, like me, working on his doctorate in Soviet and Russian studies. "Stan" (undoubtedly not his real name), over a period of time, ferreted out the fact that I was obsessively interested in travelling to Russia. He eventually told me about an American "company" specializing in research that was prepared to provide a small salary and cover the travel expenses of suitable candidates to enable them to visit this enchanting, mysterious land. "Bill, if you are so interested in Russia, why don't I put you in touch with this company?"

I was sorely tempted. As if to compensate for my protected life and timidity as a child, I lately had become something of a risk-taker – incidentally, a trait that has stayed with me. I have often dreamt that in another life I would choose to be a war correspondent.

The scoop was this: a training course would be organized in which one would learn the kinds of things to watch for, as well as the art of clandestine photography. Eventually a car would be rented in West Berlin and one would set off for a two- or three-week journey on one of the newly opened tourist routes through East Germany and Poland to Moscow and Leningrad. Was I interested? Stan, it seemed, did not propose to come along with me.

A few days later, Stan and I left the Institute at noon and walked for several blocks. A car was sitting at the curb, its engine idling and a middle-aged man at the wheel. We climbed into the vehicle and it sped away, twisting and turning – to avoid surveillance I was later told – through a maze of streets, arriving a quarter of an hour later at a small café on the outskirts of the city. There we ordered lunch.

The whole procedure by this time had definitely taken on a bizarre air, even to an innocent Canadian. The conversation was fairly general and in the nature of an interview. What was my background? Did I speak Russian? Why did I want to visit Russia? The meeting terminated on an inconclusive note with our host suggesting that he would get back to me in due course. By that time, and in spite of the lure of cloak-and-dagger intrigue, I was having serious doubts myself about the wisdom of this whole venture – even though I had no regrets whatever about having the fellow buy me a good lunch.

Back at the Institute, after exerting some pressure, I finally got Stan to admit that the whole set-up was an "enterprise" of one or other of the U.S. intelligence agencies. He would not say which, but I had little doubt that we were talking about the CIA. Stan was one of their recruiters. Fortunately, I was smart enough to resist the temptation. My literal words to Stan were: "Thanks kiddo, you go first and we'll talk about it again after you're back!"

I say fortunate because not so many months thereafter, a young American from the Institute by the name of Duncan MacKinnon was picked up on the highway to Moscow, in a rented car from Berlin, allegedly photographing Soviet military installations. He

9

was given eight years in prison. It has since emerged in the various accounts of CIA history that during that precise period the Agency was recruiting thousands of "assets" for various ill-conceived and highly risky missions in Eastern Europe, Asia and throughout the world. The grim reality is that most of these assets became casualties of the CIA clandestine service's incompetence and low or nil concern for losses incurred. Collateral damage was simply an inevitable cost of fighting Communism. Prison was the least of the penalties suffered by those foolish enough to succumb to temptation. How many other young people in the Berlin theatre had been foolish enough to succumb to my friend Stan's blandishments and turn their hand to amateur espionage I have no idea. For me personally, it was a close call.

Some weeks after I joined the Marxism classes in East Berlin, my minder, Adolph, suggested I go to the Student Affairs Office to apply for a visitor's visa, if I wanted to make a trip into East Germany proper. I made my way along Unter den Linden and into a large, bleak office inhabited by two bespectacled bureaucrats with humourless demeanour. What were my professional goals in life? Why did I want to visit East Germany? If my idea was to apply eventually for the Canadian diplomatic service – which I had frankly admitted to them, why should they help to "train the enemy" (their turn of phrase)? I had asked for a trip to Neustrelitz, Rostock and other points on the border with Poland. The comrades suggested that I return in two weeks to get a response.

Dutifully I reported back in two weeks, full of hope. But alas, I was informed that no decision had been taken as yet. As I was about to withdraw, a faceless individual behind the counter beckoned to a chunky fellow in a black overcoat and blue felt fedora who was sitting along the wall. He said, "Oh, I want you to meet this gentleman, who is the Berlin correspondent for a Soviet cultural newspaper." The man, who spoke good German, introduced himself as Vasily Mironow and said, "How nice to meet you. I have always wanted to meet a Canadian." Meeting a Russian in those days was about the same as running into a Martian and I was delighted to accept Mironov's invitation to meet for coffee the following week on Unter den Linden — notwithstanding the fact that by his dress he could have been taken straight out of a John le Carré spy novel.

Vasily and I met a number of times. He was an affable, good-humoured type, always paying for the coffee and cake with *Schlagsahne* (whipped cream), almost enough in themselves to make a penny-pinching student defect. Our conversations were not so profound, and I had the distinct impression that he was genuinely enjoying his contact with someone from "the other side". We talked about politics and culture and student life. Vasily asked many questions and told me about his work as a correspondent. He was particularly interested in the fact, volunteered by me, that I had been a Second Lieutenant in the army and had served for a short time in the Ruhr district of West Germany in 1955. Like Adolph, he continually deflected invitations to meet me in West Berlin.

After a few coffee meetings, Vasily's horns began to emerge. With increasing insistence he asked me to write a piece for his Moscow paper. Although the paper was supposedly cultural, his interest, curiously, was mainly in having an article about the intentions of NATO forces in West Germany. He assured me I would be well paid. I have always had a pretty good "sense of smell" and at this stage the odour was beginning to turn a little sour. Even in my naïveté I began to realise that I was a recruitment target. My adrenaline was given a further boost by the fact that about this time the Director of Berlin's Department of Education, which was paying my stipend, summoned me to her office to say that she had learned I was taking courses at the Humboldt University. From whom she had garnered this information she did not say. The Director did not mince words. "*Du lieber Gott,*" she asked, "have you taken leave of your senses? Don't you know how dangerous this game is? Do you know how many students from this side have ended up in Communist jails?"

In the meantime, my father had written to say that two RCMP officers from the security service had called on him at our home in Niagara Falls asking questions about why I was spending so much time in East Berlin. The espionage networks, it seemed, had their tentacles in every corner. I decided to call it quits, but not before one last *Kaffee und Kuchen* with Vasily.

And so I found myself on a corner outside the café on Unter den Linden when the black Wartburg pulled up and discharged its load of security people. A totally false alarm, it turned out, but enough to send the adrenaline surging and make me sweat. Vasily and I met, had our usual pleasant chat interspersed with occasional references to the article he wanted me to write, and agreed to meet again in three weeks. I returned to West Berlin and made a point of never seeing Vasily again.

I returned to North America in early June of 1959 and married my sweetheart Laine in September. We spent the first several months of married life in Laine's hometown of Knoxville, Tennessee, where I pursued a Master's degree at the University of Tennessee. This was the age of the civil rights movement, Martin Luther King, black sit-ins and white backlash across the South. A few token African-Americans in the graduate school were all Tennessee could muster to demonstrate "progress". The sports stadium still displayed a prominent sign in a seating section up in one far corner reading "For Coloreds Only". We counted among our friends in Knoxville a newly-married African-American couple of the same age, Jimmy and Nancy Wright, but the only possibility for getting together socially was in private since lounges and restaurants still served black people only through a window at the back. The good Christian folks at Second Presbyterian Church where we had been married also made it clear that bringing the Wrights to church with us would seriously disrupt other parishioners' ability to worship the Lord. We reluctantly abandoned any thought of doing just that.

It was in Knoxville that I first began to focus more clearly on the discrepancies between the images of America the Good and America the Ugly. In confronting Communists on the streets and classrooms of Berlin, we only spoke of the former. But here in the heart of America, the beauty of the magnificent dogwoods in spring contrasted sharply with the ugliness on West Clinch in front of Rich's department store where blacks paraded in silent protest while whites spit, whistled and jeered, policemen with their dogs standing mutely by. The seeds of doubt and cynicism began to sprout in my mind, but at that point they were still far overshadowed by the overriding menace of communism and the Evil Empire.

Armed with a fresh, multi-year scholarship from the German government, Laine and I returned to Berlin in the summer of 1960, where I intended to work much more seriously on my doctorate. Travelling was fun in those days. It was mainly by ship, and we embarked on the old SS Arkadia of the Greek Line in Montreal. The start of the journey was inauspicious. A friend took us to Montreal, where his car was stolen on the eve of our departure. Aboard the ship, on which I had managed to secure free passage in exchange for acting as a student consultant, I was promptly laid low by a severe attack of sciatica, and spent the entire voyage on my back. Transported from the ship by ambulance to a clinic in Rotterdam, I recovered, and we then took the train to Berlin.

Tension in Berlin continued to mount throughout the autumn and into the wet, grey winter. West Germany continued to rearm, and to prosper, while in the East life was bleak and cheerless, the cities still dominated by the horrendous devastation wrought during the war. The East Germans were restless, as reflected in the increasing flood of refugees crossing daily over the still-open border between the Russian and Western sections of Berlin. Leaving the so-called

German Democratic Republic was still relatively easy. It worked like this. Manfred Korn, my former roommate in the student hostel, had decided one day that a future in Karl-Marx-Stadt offered him nothing. He simply packed a small suitcase, and took the train to East Berlin. The only obstacle was to convince the border guards controlling access from the countryside into East Berlin itself that he had relatives to visit there. Once in the Russian sector, it was simply a matter of hopping onto the underground or elevated railway, which still operated in those days throughout the entire city, and riding it to the West and freedom.

Huge refugee camps were set up in the Western sectors, and nothing was done to discourage the river of humanity. We visited the main camp at Marienfelde one afternoon and there talked to some of the recent arrivals, who had simply abandoned everything in the hope of a better life in the West. As the grim days of winter turned into the promise of spring on the broad boulevards and along the canals, it became evident that something was going to have to give — otherwise the entire productive population of the East would be moving to the West. The East German press became more and more strident, accusing the Western allies and its "puppet" government of intentionally destabilizing the East. Moscow flexed its muscles, deliberately fanning fears of a renewed Berlin Blockade.

I could not have imagined a more fulfilling life as a student. One day it was a political rally, the next a 20-cent train ride to the Soviet War Memorial in Treptower Park in the East, and after that a lecture in history or politics. Interspersed were hikes through the Grunewald, forays to buy our *wurst* and deliciously fresh bread, and endless get-togethers with friends in the nearby cafés. Our economic circumstances having improved somewhat, we purchased a used Volkswagen, which increased our radius of operation significantly. In the spring of 1961 it carried us to Paris for my Foreign Service interview following which, much to my surprise, I was offered a job to commence in the summer. Of Vasily, nothing more was seen – fortunately. I was reminded of him, however, one day when a plain envelope arrived at the hostel where we stayed, inviting me to meet at our 'usual' watering hole. Having recovered from my surprise – after all, more than a year had passed since our last and 'final' meeting – I wisely chose to ignore the invitation, and simply hoped he would go away.

On the evening of August 9, 1961, Laine and I travelled the elevated railway one last time to the outer reaches of East Berlin. There we met with some East German student friends at their home in order to take a glass of wine and say *auf Wiedersehen*. The mood was sad and gloomy. Sad because we were to leave Berlin for good the next day. Gloomy because the future was so uncertain – that was the way most people felt in Berlin in those days. Khrushchev was rattling sabres even more ominously and threatening to shut down West Berlin once again. Refugees continued to pour over the border. How long could it go on like this?

On August 10, we left the city that had come to be our home for much of the time since 1958, destination Ottawa and the Department of External Affairs.

Three days later, the infamous Berlin Wall was erected in the dead of night, cutting the city in two, creating immense hardship and humanitarian trauma. Safely back in Canada, we were chilled to the quick as we watched TV images of the events taking place. What of our student friends, now cut off from their studies? And we contemplated the vagaries of fate. What if the wall had gone up three days earlier? We ourselves would have been trapped in East Berlin and almost certainly would have faced serious problems getting out. How long would this monstrous wall remain? At the time, we saw not even a pinprick of light at the end of the tunnel.

Bill as a student in Berlin, 1959.

Bill, 1959, Berlin.

Bill and Laine riding bikes in Berlin, 1959.

Bill at the university in Berlin.

Bill with his American military friends in Berlin.

Chapter Two

AN INNOCENT IN OTTAWA

Travelling to Ottawa in search of adventure might strike one as a contradiction in terms. Indeed, if there were any bland parts in my nearly three decades spent in the Foreign Service, these were the periods spent in Ottawa. Looking back, I have an overriding recollection of the capital as a beautiful city improving with age thanks to the taxpayer's generosity, but of a city reeking of hierarchy, petty politicians and jumped-up bureaucrats lusting after power and influence — and of generally boring assignments. I had one aim and one aim only in joining the Service: to get out and see the world, something that was not so easy in those days. Of twenty-seven years of government service, I considered my crowning achievement to be managing to stay away from Ottawa for most of them, including the final ten.

Perhaps it was because until age seventeen I had scarcely travelled more than a hundred miles from my hometown of Niagara Falls that I developed such an obsession with travel. The bug hit the day I finished college – and it never left me.

My first stop was West Germany, in 1955, for a delightful summer with the Canadian Officers' Training Corps, of which I have little recollection apart from the weekend trips to places like Heidelberg and Cologne and foaming mugs of beer. From there I headed to London for demobilisation and then on to Scotland, birthplace of my mother, intending to stay no more than a year. In fact, I stayed for three, studying theology and history at the University of Glasgow. Berlin and Tennessee were next, to pick up a Master's degree, make a start on a doctorate, and meet and marry Laine, who was to be my loving, lifelong companion.

Joining the Foreign Service had been a distant dream through much of my college days – although one I never seriously envisioned turning into reality. Back in those days when life was a lot simpler and people much less travelled, the Foreign Service held an intense fascination. If you wanted to travel the globe, the Service was the best and most glamorous way to do it. Moreover, with the world firmly caught in the vice-like grip of the Cold War, it was an exciting way for a young and idealistic Canadian to serve one's country and at the same time do battle with what Ronald Reagan was eventually to call the "Evil Empire".

Getting into the Foreign Service has never been easy. The late 50's-early 60's were no exception. You threw your hat into the ring by writing two examinations. If the gods of fortune smiled on you, you, along with other aspiring diplomats, were called to an interview. The written exams I took in Berlin in the fall of 1960 at the Canadian Military Mission.

The subsequent summons to the interview took me completely by surprise since I had been out of Canada for more than five years and figured that my lack of knowledge of Canadian current events would have scuppered me in the written exams. The other hard fact was that I was in the middle of my doctoral studies and had no intention of giving them up. I had written the exams more out of curiosity.

So much for good intentions.

My oral examination was to be conducted in Paris and there was no resisting the temptation to accept an expense-paid trip to the French capital. Laine and I drove to Paris, I somehow got through the interview, had all my clothes stolen in Metz on the way back through France — and was duly offered employment. With a hard offer in hand and our first baby due the following December, the siren call of the Foreign Service was not to be declined. I tried to have the job offer deferred for a year or two to enable me to complete my doctorate in Russian history, but the Department's response was unambivalent. Join now or start again later from scratch. Torn between two options, we finally decided to take the bird in the hand, drop the studies and join the ranks of budding diplomats.

Looking back on that decision some five decades later, I have to say that, given the possibility to rewrite the scenario, I would not change the course of events. This is not to deny that I am a lot smarter now – something of an old fox – in the ways of the bureaucracy, and that there are some things I would do quite differently if I had those years to live over again.

I joined the Department, still a Canadian of humble roots, believing not so much in original sin as in the essential goodness of man, at least when it came to public servants. Later on as I climbed higher up the ladder, I learned that this was a fundamental error – particularly when dealing with senior levels of the bureaucracy. As the Public Service became progressively more politicized under the regimes of prime ministers Trudeau and Mulroney, it became clear that the road to the top, far from being paved exclusively with merit, integrity and strong performance, depended just as much on having the right connections, the right politics, keeping unpopular views to oneself, cosying shamelessly up to the right people and occasionally sticking a quiet knife into a colleague, thereby enhancing one's own career prospects. But that was in the future.

When I arrived on Parliament Hill in September of 1961, the world of External Affairs was rosy indeed. Autumn was on the doorstep, the Ottawa air crisp and clear, the view of the river, and the crimson and gold Gatineau hills breathtaking. We who were born in the 30's and joined the Department in the 50's and 60's were fortunate indeed. Canadian diplomacy was on a high. Lester B. Pearson had won the Nobel Peace Prize. The Service was expanding and new missions were being opened. Canada's ambassadors were listened to, and their advice highly valued. The country was highly regarded in international circles and its voice was heard. All of us new recruits were fresh faced, well intentioned and highly motivated as we sat under the trees behind the East Block eating our bag lunches, discussing the state of the world, how long we would have to wait to get out on our first posting and where we would like to go. Those first two years were exhilarating. The twelve of us were the Class of '61, a rather intellectual bunch, and we debated each other, partied together and enthusiastically shared our hopes and aspirations.

I have to admit though that I never did reach the point where I felt myself fully at home in the world of External. I was neither sophisticated, overly intellectual nor from the side of the tracks that many of my colleagues came from. My background was very modest. For the family I grew up in, having sufficient resources to go out and buy Sunday dinner was a rare treat. My mother, with whom I always felt great affinity, was always most comfortable in the back pew of the church, away from the limelight. Those genes she must have passed on to me. There were others among our class of '61 who came from similar modest origins, but who nevertheless easily made the jump. I never did.

As such I always carried inside me something of an inferiority complex, and this was to stick with me throughout the career. Years later as ambassador, there was always a part of me that was quite out of place in the world of the affluent and the urbane – and indeed the often superficial – in which ambassadors move. On one occasion after leaving the Service, I was reminiscing over lunch with Joe Clark about his time as Minister of External Affairs, when he observed how the British made such excellent diplomats. I personally was not so impressed, but Clark certainly was. Like any other Service, the British had some first-rate people, but also its share of disasters. What I suppose Clark had in mind was, apart from their upper class accents which were usually enough to flummox any Canadian, the private school sophistication and Oxbridge sense of superiority with which the British Service was still imbued and which on occasion tended to spook us 'colonials'. Indeed, when I finally left the Service twenty-seven years later, there was nothing I welcomed more than the opportunity to move back into the relative obscurity of the last pew.

The Public Service of the immediate post-war era tended to be just what the term implies: a group of men and women who saw themselves as serving the citizens and government of Canada. Salary for most was not the first consideration. In fact I myself had been considerably better off financially as a scholarship student in Germany than I was during my early years with External. Nor were we concerned about working conditions. My first few months were spent in the East Block of the Parliament Buildings sitting at a table in a dark and dusty alcove in conditions that would have generated all sorts of grievances from employees today. However, the standard for us then was to accept whatever came our way. We might have been elitist in attitude, but as new Foreign Service Officers we had no delusions of grandeur. Looking back on those months I treasure the memories of being part of the last External contingent to occupy those historic surroundings, to walk the corridors and rub shoulders with the grand old men and women of the Department's early years.

I was quickly conditioned to the fact that I had become a member of 'the' Department, the elite of the Public Service, and that I was expected to act the part. We were imbued with the sense that we were the superior branch of government. The only reason people joined other departments was because they didn't have the 'smarts' to get into External. In particular, we put ourselves a notch above our colleagues in the Trade Commissioner Service. We were supposed to look on them as rather boorish and unsophisticated, mere merchants as opposed to philosophers and policy-makers. This was the ambience in External in the early 60's that shaped our young and willing minds. Had we been prescient enough to foresee the rising importance of trade and the Department's comeuppance in the 70's and 80's, we would have savoured our moment in the sun with far greater zeal.

From the day I joined External, I pursued one goal relentlessly: assignment to Moscow. Russia was still a dark mystery, an enigma, an enemy not much less loathed and feared than Hitler had been. It was a land cut off from the outside world. Meeting an extra-terrestrial in those days would not have generated much more interest than meeting an honest-to-goodness Russian. The forbidding Soviet Embassy on Charlotte Street with its heavy iron fence, shuttered windows and antenna forest on the roof embodied all the intrigue and suspicion associated with the Communist menace. The knowledge that the RCMP's Security Service was lodged in the nondescript house across the street, from where all comings and goings were monitored, simply added to the aura.

The standing joke in External was that the best way to guarantee *not* to be posted to a given country was to speak the language or have some knowledge of the place. I arrived in Ottawa with a reasonable knowledge of Russian acquired in Berlin, but was quickly led to believe that neither this nor my doctoral studies in Russian history would guarantee a ticket. The only thing left to me was to lobby. And I lobbied hard. This was my introduction to Departmental politics.

The upshot was that in the late summer of 1962, I was given wonderful news. Moscow was to be my assignment in the summer of 1963. I was duly assigned to the Tri-Services Language School for a year of intensive language training. Spare time, such as it was, was to be spent on the Soviet desk of the East European Division.

These were heady days for anyone involved in Soviet affairs. This was where the action was. The future of the so-called 'free world' depended on our ability to contain the Soviet menace, and for a junior officer the excitement of being part of this effort was stimulating in the extreme.

As a trainee, during the time spent in the Soviet affairs office, I was more a silent shadow than an active player, but it was sufficient to give me a reasonable overview of what was going on in Canada-Soviet relations and, more importantly, a comprehensive idea of the challenges a diplomat in Moscow could expect to face. On the Soviet desk we lived in a world of Secret and Top Secret documents, and we became thoroughly conditioned to the James Bond world of espionage and counter-espionage.

A constant refrain was that Canada indulged only in counter-espionage. We did not spy. This state of affairs was somehow cast as a reflection of our moral superiority, rather than of our naïveté ... a typically Canadian rationalisation! There were a few discordant notes. One of these was the fact that the air, naval and military attachés with whom I laboured through Russian classes each day were at the same time undergoing training in clandestine photography and such. I was also aware that diplomats in the Embassy in Moscow, when they travelled, reported on matters such as troop movements, missile sites and social developments, and I never could figure out what category of activity this fell under, since we did not spy!

At my desk in a corner office in the Langevin Building, I looked out on Metcalfe Street and up to the Parliament Buildings. Here I rubbed shoulders with former ambassadors (including John Watkins, former ambassador to the USSR, who in 1964 died while under interrogation by the RCMP, who suspected him of having been recruited as an agent of influence), and with officers recently returned from the Embassy. They would tell tales that only served to whet my appetite for the experience ahead.

The splendour of the autumn in 1962 was interrupted by the high drama of the Cuban missile crisis in October of that year. Since part of my assignment at the time was to master dreadful Russian verbs and conjugations, I was only a bit player on the political scene. Mornings of language lessons were followed by afternoons of sifting through documents, sorting telegrams and carrying messages. It was terribly exciting and suspenseful to sit in the centre of the action and watch reports on the rapidly unfolding events flow in from Moscow, Washington and Havana. Nail biting was hardly a term sufficient to describe the electric atmosphere. It was as if the world had stopped. In some ways I felt myself to be a spectator watching a surreal drama as the world edged to the brink of nuclear war in the showdown between Kennedy and Kruschev over the placement in Cuba of Soviet nuclear missiles aimed at the United States. The apprehension became almost unbearable when Kennedy announced the military blockade of Cuba and a set of ultimatums. Life as we knew it hung in the balance as we braced for the real possibility of nuclear confrontation between the two superpowers.

Whether humanity was spared by divine intervention, chance or good sense on the part of Kennedy and/or Kruschev, we will never really know. However, I can still feel the physical memory of the tension of the conflict whenever I think about it, and I can sense my blood pressure rise each time I project myself back to the corner of Metcalfe and Wellington in the glorious fall of 1962. It was only in later years, as documents on the crisis were released and as the main players in that drama, such as Fidel Castro and Robert McNamara, began to speak out, that I and the other officers inhabiting the diplomatic corridors in those days came to realize how very close to the brink we had actually come.

Two weeks after the missile crisis began, the tension over, we all relaxed and returned to the more normal pursuits of learning Russian, studying the entrails of Pravda and Izvestia to try to determine what was going on in the Kremlin and managing the day-to-day business of keeping the mysterious Soviets in check. The days of *perestroika* were so far off as to not be even the slightest glimmer on the horizon. On the contrary, the dark days still shrouded a sizable portion of the world, and the outcome of the battle between good and evil was still very much up in the air.

And so, in preparation for our first overseas posting, in the summer of 1963 we packed our bags and bid farewell to the green hills of the Gatineau, the sparkling Ottawa River and the gloomy precincts of the Langevin Building and the East Block to begin the long trek east. Ahead of us lay another twenty-five years of excitement, hard work, enlightenment and satisfaction occasionally tinged with frustration.

Still young and foolish, we naturally chose the hard route to Moscow. With two babies of eighteen months and six weeks in tow, together with suitcases, we climbed aboard the Montreal Express at the old Ottawa railway station. At this point Murphy's Law took over. Because of engine problems with the Cunard liner we were to take to Scotland to visit friends, we had to go on to Quebec City by train. No sooner on the ship, we were informed that the Scottish port of call had been cancelled and that all passengers would disembark at Liverpool. From there we took the train to Glasgow, and then rented a tiny car, in which we stuffed our possessions and screaming progeny. Much squawking, diaper changing, one week and two weary flights later, we arrived one dark night at Moscow's dimly lit Sheremetyevo airport.

Bill at the UN (seated with arms crossed, back row middle), 1962.

Chapter Three

COLD WARRIOR

Moscow 1993. How the city has changed. Thirty momentous years have passed since that late evening in 1963 when the Warden clan arrived at Sheremetyevo airport. I remember at the time that it seemed black. The airport was dimly lit, the immigration officials cold, unsmiling and unfriendly – as if characters from a James Bond novel. Even our driver, Vanya, was clad in dark blue. My recollection is that the air outside was cold, but it couldn't have been. Nor could it have been all that dark. After all, it was late summer in 1963 when the sun is still far to the north. I guess in my mind I am confusing the bleak political climate with one that we could see and touch.

For the decade following the collapse of the Soviet Union in the early 90's, I travelled to Moscow frequently. I found it absolutely fascinating to watch the metamorphosis in the appearance of the city and its citizens. Back at the height of the Cold War, the city seemed universally pale and uninviting. As we drove in from the airport along Leningradski Prospekt on that September evening in 1963, there was little traffic. Shadowy figures darted along the street. Some grocery shops, unadorned by neon, were still open and line-ups of customers patiently waited on the pavement for admittance to the premises for their meagre offerings. Propaganda and portraits of Lenin filled the few lit billboards along the way. "Electrification plus Soviet labour equals Communism!" I never did figure that one out.

When I returned to Moscow in 1992 for the first time since our initial posting there in the 60's, the first thing I noticed at the exit from the terminal was a young man selling posters, among them one of Lenin giving the finger to the crowd in front of him. That was just the start. The mighty ruble, for example, once maintained on par with the American dollar, had fallen. The precious currency in the early 90's was a carton of Western cigarettes. You could get almost anything for it. Once, some of my friends and I diverted a bus and had it deliver us to the Circus for a few packages — and come to pick us up after the performance for a few more. Another time we suborned the driver of a Mercedes limo that was waiting on the street. To whom it belonged we had no idea.

Moscow was not the only thing that had evolved by 1992. In 1963, I arrived as a passionately dedicated young cold warrior, committed with a sort of religious fervour to bringing about the downfall of a pernicious system. By the 90's, I was older and wiser and no longer so sure of possessing the absolute truth. The armour of the shining knights of the 60's had become tarnished, and the erstwhile champions of freedom and democracy were gradually being unmasked for hypocrisy, flouting of law, lack of concern for lives sacrificed, and even assassination and overturning of democratic governments. But in 1963, my vision was unblemished by such concerns and, looking back, how delightful it was to be able to see the world in black and white.

Vanya, the driver, delivered us to the former aristocratic mansion in Old Horse Lane that now served as Canada's embassy and residence for the ambassador. There we stayed in the old guesthouse for a couple of days before being shipped out to our new digs. Our Embassy administrators obviously had been in Russia long enough to adopt Soviet habits and really gave us the impression of not caring much about the average working bloke. We were unceremoniously dumped one morning in an apartment on Lomossovsky Prospekt behind the university together with our babies and unpacked cases of furniture.

Our personal lifestyle in Moscow in comparison to that of the Russians around us was extremely comfortable. In Canadian terms, it was, well, lousy. There was no other word for it. We occupied two small apartments, one of which we used for day living and the other for bedrooms. As the first tenants in the place, we should have come to a spic and span, freshly decorated dwelling. Far from it. A dairy barn in Canada was much better constructed than our shoddy new Moscow home. The building entrance was crude, the lift archaic.

In the flat itself, the wallpaper was poorly applied, badly stained by leaks, and the kitchen was a disaster. There were no curtains and the wind straight out of Siberia poured in through the cracks. One consolation was the thought that if our place was this bad, what must the dwellings assigned to average Russians have been like?

How could we complain? The whole building was filled with diplomatic families from all over the world. The only ones who were better off were the ones who had been living there for a few months and had had time to practice their decorating skills. We had a Japanese family below and one from Mongolia above. Every evening at mealtime, the aroma of Mongolian dishes mixed with those of Japan as the air currents moved freely up and down the vents. And they weren't the only things that moved. Scarcely were we in the place than we discovered the apartment had other occupants. These were enormous cockroaches, the size of small mice, which scuttled about, sampling the various national cuisines being prepared on the different levels. Neither trampling the beasts nor dangerous levels of fumigation helped much. Cockroaches supposedly have been on the planet for millions of years; three years of attack in our small apartment certainly wasn't going to get rid of them. Their time of choice was the middle of the night. A midnight visit to the bathroom was always an adventure. Suddenly turning the light on would precipitate a mad cockroach scramble, as the horde of little beasts would stampede to reach the safety of the various drains and cracks in the tile. In a word, we got used to it.

I remember our first day in Moscow quite well. The sun still comes up relatively early in Moscow in September, and our day started as soon as the light poured in through the uncurtained windows. The scene outside was bleak. Our living room window in the front gave onto a broad, unattractive boulevard, and the bedroom in the back onto a similarly austere courtyard surrounded by a high wall intended to fence us off from the real world outside. The only thing worth looking at was the remnant of an authentic Russian village just across the street to the west that had not as yet fallen victim to the 'plan'. It could have come straight out of a Tolstoy novel, with its wooden huts and tiny framed windows, and the occasional peasant emerging into the next century. Inside the apartment, between trying to pry open wooden crates and keep track of babies amid all the debris, I studied the walls rather expecting the microphones that were surely there to reveal themselves.

The extent of the domestic chaos for the first few weeks reinforced a strong conviction on my part that virtue lay in spending as much time at the office as possible. I was able to find all sorts of reasons why my presence was required in the Embassy from early morning till well into the evening hours. These were the days when wives were not expected to seek independent outside employment, but rather to provide unstinting support to their husbands labouring out there on the front lines. If we had any doubts about the role of wives, these were to be clarified shortly. But more on this later. Laine thus devoted her days to making the place liveable, while I devoured reams of reports on politics, looked after visitors, worked on exchanges, embassy security, and so forth, all of which clamoured for the attention of a political officer in a relatively small post such as Moscow.

Laine and I had always lived with animals in our lives, before we got married and afterwards during our student days in Tennessee. The most natural thing in the world, therefore, was that for our first Christmas in cold and snowy Moscow, I should present the family with a bouncing baby puppy, an Airedale terrier that I procured from the Moscow Dog Club – and that she should be named *Sasha*! Local *babushkas* on the street were insulted beyond words when they heard us addressing this furry bundle of energy by the same appellation as that of their beloved grandchild. Bill, Freddy, Tommy? No problem. Many Russian dogs bore these names. But Sasha? Sasha brought us enormous pleasure and brightened up our lives immeasurably. She bestowed particular canine enthusiasm on anyone who differed in appearance from us. Thus, whenever she managed to get loose in the courtyard and spotted a Japanese, Chinese, Sikh or Nigerian, she would roar her greeting and make a concerted rush, much to the dismay of the target. The uniformed and uniformly unfriendly militiamen at the gate to the complex were singled out for special treatment, which we found considerably heart-warming. These she universally despised and distrusted. They all came to know her by name, and with her antics and bluff charges, she even managed to get an occasional smile out of them. But Sasha also embarrassed us acutely on a regular basis with her incorrigibly undiplomatic behaviour.

The previous ambassador, Arnold Smith, had completed his assignment in the summer and the embassy was enjoying a period of relative calm as the mice played and awaited the arrival of his successor. If we had known what lay ahead, we would have savoured the interregnum much more fully. The new ambassador was duly announced in late autumn of 1963 and was to be Robert Ford, an old Soviet hand, currently serving in Egypt. The news sent chills down the collective spine of the staff, not so much because of Ford, who was widely respected, but rather because of his wife, Teresa, who had been terrorising the foreign service for a number of years. In due course, on a frosty January night, we all, diplomats, wives and various other hangers-on, lined up on the tarmac to receive Their Excellencies who were arriving from Cairo. Ford was paralysed from the waist down by a bout with polio a number of years earlier, and so the Canadian government had eased the journey by providing a C-130 military aircraft to transport the Fords and their personal effects. The arrival went off without a hitch. We all gathered at the official residence above the embassy to extend a welcome to its new occupants over a glass of champagne. The only unusual feature of the occasion was the discovery by the administrative staff upon unloading the aircraft that Ford had absconded from the Cairo ambassador's residence with everything but the proverbial kitchen sink; that is, anything he considered might be of value in Moscow, including, literally, the grand piano.

Over the succeeding three years, Laine and I got to know the Fords very well. Our main advantage was that we occupied a position at the bottom of the diplomatic heap, which provided a welcome buffer between ourselves and the frequent lightning bolts launched from on high. I nonetheless felt somewhat exposed because it usually fell to me to accompany Ford to various meetings in the Kremlin and elsewhere. It was my job to assist the ambassador discreetly, hoisting him up and letting him down by his reinforced back trouser pockets. Fortunately, I never let him drop in the presence of such notables as Khrushchev, Alexei Kosygin or Anastas Mikoyan. Actually, I really valued these special assignments. How many other people in those days penetrated the depths of the mysterious Kremlin in a big Lincoln limousine, taking the salute of members of the Kremlin's special guard and passing spectacular historic cathedrals, the Canadian flag proudly flying? Laine and I survived mainly by speaking when spoken to, agreeing with all the ambassador's frequent pontifical observations and, in particular, dutifully accepting whatever summons or instruction emanated from Madame. Not so fortunate were those who moved in the upper circles of the Embassy hierarchy. Bert Hart, a quiet and capable officer with a facial quirk that made you think he was smiling when in fact he was about to bite you, was number two in the mission. Bert was the ultimate diplomat who managed the Fords splendidly by keeping a sense of humour and not shying away from serving as a doormat at the appropriate moment. He was replaced a year later by Gordon Brown, a much different sort, who was not about to be walked on. Gordon's major accomplishment on the personal level was to annoy Ford so much that he made backroom arrangements to have Brown booted upstairs before his posting to Moscow was officially over. Brown duly went off as ambassador to the Congo, which for Ford probably represented the ultimate punishment.

Both Ford and his wife have long since passed away, but their influence extended well beyond the grave. The various tomes produced by foreign service officers who worked under Ford have been very generous, generally giving his regime a complete bye on the 'reign of terror' (I am being facetious) while focusing exclusively on the positive aspects of his career – of which there were plenty. I can only think that Ford's intimidating spectre still lurks above the pens of those who write, promising retribution to any who might dare to venture beyond words of homage. Why, thirteen years after leaving Moscow, I was serving as Commissioner for Canada in Hong Kong when I received word from Robert that Teresa (the Fords were still in Moscow!) was planning a visit to the colony to do some shopping. I immediately froze, and during her three-day sojourn regressed totally into the slathering, blubbery third secretary persona of my Moscow days. Teresa was much offended by her treatment as just another 'foreign devil' by the Chinese officials she encountered ("The Chinese are so ugly"!!), and she left Hong Kong yearning to reach Beijing as quickly as possible where she would board Aeroflot for the return journey to Moscow. Having been in the Soviet Union for some fifteen years at that point, Teresa had succeeded in terrorising the entire Soviet airline system, and even the surliest of Soviet flight attendants was as malleable clay in her hands.

Mrs. Ford was the last bastion of the 'divine right of ambassadoresses'. She disposed of her army of wives, summoning whom she would to decorate the residence Christmas tree, others to act as robotic hostesses at her various parties. If you were showing too much leg, you were sent home to change. If the costume you wore to the party was not appropriate or if a mistake in numbers had been made, you were dismissed forthwith. I recall an occasion on which wives were told to appear with hats. One unsuspecting new arrival showed up *sans chapeau*, saying that she didn't own a hat. Without batting an eye, Mrs. Ford replied in her inimitable heavy Brazilian accent: "Well go home and make vun, my dear. Your hair, she looks terrible!"

Talk of polar opposites. Where Teresa was Brazilian dynamite, explosive and temperamental, Robert was reserved, personable on appropriate occasions but cold as ice on others. His natural workaholism was accentuated by the paralysis that left him little focus but his work. Fail to show at the Embassy on a Saturday morning and a political officer (the only kind who really counted in Ford's eyes) could expect to receive a terse phone call: "Did you see such-and-such article in Pravda this morning?" Meaning, get in here and start writing.

Thursdays were days of much tension. That was the day the weekly diplomatic bag with all the classified dispatches went out, usually around four in the afternoon. We political officers were on the second floor, our offices arranged around a quadrangle. Ford's office was in the corner, and beside the stairs a noisy elevator had been built to accommodate the ambassador's mobility constraints. Every week, we all had our dispatches to write, assigned by Ford as easily as if he were passing out peanuts. Not infrequently, one might be instructed late on a Wednesday afternoon to write something for Ford's signature on some obscure piece in the Soviet press in time for Thursday's dispatch, the expectation being that come storm or pestilence or other commitment that might tie you up till midnight, the report would be ready. Well, it wasn't always – and on Thursday afternoons we would cower in our dim offices, waiting for judgement day. Around three, the ambassador's door would usually open and there would be the tip-tap of the cane as he emerged. Sweating profusely, we would sit transfixed in our respective offices as the tip-tap drew closer. If we were lucky, the elevator door would open and clang shut and we would all resume normal respiration. Otherwise, Ford would appear at one door or another, literally white with rage, demanding to know what had happened with the report on Khrushchev stubbing his toe – or some such triviality. I went through this several times during my posting, but am quick to add that more often than not Ford would appear the next day and apologise for any harsh words uttered.

In reality, most of us took it all in good humour. Personally, both Laine and I valued highly the discipline and rigour imposed, which served us in good stead in years to come. Apart from anything else, the experience was unique and provided untold opportunities in later years for laughs and exchange of stories with colleagues. Of course, the stories tended to grow with the years and undoubtedly some of them were apocryphal – such as the one told to me by a secretary who described Mrs. Ford's anger one day with the local administrator having reached such heights that she threw a chair at him, which missed and, sailing through the front window of the residence, fell two stories barely missing the Soviet militiaman on guard below. Not apocryphal at all was the story of Mrs. Ford's brilliant success in commandeering two of the KGB's clumsiest common labourers from the Embassy's maintenance staff and converting them into polished, white-jacketed and gloved waiters serving distinguished guests at Their Excellencies' dining table — where the opportunities for gathering juicy tidbits to pass on to their masters were undoubtedly much greater than on the end of a broom in the courtyard.

On one occasion I accompanied the Quebec theatre group, *Théâtre du Rideau Vert*, to Leningrad (now St. Petersburg) for several performances. Shortly after my arrival, I received a call from Robert informing me that Teresa had decided to take in a play and that she would arrive the next morning by overnight train. Would I please arrange an 'apartment' for Madame at the Astoria, Leningrad's finest hotel? Although it sounded easy, the complication was that the next day was May 1, a major holiday in the workers' paradise, and every last room in the city was booked. However, driven by the fear of death by a thousand cuts, I begged/cajoled/threatened the unaccommodating Astoria manager until he agreed to come up with a suite. Mrs. Ford arrived early the next morning on the Red Arrow and I accompanied her to the hotel. We obtained the key and together with an entourage of hotel staff proceeded ceremoniously to the room. About thirty seconds later, I heard a shriek, "That seelly beetch!!" It turned out that in honour of May Day, a giant portrait of Valentina Tereshkova, the country's first and most revered woman cosmonaut, had been hung on the outside of the sitting room window, completely obscuring the view of the square. The intent may have been to have the good Valentina look outwards, but there was no preventing her visage on the canvas from looking inwards as well. The Soviet maid and valet emerged, horrified at this desecration of their national hero. To make a long story short, followed by imprecations and a litany of aspersions cast on the parentage of the heroic cosmonaut, I persuaded the manager to find another suite. We moved everything over to the new digs only to find this time Yury Gagarin, the very first cosmonaut, peering in socialist realist splendour down on the square, as well as in on Mrs. Ford's sitting room. It was perhaps the only time I saw the Ambassadoress retire from the field of battle in defeat.

Lest the above sound too critical, I should be quick to affirm that we left Moscow with the greatest of respect for the Fords and even some affection. They forgave us for the one or two occasions when our good dog Sasha, in her enthusiasm, just about knocked His Excellency off his pins. The Fords served Canada magnificently in Moscow, and whatever their foibles, these were more than compensated for by the standards of excellence which they set for themselves as much as for others. Ford was a superb representative for Canada, of the kind scarcely seen in the present day. Mind you, my affection had its limits. When in 1972, after our return from Havana to Ottawa, Ford came to my office one day to ask if I would accept an assignment to Moscow as his number two, I quickly contrived all sorts of reasons, from failing health to domestic crises, to explain why Moscow 'most unfortunately' was out of the question. Having passed through the trial by fire once, I was not about to venture into the furnace again.

⟫◆⟪

In 1963, the Cuban missile crisis was barely a year old, and the Soviet authorities had us Western diplomats well isolated from the local population. We lived in a walled compound with guards at the gate. Movement even within Moscow was severely restricted. There was a police post at every main intersection and our licence numbers would be called into central control every time we passed. Travel outside Moscow was subject to 48-hour advance authorisation, and more often than not permission would be refused. Much of the country was designated as 'closed'. However, the most effective measure cutting us off was the local population's fear of being seen communicating with foreigners. Stalin's tyranny was not long past and Khrushchev's reforms had not changed anything in this respect. Most effective, of course, was the fact that the KGB was omnipresent and still very much in the business of detaining errant citizens on the slightest pretext.

It must have been a perverse element in my nature, but I have to admit that the KGB provided me with a lot of light relief. Apart from the ubiquitous mics in the wall to which we addressed frequent epithets as an antidote to frustration, I found in my own case that frequently the KGB 'goons', as we called them, would put me under intensive surveillance. I don't know whether this was the case with everyone, or whether I got extra attention because I spoke Russian, and had responsibility for visiting Canadian delegations coming in, or because my Berlin file had surfaced. Whatever the reason, intensive surveillance meant that my movements would be subject once or twice each month for a period of four or five days to physical observation from the moment I left the apartment until the moment of my return. On foot there would be as many trackers as required. Following my car, our 'friends' would normally use a minimum of four vehicles constantly changing position. It became quite a game keeping track of them, trying to lose them or otherwise being an annoyance. In my petulance I have to admit that I even stooped on occasion to giving some particularly obnoxious type the appropriate finger. It was probably foolish of me, but at least the games provided some relief from the gloom.

In retrospect, it is quite amazing how pervasive and intrusive the presence of the KGB was in the days of the Cold War. Mind you, from what one reads and observes in the new millenium, it seems that after a brief respite in the 90's, the organisation has been rapidly regaining its old repressive powers. I suppose it is not so surprising when you have a former KGB agent running the government.

I recall on one occasion accompanying *Les Castors de Sherbrooke* to Smolensk for a hockey game. This was back in the days when the only Canadian teams visiting Russia were amateurs – and not very good ones at that – whom the Soviet squads routinely gobbled up and spit out without a hiccup. The team, including myself, went for a walk in the afternoon through downtown Smolensk where, as usual on my out of town trips, I was accompanied by my shadows. One persistent fellow followed me into a department store, keeping a distance of about fifty feet. I sauntered along until he was passing a table of lingerie, at which point I suddenly turned and retraced my steps. The Soviet goons all seemed to have a pathological fear of being confronted by their quarry. This fellow was faced with the choice of either meeting me face to face or of feigning profound interest in women's undergarments. He, of course, chose the panties and bras. I thought it only reasonable to give him adequate time to make a selection, so I stopped immediately behind him and waited there for some two or three minutes. He didn't move a muscle for the entire period, at the conclusion of which I muttered into his ear in Russian, "amateur", and moved on.

My newfound companion, however, had the last laugh when at the hockey game that evening in the local outdoor arena the Soviet squad defeated the Canadians by a score of something like 10-0. The only light relief for the Canadian side was provided by one of the Canadian players who, frustrated at his impotence and when the referee wasn't watching, chose to sweep the feet out from under a Soviet player during a break in the play. Against the backdrop of shrill whistles from the sell-out crowd, the offended Soviet player followed the Canadian to the bench and, with about one inch separating the two noses, roundly berated the *nekulturny* (uncultured) Castor. Our defender of capitalism, standing tall and cool as a cucumber, heard the Soviet out and then just as calmly planted a great gob of spit directly on the Soviet schnozz. The crowd, most of whom had never witnessed a game against a foreign side, were delirious with delight and thought the whole show wonderful. Not only did their side win decisively, but at the same time they were able to witness first hand a bunch of uncultured capitalist ruffians act out the role in which the Soviet media had long been casting the Western world.

The creativity of the goon squad was remarkable to behold. In Kiev on one occasion, to attend the trial of Canadian tourists who had run over and killed a young girl, I was walking down one of the city's broad sterile boulevards. I sat down on a park bench. The only place my shadow, left in mid-creek without a paddle so to speak, could disappear was behind a sandwich board on the sidewalk. Patience was always a virtue, I determined, when trying to ascertain the enemy's moves. So I sat there – and I sat – for at least ten minutes. The fellow had most certainly disappeared behind the sandwich board and must have been extremely uncomfortable scrunching down behind it. I had just about decided that he had either been an illusion, or had perhaps popped down a manhole, when suddenly he emerged – but in a new incarnation. Instead of the tall athletic type who had seemingly stooped to tie a shoelace or adjust his socks under cover of the sandwich board, there emerged a cripple. The makeover would have been quite convincing, except for the fact that we were the only two people on that particular section of street, and the goon with his government issue outfit of blue pants, blue jacket, scruffy shoes and crumpled shirt, was scarcely equipped to change his appearance. Out he came, crouched way over and dragging one leg behind him, as he slowly and painfully beat a retreat. I could only sit, open-mouthed, and marvel at the ingenuity and innovativeness of the fellow, as he made his way down the endless expanse of dreary boulevard into the late afternoon sun. By that time, of course, I had three or four other 'friends' on station at various points of the compass.

Goon stories were endless and good fodder for cocktail conversation. Every Sunday afternoon in the winter, we Canadians played the Americans at hockey in an outdoor arena. The only spectators in the frosty place were the ten or twenty odd goons who dutifully observed their quarry and enjoyed the occasional scrap between two allies. I recall a Colonel Landrigan, a big marine attaché at the U.S. embassy who lumbered around the ice, laying low with a contented smile on his face any Canadian who came within reach of his stick or any other appendage. I once shouted at him from my position flat on my back, "If you do that one more time Colonel, I'll wrap my stick around your neck!" The goons loved it. And then there were the goons who once followed my wife and me into a cathedral in Riga. Their method of fitting into the surroundings on this occasion was to drop to their knees, as if in deep prayer, as we retraced our steps from the altar down the aisle. It was rather fun to drop down into the pew behind them for a few minutes to allow them plenty of time to get through their very long list of sins.

All was not fun and games, however. There was indeed a dark side, a very dark side to the KGB, and it behoved one at all times to be aware of this. We always felt like we were prey amidst a pack of predators. To hold any kind of a political conversation in our offices, we would mask our voices by switching on a sound box that turned the place into an instant cocktail party. If the discussion were on a more sensitive topic, or if we were holding a staff meeting, we would retire to a 'safe room' in the bowels of the building where enemy mics could not reach. That strategy seemed quite secure until we later learned that the KGB had mounted an operation to tunnel under the Embassy and come up to the safe room from below. Every once in a while, a member of the Canadian staff would disappear on short notice and we simply assumed that the person concerned had been compromised in one way or another and sent back to Ottawa. Maybe he was gay. Maybe she drank too much. Maybe he beat his wife. Confession or discovery meant an end to one's career.

Ironically, we were surrounded on all sides by local staff recruited by the KGB. That was just the way it worked. It was too expensive to bring Canadians out to carry out all the tasks of the Embassy, so instead we hired local staff through the official service provider, UPDK. As a result, we had several dozen KGB agents to look after administration, to perform some of the consular work, to organize the social calendar, to sweep and clean and serve cocktails. There was the gorgeous Tatiana, blonde, voluptuous, bait for the unwary or the over-sexed. Then there were the silent moles, quiet and barely noticeable except for those times when you would feel eyes on the back of your neck and, turning suddenly, would find yourself under minute examination. These agents, obviously under instruction to note any weakness or aberration on our part, were debriefed regularly by their KGB handlers. The same thing in our apartments. Any Russian nanny to look after the children, any cook or maid or handyman, was similarly hired through UPDK. It was no wonder that at times we felt paranoid!

The KGB could be vicious. Shortly after we arrived in Moscow, a technician with the West German embassy was visiting the historic Holy Trinity Monastery of Zagorsk (the original name of Sergiyev Posad was restored in 1991), north of Moscow. Mingling with the crowd in the dark interior of the main cathedral, he suddenly felt something wet go down the back of his leg. Later on he began to feel ill. The blisters on his leg were determined to be the product of mustard gas poisoning. The Soviet authorities put all possible administrative obstacles in the way of his being evacuated. The only thing that saved him was the expert ministrations of the American Embassy doctor. Two theories for the attack emerged. One was that certain elements in the KGB were attempting to sabotage a forthcoming summit between Khrushchev and German Chancellor Willy Brandt. The other was that the technician had uncovered a hidden microphone in one of the German residences and had hooked it up to a strong electrical current – which in turn had fried the person servicing the mic at the other end. Who knows? Such was the world of speculation and intrigue in which we lived. The story was particularly vivid for Laine and myself because on that precise afternoon we ourselves had visited the same Zagorsk cathedral.

Personal contact with Russians was a rare occurrence. The reason for this was simple. Average Soviet citizens were under a blanket prohibition to mix with foreigners – such as the young man from the countryside whom I met on the street one day who, in spite of my efforts to dissuade him, insisted he would come to my apartment to visit me. An hour or so before he was to arrive, he called the telephone number I had given him to report that something "unexpectable" had happened. Ya right! In Moscow, it was a simple proposition. Any 'casual' Russian you met who showed an interest in getting together, and who actually managed to pull it off, was automatically a KGB plant, with no exception.

Once in January, Godfrey Hearn, the First Secretary, and I flew to Murmansk to get a feel for life above the Arctic Circle in the dead of winter. As usual we were seated above the wings in aisle seats to prevent us from catching a glimpse of any military or industrial installations we might pass over. Beside me, a middle aged-gentleman struck up a conversation, identifying himself as a merchant marine captain who sailed frequently to Western ports. Within three or four minutes, a flight attendant leaned over and whispered in his ear. The good captain with a smile said that he had been instructed not to talk to me, which did not deter him. Shortly thereafter he was summoned to the cockpit to receive a lecture and a warning from the captain of the aircraft. He shrugged it off and we continued for the rest of the flight to have a pleasant conversation about his life as a sea captain and his visits to Montreal. He said he found it insulting that he, a sea captain, should be able to take a ship to Canada, but not speak to a Canadian in Russia. He said he would have liked to be able to entertain us in the city. My last sight of the captain was at the bottom of the steps as we deplaned, where he had been intercepted and pulled aside by three of the KGB's finest, readily identifiable by their dark fedoras and navy blue overcoats. Such was the state of paranoia within which we made our every move.

We met Rita and Sasha Sovtsov, a delightful couple, at the home of some American friends. In time, we went with them on picnics to the Moscow River; they came to our apartment, and we enjoyed their company thoroughly. Of course we knew, and they knew we knew, that they were KGB. In spite of this, we managed to have a fairly normal and amicable relationship with them and, just by being together, learned quite a bit about the Soviet Russian way of looking at things – for example, their insatiable desire for Western consumer goods. Before coming up to our place, Rita and Sasha always went through the charade of calling to say they had parked their car a few blocks away in order to avoid having the police at the gate take their licence number. The small issue of how they intended to get through the gate with the militiaman scrupulously controlling all passage was left aside. They never had a problem. One night they invited us and the couple from the U.S. embassy over to their place for a party. There were about forty or more Russians there about the same age, no doubt all KGB agents. The notable feature of the evening was the string of types continuously sidling up to me, confiding in low tones that he or she was involved in this or that secret kind of work, and that they should *really* not be talking to a foreigner. This was known as 'the troll', aimed at getting a foreign diplomat to bite and try to exploit the contact for information. Tempting as it might have been, I didn't bite. Not too many weeks later, we learned that our American friends, who had been at the same party, had been declared *personae non grata* and hustled back to Washington on forty-eight hours' notice. As for Rita and Sasha, we continued to see them off and on right up to our departure in 1966. Sasha, who had a mechanical flair, was salivating over the possibility that I might turn over to him, when I left, a decrepit wood-panelled Ford station wagon purchased from an American. I would have been glad to do this, but unfortunately regulations made it too difficult. We lost track of them after that. It would have been fascinating to look Rita and Sasha up in the Russian 'spring' of the early 90's and I was always sorry that I had misplaced their address.

The one thing that impressed me about not only Sasha and Rita, but also about the other KGB people of junior and mid-officer level we met through them was their urbane and 'with it' approach. These were people who were well dressed, savvy in the ways of the world, and very up to date with life in the West. They were also people confident of themselves and more than willing to discuss relatively freely the issues of the day. At the time I found this surprising, but it should not have been. Obviously the KGB was a collecting ground for some of the Soviet Union's brightest and best and, for the country's young people, the secret police, like the Communist Party, was one means of climbing the ladder to power and privilege.

Such personal contacts were never really benign. A British ambassador of the time became smitten with the laundry maid assigned to the official residence. It emerged some years later that he had arranged a tryst in Leningrad where the KGB just happened to appear, interrupting a good frolic and throwing a wet blanket on the whole affair. I am not aware of the final outcome of the whole matter, but it undoubtedly did not lead to the ambassador's promotion to bigger and better things!

One of the toughest parts of my work was dealing with the occasional defector who managed to penetrate the KGB screen around the Embassy. It was a difficult feat. Uniformed militiamen were on duty twenty-four hours a day at the vehicular entrance beside the building, and also at the solitary door leading into the Embassy. The only possible way to make an unauthorised entry was to watch for a momentary lapse in the guard's attention and then to rush the door. Amazingly enough, some poor souls did manage it. I say 'poor' because the convention in those days was that political asylees were not accepted by any of the embassies. The practical reason, and the one we used to salve any bad conscience over our treatment of the would-be defectors, was that under no circumstances would the Soviet government of the day ever agree to grant safe passage out of the country.

Yet they came. I don't remember how many arrived in the foyer during my three years in Moscow, but perhaps a dozen or more, most of them genuine but with the occasional provocateur thrown in. It generally fell to me to deal with them. The routine was straightforward. The intruder's first utterance almost always was a relieved "Thank God I made it here." The would-be asylee would be conducted to a room in the basement where he would be given some refreshment and time to calm down. I would listen to his story, then explain the realities of the situation to him and suggest that he leave peacefully as soon as possible and try to convince the authorities outside that it had all been an innocent mistake. Most took the advice. Others did not and these were the ones that have always weighed heavily on my conscience.

I can recall at least three who remained for several hours begging for asylum. One was a Ukrainian nationalist just released from the gulag who had with him a large volume he had written about his experiences. He eventually agreed to leave – as an alternative to being forcibly removed – although he left his papers with me. They were forwarded to Ottawa and never heard of again as far as I know. Another was a Jew out of the notorious gulag in Potma, southeast of Moscow. He entered the embassy in the early afternoon and was with us till near midnight. After finally realising that there was no future inside, he agreed to leave. I escorted him to the front door. The image is still clear in my mind. He went out, turned right and began to run up Starokonyushenny (Old Horse) lane. Several KGB agents who had been patiently waiting in the dark alley across the lane gave chase. A Volga sedan pulled up and he was shoved inside in the best tradition of a Stalin spy thriller. Yet another case I clearly remember was a man who similarly refused for several hours to accept our counsel to leave. Towards midnight, I backed my own car up to the rear entrance of the Embassy, got him onto the floor of the back seat as surreptitiously as possible and drove him out the gate past the ever-present militia to Kievsky train station. I was not aware of anyone following us, but was not naïve enough to believe we were not under surveillance. He walked away into the darkness. I am under no illusion as to what the fate of these would-be asylees must have been. Although the gulag system had eased up somewhat ten years earlier after Stalin's death, it still held under the harshest of conditions millions of the condemned throughout the 60's as testimony of man's inhumanity to man.

In retrospect, I have no pride or satisfaction in how these cases were handled. At the time I accepted without question the policy under which we expelled these people from our premises. While we tersely reported most cases to Ottawa, we never asked for instructions or argued the possibility of making an exception in the occasional extreme case. Was our action any less cowardly than that of embassies in previous times who had denied visas and other assistance to Jews whose lives were threatened? Should we have taken deserving persons in on principle even though this might have meant having to accommodate them in the Embassy itself for months or years while attempting to get permission for them to leave? At the end of the day, I am certain that no amount of argument would have moved Ottawa off the established position. I sometimes wonder if, at the very least, I should not have refused to be the instrument for the execution of the policy.

A lot of visitors came to Moscow in those days as an expression of the cautious attempts on both sides to flirt with détente, and one of my principal duties was to look after them. The first batch of Canadian students came in 1964 under an official exchange agreement, and we did our best to provide something of a second home to them. One of them married a Russian student and, to our enormous surprise, succeeded eventually in getting permission for her to accompany him back to Toronto. The greatest opposition to the marriage came from an unexpected quarter, the office of our military attachés, where unholy union with a Russian was considered a treasonous pact with the devil.

The ongoing visitor flow, of course, included scientists, journalists and the usual crop of peaceniks. Among the latter group was a prominent editor of a well-known publication who arrived in the country courtesy of the Canada-Soviet Friendship Society. He showed up in my office late one afternoon to make contact before setting out on a countrywide tour courtesy of the Society. I gave him the usual 'fear-of-the-devil' briefing during which we outlined the perils of consorting with Ivan and Natasha. I could tell his impression was one of: "You people have been reading too many spy novels!"

Some two or three weeks later, once again in the late afternoon, the same Mr. X showed up in my office, but this time looking rather dishevelled. His tie was askew, his shirt collar was dirty and he hadn't shaved for a couple of days. His story went something like this: after leaving the Embassy, Mr. X had gone off to various cities where he had been treated royally. Eventually they arrived in Siberia. Ivan, of the local Friendship chapter, arrived at the hotel and suggested that the following morning, a Sunday, they go out into the countryside for a picnic. Sounded like a good idea. Ivan showed up the next morning in the company of two delectable young Russian women, with a hamper of food and drink. No sooner did they reach the depths of the Siberian forest than Ivan produced a bottle of vodka, suggesting they drink a toast to friendship. No matter that Mr. X was in real life the Reverend X who had taken a temperance oath. Worn down by his host's insistence that he not violate 'Soviet hospitality', the good Reverend first took one, then another and another — until, to use the colloquial term, he was more or less pie-eyed. At this point Ivan announced he was going off into the bush with one of the female companions to conduct hanky panky, intimating that Reverend X might like to try his hand with

Natasha. Shortly thereafter, he remembered that the young lady began screaming, whereupon Colonel Sergei with his merry band of KGB men, who opportunely happened to be in close proximity, emerged from the dark Siberian forest, intent on saving a damsel in distress. The Reverend was conducted to a cabin conveniently located nearby, interrogated, and told that he would probably be charged with attempted rape.

Taken back to his hotel, Reverend X was advised to continue on his Friendship tour and that he would be later contacted to know his fate. By this time, he was gradually turning into a quivering mass of jelly as he contemplated headlines back home, to say nothing of the shock to his wife, children and abstemious church elders. Colonel Sergei duly turned up in a southern Soviet city, where he suggested to the Reverend that in return for writing articles favourable to Mother Russia (becoming a Soviet agent in other words), the attempted rape charges would be dropped. He was told to carry on to Moscow, to scrupulously avoid the Canadian Embassy, and thence to Leningrad where he would receive his final instructions.

Back in Moscow, the Reverend made the first sensible move of his tour and came directly to the Embassy. That is how he happened late one afternoon to show up again in my office. We took X under our wing, immediately secured an airline ticket to get him out the following day, collected his things from the Ukraine hotel and arranged for him to stay overnight in our apartment. The KGB were thick as I accompanied him to the hotel, crowding the lift in such a way as to intimidate. From that point on, we were followed every step of the way. Before leaving for the airport, I briefed him on steps to follow in case the authorities should decide to arrest him, which at the time seemed a not altogether unlikely possibility. The airport waiting room was thick with goons, and it was with considerable trepidation that we waited for X's documents to be processed and returned to him. The system in those days was for all travellers to turn in their papers. They would be called up one by one to get them back, and would then proceed to the departure gate. We waited and waited, until we were the only ones left in the room. I actually thought, "This is it. He's not going to make it." Finally his name was called and we went up to the window where three goons were studying his passport, smirking and sneering. They looked at me and demanded my ID. After a moment, I put my hand through the window and jerked my ID back. The whole thing ended quietly. They handed the Reverend's passport to him. I said to them in Russian, "Thank you for your Soviet hospitality," and accompanied X to the plane.

That was the end of it. The Reverend, so far as I know, went back to Canada and on to bigger and better things. No more of the matter was heard from the Soviets, who simply had to eat their defeat, knowing that if they made any noise about it, it would have had a seriously damaging effect on Soviet-Canadian relations. So they lost this one. In the Embassy, we asked ourselves, "How many other such encounters did they win?"

The Cold War notwithstanding, relations were showing the tiniest signs of thaw. This was reflected in the increase in exchanges of academic, scientific and governmental individuals and groups. In June of 1965, Canada's Minister of Northern Affairs, Arthur Lang, accompanied by his Parliamentary Secretary, John Turner, came to the Soviet Union at the head of a small delegation headed for the Soviet north. This was to be the first chapter of an exchange that would see the Soviets send a similar group up to Canada's Arctic. Arthur Lang was a kindly old gentleman who believed in the innate goodness of mankind and who could not conceive of the Soviets doing such things as putting a microphone in his room or a young maiden in his bed. Our security briefing was entirely lost on him. Fortunately, John Turner was the exact opposite, hardheaded, articulate and not about to be taken in by the various tricks in the Soviet bag. Where Minister Lang would nod agreeably as his hosts employed various impolite descriptions of our American allies, Turner would stand his ground and reiterate the strength of our commitment to NATO including the U.S. Nothing could persuade Lang of his hosts' ulterior motives: not the bogus delays as they attempted to prevent us from reaching our various destinations, not the copious quantities of vodka trotted out for breakfast, lunch and dinner, nor the surveillance cameras poking out the windows of all the buildings surrounding our hotel in Norilsk, the northernmost city in Russia constructed entirely with slave labour. The most indelible element of the journey was a river voyage from the small town of Khandiga, far to the east of Yakutsk, down the Aldan to visit an operation, again constructed by captive labour under horrific conditions, where coal was mined amid permafrost. The trip was memorable. Most of our group were totally in their cups as we made our way to the wharf and were poured onto the steamer.

Two or three hundred people, probably all of whom had never seen a foreigner before, let alone a Westerner, streamed along the bank for a kilometre or so, waving goodbye to the Canadian visitors.

Meanwhile, on the boat, the Soviet comrades had more important things to attend to. They busied themselves propping Lang up on the deck, adorning him with a red Young Pioneer scarf and other Soviet paraphernalia, and snapping photos for propaganda purposes. At this point I intervened and told the leader that under no circumstances should they even think of publishing the photos unless they wished to seriously embarrass the Minister and undermine the goodwill created by the visit. Everyone then retired to their cabins to try to sleep it off, including myself and Jack Best of the Canadian Press in Moscow. No sooner had we lain down on the bunks than there was a loud knock on the door and six comrades, four men and two women entered. With them they had bottles of vodka and cognac. "Come," they said, "We want to drink a toast with you!" Jack, who could hold his liquor better than most, was all for entering the fray, but I smelled a rat immediately. "Not with me", I said. I categorically refused to take a drop and rather filled a glass with water and raised it. The comrades of course in the classic Soviet pose claimed offence and sent for the captain of the steamer who arrived on the scene to propose a vodka toast to Canada-Soviet friendship — in which, I suppose, he figured we could not refuse to join. He figured wrong. I steadfastly refused to touch a drop. My assumption all through this episode, probably correct, was that the main target of our friends was to get hold of the notes I had been taking all through the trip, some of which related to military targets.

I digress here to touch on the subject of espionage. Did Canadians spy? After all, the staff of the majority of embassies in Ottawa included intelligence agents. And we Canadians? Were we naïve? Generations of diplomats and officials have proclaimed with as much virtue and self-righteousness as they could muster that Canada did *not* spy. Yes, we did have the Royal Canadian Mounted Police Security and Intelligence Service, but Canadian activity was 'purely defensive' in nature. That line, of course, was pure bunkum and self-delusion.

Espionage back in the 60's and earlier was largely primitive by today's standards. Yes, even the communications of other states in those days could be monitored, even if not necessarily successfully. But espionage could also entail the simple act of venturing forth to collect information secretly. From the perspective of the KGB, some Canadians attached to the mission certainly were regarded as spies and treated as such by Soviet counter-surveillance. The Soviet state in those days was closed tighter than a drum. We knew little of what ordinary people in Moscow, let alone in the countryside, were thinking. Google Earth had not arrived to give us a street-level view of cities around the world. The job of the KGB was to do everything possible to prevent its 'enemies' from penetrating that secrecy, but try we did.

The Naval, Air and Military attachés attached to the Embassy travelled as much as possible to see what they could see. This normally was not very much, since the Soviet authorities controlled their movements so closely. Occasionally, one or other would overstep the limits of the acceptable and be declared *persona non grata*. We civilian political officers would also travel when possible, but had considerably more latitude given that we could cast our journeys as cultural, or consular, or for the purpose of meeting specified organisations. The deal was that we had to request permission forty-eight hours in advance in order to travel more than twenty-five miles outside Moscow (in reality, more than one-third of the territory inside that circle was also off limits). The game was, in consultation with External, the RCMP and National Defence, to keep a steady flow of travel requests going to the Soviets, including requests for places from which we knew foreigners were excluded. This ensured that our own people in Ottawa had a ready file of Soviet refusals to use as tit-for-tat for barring Soviet Embassy people from visiting certain areas in Canada.

And so it was that before undertaking a journey outside of Moscow in those days, we political types would also consult the voluminous files of the Joint Intelligence Committee, based in London and Ottawa, from which we would obtain a detailed layout of the town to be visited, as well as a list of outstanding questions relating to the precise location of military, police, security and other government buildings. We would then, in addition to whatever the formal mission of our trip was, scour the town on foot, dutifully noting the desired addresses when we could find them. We would also note the insignia of troops we encountered, since these could give an indication of the type of activity in the area, take note of the availability of consumer goods, check on the state of the harvest and so on. Did this constitute spying? Of course it did by every definition in the Soviet dictionary, and perhaps a few others, even if the efforts were rather amateurish. Only in the last decade or so as the spies of the Cold War have turned their hand to writing, have we learned how very little of what went on in the Soviet Union we actually knew, how shallow our penetration of the minds of the Soviet top brass, how flawed Western intelligence analysis was. But in the frigid atmosphere of the times the Soviets regarded our activities as espionage. We, in turn, felt virtuous as we tramped the blustery streets in the service of democracy.

Returning to the trip with Lang and Turner, as we ventured into places like the uranium-mining city of Norilsk above the Arctic Circle where no Westerners had previously trod, I kept meticulous note of what I saw, carefully writing this down and securing the small sheets in a belt worn around my waist under my clothes. I had no doubt that the belt was what our would-be drinking companions from the ship's crew were after. Jack Best and I put an end to the whole charade when we both picked up glasses of water and drank a toast to friendship, with the comrades abstaining. I opened the cabin door and said 'do svidanye' (goodbye). They abruptly filed out, unsmiling; I locked the door and we turned in.

The rest of the journey passed in something of an alcoholic fog, interrupted periodically by a dreadful hangover on the part of delegation members. I'm not so sure that these scientific exchanges produced any immediate scientific gain, but I suppose that over the long run they were politically useful and did serve to tear a small rent in the veil of secrecy surrounding the workers' paradise.

I was always delighted to make these excursions. They provided an unparalleled opportunity to see aspects of Soviet life that few others managed to see in those days. When a Canadian parliamentary delegation arrived in 1965, I accompanied members in their call on Soviet Premier Alexei Kosygin, who personally authorised two of their number with roots in Soviet territory to visit their ancestral villages. So it was that I rode an overnight train together with former Conservative minister Michael Starr deep into 'closed' country (closed in the sense that foreigners were not normally permitted to travel there) in the Ukraine south of Kiev. Then further by automobile for several hours along gravel roads, to be greeted at the end of our journey by a large and joyous crowd of Starr relatives, all ecstatic at the chance to greet this native son who had made good in far-off Canada. However, it was not clear whether the crowd was more amazed by the sight of Starr speaking to them in Ukrainian, or of the massive tables groaning under the weight of cold cuts, salads, caviar, vodka and all manner of luxury items obviously imported for the occasion from some commissar's store, but more specifically intended to give Starr the impression that this was how happy Ukrainian peasants normally lived. Actually the occasion was a bit of a tearjerker, for me as much as for Starr, as this emotional and never-to-be-repeated encounter wrapped up and farewells were said.

A few days later I set off with Senator David Croll, whose roots were in Byelorussia, for his village. This time we made the lengthy journey entirely by car, accompanied by our minders. The outcome was not quite as well orchestrated as that set up for Starr. Arriving in the dusty little village where the inhabitants seemed to be spending more time lying about than working in the communal fields, we located with some difficulty the small house of Croll's aunt. Word had not gotten through about our visit and she, to put it mildly, was totally taken aback to have this apparition from the outside world descend on her. The conversation was a bit painful as the good aunt, not having been briefed as to what was permissible and what was not, kept looking to the minders for some kind of psychic guidance. Croll's several queries about his uncle were ignored or turned aside, and envoys sent out to locate him returned empty-handed. Auntie eventually confided, "He takes the money every month and spends it on booze." She allowed as to how Uncle was a no good bum who drank up every kopek he could get his hands on. The conversation was taking a decidedly unintended turn and the minders applied themselves furiously to returning it to a recital of grain production figures and other healthy Soviet themes. Just as they began to succeed, the door banged open and in lurched Uncle himself, totally in his cups, at eleven in the morning. A rather incoherent exchange followed, Uncle inviting the good Senator to have a little snort. Now this was rather ironic. Under normal circumstances, it was the Soviet minders who insisted on plying their visitors with vodka, whereas on this occasion they were doing their absolute best to banish both Uncle and bottle from the scene. Uncle, of course, in his condition was unable to comprehend who

Senator Croll was or whether Canada was a country or a nearby planet, and the minders decided that our visit should be cut short. Minus the happy peasant-table-groaning-with-goodies routine, we headed back to Moscow.

Those were exciting days. Even then, but especially looking back, we consider ourselves to have been privileged to spend our first assignment in the Soviet Union. The Cuban missile crisis was just behind us, the Cold War still in deep freeze, but the first tentative signs of détente were in the air. We followed the politics closely; we painstakingly scrutinised every announcement and official photo to come out of the Kremlin in an attempt to detect any change in the power structure. We tried, mainly without success, to burrow into the minds of the political leadership hoping to divine their thinking and goals. In the 60's, the country was pure enigma, shrouded in mystery and speculation. Travel was severely restricted. How did Ivan and Natasha live? What were their thoughts? Did they really believe the propaganda they were constantly fed? What was the state of the harvest? How were the collective farms functioning? Were there any signs of unrest? We ourselves lived and moved in a diplomatic bubble, but nonetheless, you can't rub shoulders with people on the street or ride the crowded subway to work without something rubbing off. Our biggest challenge was to try to penetrate the mask. And so we grasped at the slightest opening and tried to drive in a wedge.

Travel formed a good portion of my duties in the Embassy, either simply to observe the political and social scene around the country, or to deal with consular cases. This was paradise for me, the most memorable and fulfilling part of my time in the Soviet Union. I was privileged to make a number of these journeys with Godfrey Hearn, senior to me and an absolutely first-rate officer. We had a marvellous time, trekking through the gloomy streets of Archangel and Murmansk in the middle of January where the cold froze the tears on your eyelids, and keeping our blood moving with the occasional draught of vodka from a hip flask. We checked the shops for the availability of foodstuffs and other supplies, tested security in the vicinity of various naval installations and paid official visits to several Soviet institutions. In our three or four free evenings, we dined at the hotel restaurant where there were no redeeming features in terms of décor or menu. The main value, however, was in the opportunity to sit at the same table with other hotel guests where eventually an overdose of vodka served as an icebreaker.

The routine went like this. Soviet dining rooms were set up in tables of six or eight, and the idea was that each table would be fully occupied before diners could sit down at another empty one. From our perspective, this was ideal. We would hover around the entrance, where we waited until we spotted a table partially occupied with congenial and interesting looking types, whereupon we would enter and claim two seats. This was the one contingency that the KGB had not prepared for. Soviet dining room service being as dreadful as it was, one could count on a good three to four hours to get through the full meal. This was more than adequate for our purposes.

We would usually start things off by ordering two hundred grams of vodka for ourselves. The process of icebreaking thus begun, it was further accelerated when we pulled out packs of Western cigarettes and lit up. Neither of us had ever smoked, but there was nothing like passing the pack around the table to dissolve the remaining reserve. Copious portions of vodka and cognac, this time for the whole table, did the trick, and we were able to settle down to a full evening of discussion with our newfound friends. In fact, these sessions provided us with delightful and valuable insights into everyday life in whatever area we happened to find ourselves. The only damper on the evening was the invariable presence of KGB agents at a nearby table of whom we were very conscious even if our dining partners were not. People, when loosened up, were invariably very friendly and excited to meet foreigners, so much so that not infrequently one or other would invite us to visit their home. The temptation to accept was almost irresistible, but we seldom succumbed, simply because we were always conscious of the grilling by the KGB our contacts would have to endure after our departure.

Of course, the table arrangements could work two ways. On one occasion, in the grimy little town of Tula, south of Moscow, we had just seated ourselves with one chair still unoccupied, when a voluptuous blonde appeared at the dining room entrance. Godfrey looked at me and said, "She has to be for us!" Sure enough, she marched directly to our table. This was such a textbook manoeuvre that we could scarcely contain our smirks. We actually had a rather enjoyable evening. Although little doubt was left as to her employers or her intentions, the lady was quite entertaining and we enjoyed the evening thoroughly.

What did we learn? We heard a great deal of grumbling about the poor harvests, the scarcity of foodstuffs and other consumer items. We experienced the frustration of average Soviet citizens with their system, and particularly with their inability to see the outside world for themselves. We learned of the deep-seated hunger for material goods and dissatisfaction with shoddy materials. These trips provided a window on everyday life in the Soviet countryside and in the far-flung republics. This today might not seem like such a big deal, but in the era of the 60's, such journeys and contacts provided us with insights in living colour that were otherwise impossible to come up with.

Once when driving our Russian Volga to Helsinki, I made an involuntary stop in the small town of Chudovo when the screws holding the carburetor together all popped loose and the car ground to a halt. The small crowd that gathered to deal with my predicament could not believe that I would have purchased a Soviet vehicle when any other choice was available to me. The militarisation of society was everywhere apparent, as was the all-pervasive influence of the KGB, even in the tiniest hamlet. Evidence of ethnic discontent and anti-Russian feeling was present in spades in the Baltic states and Central Asian Republics. I vividly recall mixing with Soviet officials from Georgia and Azerbaijan who always protested far too loudly and without provocation of the depth of Soviet solidarity in their respective homelands. I also recall the not-so-subtle grumbling of Latvians and Estonians during our visits to Riga and Tallinn regarding the loudspeakers blaring in Russian on their main streets. But we were, all us Westerners, too blinded by what we perceived as the invincibility of Soviet power and control to read the signs and foresee with any clarity the utter collapse that would occur three decades later. Not even a glimmer of the coming drama crossed our minds.

Interspersed with adventure, the political kaleidoscope continued to turn. We had arrived in 1963 on the heels of the Cuban missile crisis. The construction of the Berlin Wall was only two years behind us. Relations between the Soviet Union and the West were tense, to put it mildly. In the autumn of our first year, President Kennedy was assassinated. The moment we heard the news I recall clearly. We were partying in the basement of the Embassy with a visiting hockey team on November 22, 1963 when former Detroit Red Wing great, Ted Lindsay, arrived with the news. Interesting was the Soviet reaction, both official and on the street. Theirs, like ours, was one of absolute shock. People wept — in spite of a near Third World War as a result of the Kennedy-Khrushchev face-off over Cuba. Even the militiaman on the Embassy gate that night expressed his sympathy, as if Kennedy were Canada's president too. The Kennedy family and Camelot had caught the imagination of average Russians. Nonetheless, the sympathetic tone in the media quickly gave way to criticism, and the assassination was presented as the logical consequence of the corruption and criminality of capitalist society.

The next political milestone was the unseating of Khrushchev himself in 1964, which in some ways was just as shocking to those of us in Moscow as had been the death of Kennedy. After all, it was Khrushchev who sewed the seeds of liberalisation in 1956 with his attack on Stalin's excesses. He it was who agreed to the first test ban treaty. He it was who triggered the initial and momentous split with the Chinese. In hindsight it can be said that Khrushchev's impact on Soviet society was second only to that of Mikhail Gorbachev, whose perestroika eventually led to the collapse of the system. Ironically, it was largely Krushchev's eccentric peasant antics on the international scene that embarrassed the Soviet brass and contributed to his removal as leader of the so-called peasant and worker state. This was an event that took us by surprise, in spite of our diligent pursuit of the pseudo-science of Kremlinology. We spent hours each month pouring over group photographs in the Soviet media and in reading the entrails in an effort to stay on top of who in the Soviet hierarchy was "hot" and who was "not". Khrushchev's fall astonished us, but the subsequent months breathed new life into "kremlinology" as we tried to figure out the new configuration of power.

I remember well the day Khrushchev fell. That morning I rode on the subway, packed as always with people on the way to work. Everyone had his or her newspaper. The change in leadership was mentioned only in a brief paragraph at the bottom of page 1 in *Pravda*, but Russians were well accustomed to learning of big events in small print. Absolute silence. No conversation. No show of either surprise or emotion. And so ended the era of Nikita Khrushchev, unsung and unremarked. He reputedly had a flat in the building next to the Embassy on Starokonyushenny Pereulok. I saw him once on the street, an old man shuffling along unnoticed. He died in 1971 and was buried in a modest grave in the grounds of Novodyevichy monastery. Ironically, his son later migrated to the United States where he is a university professor.

The overall social gloom was pierced now and again by flashes of humour. Soviet society was politicised in the peculiar fashion that affects people in totalitarian states. Political jokes were common, spoken only in an undertone, and we heard most of these from contacts like Rita and Sasha who were KGB. For example, Sasha told the story of the man who was arrested while running around Red Square, shouting: "Khrushchev is an idiot!" He was taken to court and sentenced to twenty-five years' hard labour: five for running around naked – and twenty for giving away a state secret! Another one: A man is walking down Gorky Street and spies someone struggling to climb out of an open manhole. When he looks more closely, he sees that it is Stalin. He gives him a hand up after which Stalin says: "What can I do for you? Anything!" The good Samaritan replies, "There is only one thing. Whatever you do, don't tell anyone I pulled you out."

There were other, more practical events that struck us Westerners as humorous, but not the Russians. For example, after the split with China, all Chinese students studying in Russia were expelled. Travelling by special train, they disembarked at the last station on the Soviet side of the border, unzipped, and contemptuously peed on the station platform. For Russians, so attached to the idea of conducting oneself in a *kulturny* (cultured) fashion, nothing could have been more calculated to piss them off!

Such was life in the Soviet Union. As a family, we survived and thrived. We arrived in Moscow with two boys under two, and left three years later with the addition of a one-year old daughter and a two-year old Airedale terrier. Diplomatic life was new and exciting for us. Our existence was anything but dull, as we mingled with people from a hundred nations, as we picnicked on the shores of the Moscow River and as we made excursions near and far. Wonderfully preserved historic towns such as Vladimir and Suzdal, Yaroslavl and Zagorsk, were open to us and we took full advantage of such opportunities. There is nothing quite like the sight in deep winter of a *kremlin*, or ancient fortress, on the bank of a frozen river, silhouetted against the forbidding forest with snow gently sifting down, the smell of wood smoke in the air, and a Russian peasant in his padded jacket and felt boots, ear flaps flapping, driving a horse and sledge through the late afternoon gloom. In spite of everything, Tolstoy's Russia was still alive and we considered ourselves only too fortunate to have been able to add that to our treasure trove of memories.

As a junior diplomat on his first posting, I could not have wished for a more exciting or invigorating slot. The Soviet empire was at its peak and its grip seemed, at that moment in time, unbreakable.

We were locked around the globe in a life-and-death struggle with the forces of repression, and there I was in the middle of it. All the preconceived notions I held on arrival were only reinforced by my time on the ground. In interacting with the Soviet bureaucracy, I learned a good deal about negotiating in the bazaar, about navigating the twists and turns of the Byzantine world of diplomacy and about the evil and misery that absolute power can generate. I left Moscow a more committed cold warrior than ever. It was only many years later, after the collapse of the Soviet empire, that I was able to clear my mind of much debris, stand back, look at history and realise that the world does not, and never did, consist only of black and white, but of many shades of grey.

In July of 1966, we took our leave, and not without sadness. There was Anya, who so diligently helped out with domestic chores and the children; vivacious and good-humoured Natasha, who tutored us in the language; Rita and Sasha whose company we thoroughly enjoyed, and many more. We often said that Russians, stripped of the ideological veneer imposed on them by the Soviet state, were among the most hospitable people on earth. They still occupy a warm place in our hearts and time has not erased their memory. From the old days, only Natasha remains, amazingly enough (at the time of writing in December 2009) still teaching Russian to Canadians in the Embassy. There was good friend George Costakis, the Embassy's inefficient local administrator, with a heart of gold, and even more notably the owner of a most amazing collection of outstanding art, literally worth millions. (George Costakis single-handedly, and in the face of considerable difficulties, collected and saved Russian avant-garde art by painters such as Chagall and Kandinsky for the world. His paintings now form part of the permanent collection at the State Museum of Contemporary Art in Greece, the State Tretyakov Gallery in Moscow and have been displayed in museums around the world.) And there was the smoothly functioning team at the Embassy under Ford's leadership.

From Moscow we flew to Amsterdam, where we boarded the good ship *Nieuw Amsterdam* en route to Halifax. The end of another era. This was the last sea cruise we would take at government expense since, shortly thereafter, travel by air became mandatory.

Bill (right) and Laine travelling by ship to their first posting in Moscow, 1963. On the left is Tim Williams, Bill's Foreign Service colleague, on the way to his first posting in Germany.

Bill and Laine with sons Tom (middle) and Scott, and their Russian dog, Sasha, Moscow, 1964.

Bill and Scott with the trusty family VW and its diplomatic plates, in front of their Moscow apartment, 1964. Bill marked the Warden apartment windows with an x.

The Warden family, now bigger by one with the arrival of daughter Lisa, travelling back to Canada by ship in 1966.

*The Canadian Embassy hockey team in action in
Moscow, 1960s. Bill takes a shot on goal.*

*Bill (front row, second from left) with the Canadian Embassy hockey team.
Peter Worthington, a reporter in Moscow at the time, dons the 007 jersey.*

*Bill in Moscow at the USSR-Canada Friendship
Society, not looking particularly friendly.*

Bill and son Tom enjoying Bill's new hobby, Ottawa, 1967.

Chapter Four

HAVANA MISSION

Cuba. Gem of the Caribbean. Rogue nation. The very name conjured up all sorts of vivid images including playground of the American mafia, and domain of the dictator Fulgencio Batista. Then came the Revolution of Fidel Castro in 1959 and the failed attempt by Cuban exiles and the CIA to overthrow him two years later. But all of this was eclipsed by the drama and near catastrophe of the Missile Crisis in 1962.

After having been exposed to Soviet Communism and its East German version, it seemed only logical that Cuba should be next on our list. And indeed it was. If I had been given *carte blanche* to choose our next posting, Havana would have been it. As it turned out, I did need to lobby – but not too much. The Department, in its normally impenetrable wisdom, made the choice for me. We used to reckon that the surest way to avoid being sent somewhere was to have some expertise on a given country and, particularly, to know the language. As for Cuba, it could be said that I had neither – which qualified me eminently for the post. However, I did by then have a fair knowledge of how Communism worked, and that was an overriding factor. The other two deficiencies could be remedied.

On returning to Ottawa from Moscow in the summer of 1966, I was assigned to Defence Liaison (2) Division, which was the group responsible for processing intelligence in and out of the Department. That the job required stratospheric levels of security clearance did not prevent it from being a big yawn, sorting out reams of reports principally from the US and UK, but also from Australia and New Zealand. My job worked like this: every day in my stuffy, window-less office in the East Block of the Parliament Buildings, I received hundreds of intelligence documents, many of them actual intercepts of conversations and messages of foreign governments and individuals. I would go through these documents and try to sort out the wheat from the chaff, picking out the few of relevance to our people in Foreign Affairs. This was highly classified stuff and only a very limited number of officers were designated to see it. I would decide who among the privileged class of the 'indoctrinated' should see what, then load it up in a secure case and traipse around the various offices scattered throughout the downtown core, wait while the material was read by the designated officer, and then carry it back to my office.

Most of the stuff was a total bore, and often received too late to be of burning interest, but occasionally a piece would make my day. For example, at that time we (by "we", I mean the intelligence community at large) were intercepting messages between the headquarters of the Shah's secret police in Iran and its agents. The whole operation was rather ironic in that Savak, as the organisation was known, was largely the creation of the Americans, and was riddled with agents closely aligned to the U.S. Nevertheless, it was felt necessary to monitor their communications. I recall one message from an agent in a far-flung province addressed to the Supreme Leader reporting on a dinner the visiting Soviet Premier Kosygin was attending with the Governor of the province and his wife. The agent recounted in colourful detail how Kosygin, after drinking copious amounts, had put his hand on the thigh of Madame Governor, under the table of course, and proceeded to induce her to a state of considerable animation ("dancing with her breasts"). You have to remember that attitudes in the 60's about such things were quite conservative, to put it mildly. Titillating stuff, obviously. Otherwise how would the images and precise words be so thoroughly fixed in my memory to this day? When I, with embarrassment, showed the item to the Divisional Director, he became red in the face and said that certainly such things should not be shown to anyone else – himself excepted, of course. One can only imagine how the Shah reacted.

Another series of messages that attracted considerable interest was one generated by tapping into the communication system of the Soviet elite travelling in their luxurious ZiL limousines between the Kremlin and their *dachas*. I don't recall the specifics of the messages, which in any event tended to be rather terse and without a lot of serious content, given the Soviets' extreme devotion to secrecy. Nonetheless, it was interesting to read the casual chitchat of the enigmatic wielders of power in the Kremlin. While the penetration of this particular communications network was considered quite a coup at the time, the reality was that the product was largely useless. Indeed the likelihood was that Soviet counter-intelligence itself, which proved itself far more adept at the spy game, was fully aware of the operation and used it to feed false leads to the West.

Life for us as a family in Ottawa was very agreeable, but service at home base itself had few redeeming features. Looking back, I see my service there over three assignments totalling eight years as something of a black hole. It couldn't be avoided and one had to make the best of it. There were those among us who aspired to positions of power in the Public Service and for them time in Ottawa was the key, but others, myself included, were more interested in roaming the world, and serving abroad was our goal.

Accordingly, no sooner was I settled in DL (2) than I began to contemplate my next assignment abroad. On speculation I took up Spanish studies, which I rather more enjoyed than the mandatory French lessons. For some reason or other, the pronunciation was easier and, with Spanish, I found that if you didn't know a word, you could usually produce a reasonable facsimile of the Spanish version by adding "...*mente*" or some such. At one point I used to pride myself, facetiously, on being able to improvise a talk to a mixed group of, on the one hand, Spanish-speakers who knew no English and, on the other, English-speakers who knew no Spanish – and have them all understand perfectly well what I was saying. Apart from working on the language, preparation involved immersing oneself in the Department's Cuba files, in various intelligence reports and, of course, in discussion with those Havana alumni who happened to be in Ottawa. The whole crowd of us could best be described as 'reactionary' in the political terminology of the day, more attuned to the aspirations of the exile communities in Canada and Miami. Like the others, I myself, well conditioned by life in Berlin and Moscow, tended to interpret everything in the light of Cold War dualism; Castro was a Soviet ally and threat and, therefore, the enemy.

I was very happy when, in the middle of 1967, I was formally notified that I should begin to prepare myself for a posting to Cuba. The decision was not totally without reservations. My bosses in DL(2), for obvious reasons, were not very happy about sending a person directly from the Division to a Communist country.

One brief episode occurred just prior to our departure, which served to remind me rather dramatically that I was headed back onto the front lines of the Cold War. My habit in those days was to leave my office in the East Block of the Parliament Buildings around 5:30 pm and stroll some three blocks to where I parked my car behind the railway station. One afternoon, I left work and was about to cross the street at the intersection of Rideau and Sussex, when I noticed a black car stop momentarily. It took just a moment and it was only by pure coincidence that I happened to notice the occupant of the right front seat pick up a camera, point it in my direction and presumably snap a shot. Even then, my first reaction was to suppose that the photographer was simply taking a picture up Wellington Street, although why that perspective should have any tourist value rather puzzled me. The whole thing took about five seconds, after which the car moved on. I was interested enough to look at the licence plate, which turned out to be diplomatic and, on further checking, turned out to be Soviet. I duly reported the incident to the RCMP Security Service and was informed that, yes, I had been photographed by an intelligence agent from the Soviet Embassy and that, indeed, the RCMP themselves had been following the vehicle and had observed the incident. Presumably the Soviets sent the photo on to their Havana Embassy to include in their gallery of mug shots of Western diplomats.

Getting to Havana in those days was half the fun. With the island cut off for the most part by the U.S. embargo, there were only two practical routes from Canada to Cuba. One was via the twice-weekly flights on Cubana Airlines from Mexico City, and the other was to fly to Miami, thence to Nassau, and take the weekly flight on an old DC-3 of Bahamas Airways, chartered by the British and Canadian embassies. Nassau, of course, was the preferred route with the required overnight stay on the luxurious isle in the sun. On our first flight into Havana, on which the five Wardens, accompanied by our faithful dog Sasha, were the only passengers, we were somewhat amused, if not taken aback, when the captain climbed into the left-hand seat and was overheard to confide to his co-pilot: "Jeez, it's been years since I've flown one of these things!" Apparently the

Bahamas pilots who normally flew big jets would occasionally book themselves onto the DC-3 flight to Havana as something of a lark.

We arrived in Cuba in July 1968, and thereby embarked on what was to be one of the most enjoyable postings of my career. However, that judgement lay in the future as we rode from the airport into the city on our first day. It was mid-day and unbelievably hot and sticky. The sight of dilapidated, pot-holed streets, empty shops and buildings in dire need of repair, and people lolling about without much apparent purpose in life was rather depressing. We went straight to the home of the couple we were to succeed where we sweltered through lunch with no electricity to power the air conditioners. After that, we were delivered to the *Habana Libre* (formerly Hilton) Hotel that was to be our home for the next several weeks. Also without air conditioning and most other amenities, the hotel stay nonetheless turned out to be one of those memorable interludes, the outstanding compensation being a luxury suite at the very top of the building where we occupied a full half of the twenty-fourth floor. The views of the city and the sea were glorious. On a typical mid-summer Caribbean afternoon one could observe on one side of the hotel people scurrying for cover from a sudden downpour, while on the other *Habaneros* were basking in bright sunshine. Hotel meals were a challenge as we tried to satisfy the appetites of our 3-, 5- and 7-year-old children, since even the most elementary items such as bread, peanut butter, milk and Alpha-Bits were lacking. We explored the streets around the hotel on foot, joined the long line for the one luxury that existed in the city, Coppelia ice cream, and discovered in short order how delightful and friendly the people

could be. Our blonde three-year-old daughter was an instant hit —
even though she objected strenuously to being patted on the head
so frequently — and she opened many doors for us.

In the suite, we wished the walls could talk as we imagined the
colourful figures from days past, from Meyer Lansky to Che
Guevara, who might have occupied this luxurious accommodation.
After all, Fidel himself had allegedly lived in the same exact suite
during the first years of the Revolution. Years later, my most vivid
image of our stay in the *Habana Libre* was of our daughter Lisa's
freshly laundered bloomers blowing off the balcony one afternoon in
the gust preceding a thundershower, and floating down twenty-four
floors into the hands of some unseen but undoubtedly grateful child.

The Embassy, located in the lovely old Cubanacan quarter of
Havana, had a small staff. We led an isolated existence. Mexico was
the only other country from the Western hemisphere represented
in Havana. The British were our closest friends, while a few other
European countries had small, often one- or two-person missions,
in contrast to the enormous embassies of the communist countries
— with whom we did not fraternise. There were no tourists in those
days, and very few visitors. An occasional Canadian businessman
would show up, as would ideologically motivated travellers. The
resident Canadian community consisted of a few long-term communists as well as a handful of others who had stayed on after the
Revolution. A measure of our less than vibrant social environment
was the Sunday afternoon when all of us from the Embassy decided

for 'excitement' to attend the eightieth birthday of a Canadian communist, Bill Faulkner, who had come to Cuba a decade earlier with his daughter, Elsie, to celebrate Fidel's Revolution. Inveterate cold warriors that we were, we nonetheless saw little inconsistency in mixing socially with the ideological Canadian 'fellow travellers' whom we occasionally came across. Indeed, the latter were the ones who acquired guilt feelings for appearing on our doorstep now and then to collect whatever 'capitalist' crumbs, such as a bottle of Canadian Club whiskey, we might let 'fall' from our table.

Apart from supporting certain export interests and trying to negotiate compensation for companies whose facilities had been nationalised, Canada's focus was primarily political. The high technology of the intelligence trade was in its infancy. The way you found out what was going on in a country was, as in the Soviet Union, by getting out and talking to people, by travelling and observing firsthand. With no American diplomatic presence on the ground, the British and ourselves were the overt eyes and ears of the English-speaking West. And so we reported at length on Fidel's pronouncements, on changes in the hierarchy, on the Soviet presence, on people's attitudes and on the economy and how it was affecting the daily lives of Cubans.

There was plenty to report. The year 1968 was the summer of discontent in Czechoslovakia. Soviet forces invaded the country and, in a most uncommon scene in Castro's Cuba, the large resident Czech community mounted a protest march through downtown Havana. Both they and the rest of us were kept in suspense for several days as Castro mulled over how to react. In the end, the

Soviets' powerful economic weapon, its million-dollar-a-day aid to the island, was decisive and the resident Czechs were put firmly in their place. Interesting for us was that during that very brief interlude the curtain dropped, and we found ourselves suddenly meeting and conversing as allies and friends with the normally closed Czech community.

In terms of contact with the local community, Cuba was incomparably more satisfying to us than had been our Soviet experience. Whereas Soviet citizens posed a blank wall, Cubans were irrepressible Latinos and largely happy to talk to us. At least this was true of many in the community. For instance, there was a small group of the old guard known as *gusanos* (worms), generally anti-Castro, who had stayed on and were particularly eager to cultivate Western diplomats and coax whatever material benefits, especially booze, friendship might bestow. Then there were the artists and writers and professionals, many of them solidly on Castro's side, but who took pride in their ability to move freely among those of us from the West. There were also other avenues for contact. We, for example, faithfully attended a Presbyterian Church on Calle Santa Felicia in Old Havana, attending their services and socials and occasional weekend gatherings without impediment. This in turn generated contacts with the seminary in Matanzas and its 'progressive' clergy, who struggled to extract whatever redeeming features they could from the government's Marxist thrust. Otherwise, Cuban Christians were severely marginalised by the regime and the good people of Santa Felicia were delighted to welcome us to their congregation. Ordinary citizens were usually approachable, although such contacts were hampered by the pervasive awareness of the ever-present Committees for the Defence of the Revolution in virtually every block of the city. Senior government officials we met only as necessity dictated and never socially in their homes. For example, the Vice-Minister of Foreign Affairs, Antonio Carrillo, lived a few houses down the avenue from our home, and our children often played together. We tried on a number of occasions, unsuccessfully, to strike up a social relationship with Carrillo and his wife.

The children had perhaps the most normal existence of any of us since they were able to play with whatever Cuban children were in the neighbourhood. Occasionally this deteriorated into warfare, as on the occasion when we found our boys engaged in a rock-throwing melee with the Vice-Minister's son. In the heat of the battle our by then six-year old, Scott, was overheard uttering the prayer, "Jesus help me! Jesus help me!", whereupon the next rock he launched found its mark right on the forehead of Carillo's son – score one for the Christians – thereby threatening to precipitate a diplomatic incident.

Ours was a curious existence, rather one of love-hate. We were 'loved' by the Cuban state because we had maintained relations with them in defiance of the American embargo, but at the same time 'hated' because we were capitalists and representative of a system the Cuban Revolution was even then trying to destroy through its material support of guerrilla movements in Latin America and other parts of the world. The whole relationship was unusual, if not at times unsettling, in that we might go through several incarnations in the same day: attending an official cultural event showcasing the Revolution, followed by a visit to a Canadian, Ronald Lippert, incarcerated in La Cabana prison for anti-state activities, followed by a meeting with a Cuban dissident who wanted to pass on sensitive information.

Two welcome changes from life in Moscow were the much less intrusive surveillance, and the freedom to travel anywhere. We took good advantage of this and lost no time in getting out to the countryside and the gorgeous beaches as yet untrammelled by tourists. It was not long before we discovered the flip side and realised that all travel was not so simple. Some months after our arrival, we set out to spend a long weekend on the Isle of Pines off Cuba's southern coast, some six hours by ferry. The return ferry left at midnight, which meant sitting up all night. Some hours after our departure we realised that we were not moving, and learned that the ship had moved no more than several hundred yards from the dock before grounding firmly on a sandbar. There we sat. No food, no drink. After sun-up, three tugs tried to pull us every which way, but the ferry would not budge. A very restless and uncomfortable twelve hours ensued (half the passengers had nowhere to sit, with the males required to stand on the lower deck in what I termed 'bilge class'), following which we were transferred to another smaller craft.

Predictably, ferry no. 2 broke down after a couple of hours. A small tug eventually appeared and then pulled us ever so slowly to the port of Batabano. From there it was a long wait for a standing-room-only bus to Havana, thence another bus across the city, and finally a fifteen-minute walk late at night, each of us dragging two large suitcases. We could not call anyone for assistance for the simple reason that the telephones did not work. A trip that should have taken seven hours stretched out to twenty-six!

One very positive outcome did emerge from the journey. Prior to our departure, the children had begged us, "Please bring us back a parrot!"[4] The Isle of Pines was well known for its parrot population, but their depleted numbers had led to a ban on their removal. At the hotel where we stayed, we jokingly said to the elderly concierge, "If you ever come across a stray parrot, send it to us." To our enormous surprise, several months later there was a knock at our door in Havana and there stood the concierge with a satchel from which emanated infant chirping sounds. He had brought with him several chicks, one of which he extracted and left with us. Promptly named *Josefina*, the chick from the Isle of Pines took up residence and became mistress of the house, greeting each dawn with loud shrieks from her wrought-iron cage in the garden and cajoling the household into carrying out her every wish. Her relationship with Laine was very loving from the get-go. Sasha the Airedale was totally intimidated by Josefina, who would wander around the house and garden freely most of the day. Suzy the goat escaped her sharp pecks by leaping into Laine's lap, while the rest of us enjoyed her company but always maintained a respectful distance. Without air conditioning, the door to the garden was usually left open and our dinner guests were often entertained by

---

4   The Wardens grew opposed to the capture and keeping of wildlife.

Josefina, Suzy, Sasha, Petunia the guinea pig, the three ducks and three rabbits, all of whom assumed they had the run of the house. Josefina, some forty-one years later is still with us.[5]

Even if surveillance was less intrusive, the Cuban security services undoubtedly did keep good track of us, but in nothing like the overt manner to which we had been subjected in all aspects of our lives in the Soviet Union. Nonetheless, we were more cautious in dealing with the Cubans. Whereas in Russia we did play 'games' with the KGB agents in the knowledge that they would never take physical action against us without direct orders, one was much less sanguine about how hot-blooded Cubans might react if provoked.

On one occasion I, together with John Hill, the commercial secretary, was driving from the southern city of Cienfuegos to Santa Clara in the middle of the island. There was a national census taking place that day and all movement was prohibited. However, Protocol had given us, as diplomats, permission to travel. We stopped to clear one checkpoint. That went smoothly. At the next one we thought the militiaman on duty was giving us a friendly wave. We waved back and breezed on through without stopping. Coming up on the third checkpoint, we were sure we had the routine down. And so we waved, again not stopping and moving even faster. No sooner were we through than John said, "Did you see what I saw?" I said, "Yeah, looked like he was holding a pistol up in the air with his finger on

---

5   The parrot Josefina died on January 1, 2011, just 10 days before Bill himself passed away.

the trigger. Just as well we were moving at a good speed!" About ten miles down the road we came around a curve and suddenly there in front of us, lined up across the highway, were four patrol cars and a squad of militia all with guns at the ready. We pulled up short and spent the next hour and a half explaining ourselves, searching for our written permission to travel that road, and waiting for the police to get instructions from their superiors. Looking back on the incident, I think we had a rather close shave. It was just as well they had barricaded the road because otherwise some trigger-happy type further along might well have blown us away.

We were never too sure how closely the Cuban G2 was monitoring our social contacts. Of course we tended to be rather paranoid. I recall on one occasion having a drink with a Cuban contact when, suddenly, a small antenna-like object popped out from the inner pocket of his jacket as he leaned forward. Naturally my immediate assumption, based on conditioning from spy movies and DL (2), was that our conversation was being transmitted to a nearby receiver, which it probably was. Certainly our relations with artists, professionals and other non-government people were fairly normal; these contacts were not constantly reminding us that Big Brother was watching, even though some of them undoubtedly were required to report periodically to G2. We spent numerous spectacular weekends at a Varadero beach house with a Havana doctor and his wife who for whatever reason were given special privileges. The tourist boom had not yet started, there was only one virtually unoccupied hotel (the *Internacional*, which still is in business today), and for the entire winter and spring we had miles and miles of beautiful sandy beach all to ourselves. The house itself belonged to a former newspaper editor who was serving time for counter-revolutionary activities. He appeared at one point for a year or so, but apparently had not learned to hold his tongue. During that year, Antonio the editor spent much of his time pounding up and down the beach in his swimsuit, training, as he was quick to say, for the next revolution. Before long he was sent back to prison.

A number of our artistic contacts did not trouble to hide the fact that their main interest in attending parties was for the access it afforded them to good booze. I recall one evening when Luis Martinez Pedro, a noted artist and well into his cups, was holding forth, glass of neat scotch in hand, chair tilting backwards, when suddenly he went completely over on his back. The most notable thing about the incident was that Martinez Pedro managed to survive without injury and without losing a drop of the precious scotch from his glass. Of course we learned from our guests all the latest rumours floating around the Havana scene, the great majority of which were absolute nonsense. The long and the short of it was that, as in the Soviet Union, this was a police state and we trusted no one.

Indeed Cuba in the late 60's was a period of curious encounters. The capital was full of the representatives of every two-bit revolutionary group in the world, and all of these religiously attended official functions hosted by the government. There were generals and colonels galore from liberation fronts we had never heard of, all splendidly outfitted, strutting their stuff. Other more shadowy types were clumped here and there throughout the halls. Even purely diplomatic functions often became something of a game, since a room could contain *Ambassador X*, who was not authorised to speak to *Ambassador Y*, and so on. I was constantly, for example, scuttling away from the Viet Cong representative, who frequently tried to approach me. I recall on one occasion chatting to the Israeli Chargé d'Affaires, Israel Peled, undoubtedly a member of the Mossad, Israel's intelligence agency, (declared *persona non grata* in Havana not so long thereafter) when who should approach but the newly arrived Algerian Ambassador, all smiles. I found myself in a bit of a quandary, even if amused, speaking first to one, then to the other, but not introducing them. After about a minute of this they were eyeing each other rather warily. At the first opportunity, while the Israeli was distracted, I whispered surreptitiously to the Algerian, "This is the Israeli." He reacted as if struck by a bullet and urgently whispered back, "Don't tell anybody! Don't tell anybody!", as he scuttled off.

That was Havana.

What of the United States, so near and yet so far? Did Canada serve as an American proxy on the island? The Swiss provided formal representation of U.S. interests. It is self-evident that Ottawa shared run-of-the-mill reports from Havana with our American and British allies, even as happened with dispatches from our embassies all over the world. But was there more?

One aspect of the Canadian presence in Cuba that has received little attention but is very much a part of Canadian diplomatic history was the close link for a number of years with the CIA.[6] Following the Bay of Pigs fiasco in 1961, and in the wake of the Cuban missile crisis in 1962, which posed a serious threat to North America as a whole, President John Kennedy struck an agreement with then Prime Minister Lester Pearson that provided for the assignment of an extra political officer to the Canadian Embassy in Havana whose primary responsibility was to be responsive to CIA tasking. The arrangement was highly secret – similar but much longer-term than the deal struck some two decades later that enabled Ambassador Ken Taylor to mastermind the ex-filtration of American diplomats concealed in the Canadian Embassy in Tehran. Whether the deal was known to the resident Canadian Ambassador at the time I am not absolutely sure since I never discussed the matter with either of the ambassadors under whom I served. It was of course known to the cipher clerk, but no one else. During the missile crisis itself and for a few years thereafter, the activity mainly involved monitoring Soviet military movements. For instance, one would park surreptitiously on side roads in the dark of night near the port of Mariel watching for Soviet troop movements or anything passing by that resembled a crated missile.

It worked like this. The CIA would forward tasking requests to External Affairs in Ottawa, who vetted the requests, removed any

6   Since the time these memoirs were written, this facet of Canadian history has been elaborated in the work of Professors Don Munton, Robert Wright and others.

references to CIA, and then forwarded them verbatim as secret External messages for the 'eyes only' of the designated officer. Responses would be filed in the same way; that is, from Havana to Ottawa and thence to Washington.

The arrangement was in place for a full ten years, from 1963. I carried said responsibility for the final three years of our four-year posting. During this period I visited CIA headquarters in Langley twice for very useful and well-attended briefing/debriefing sessions with both the overt and covert sides of the Agency. The main features of the visits were the splendid lunches invariably served up with double martinis. After dining – and drinking – I was always ready to bare my soul to my hosts and part with my innermost secrets.

The nature of the function had largely changed by the time I arrived in Havana, with less emphasis on observation of military movement and more on human intelligence. Nonetheless, as an example, in the spring of 1970 information was sent to us to the effect that the Soviets had begun to construct a submarine base on an island in Cienfuegos Bay. I was asked to see what I could. I then began to make regular trips to Cienfuegos. There I established a good relationship with a British technician and his family working on a project in the city, who lived in an apartment overlooking the bay. They were able to provide me on an ongoing basis with a good bit of useful information on Soviet comings and goings, and especially on construction taking place on the island. This I supplemented with photographs surreptitiously taken from various points along the shore. Such material was duly sent on to Langley. We watched with much interest as President Nixon eventually gave the Soviets an ultimatum to stop this construction. Having been burned once during the missile crisis, the Soviets did not resist.

A footnote to this was a final trip to Cienfuegos where I made my way, always expecting to be stopped by security, into an area where anti-aircraft missile sites were being built. The only things found were abandoned brickworks hidden among the scrub and it seemed that we may have been deliberately permitted into the area to verify that work had stopped.

Other contacts were established which served as sources for very specific sorts of information. For example, one might establish a relationship with a closet dissident with good ties to the establishment, and meet periodically. Through such a contact, one might get answers to many questions that had been passed to us via the CIA channel. For instance, in this manner one could obtain a constant trickle of information on Communist individuals or groups travelling under false cover to various meetings in Europe and Africa. It was quite useful since this was still a period in which the Cubans were involved in subversive activity abroad. By this time I was anything but naïve, and with my cynical mind I always viewed a contact of this sort with suspicion, not knowing for sure whose side the individual was really on and whether he or she was a G2 plant. Not to have treated all contacts with a large element of cynicism would have been the height of folly. After all, as the world now knows, this was the period when the CIA was making attempt after attempt on Castro's life, and the G2 was probably one of the most effective intelligence services in the business.

The idea was that the relationship with the CIA should be closely guarded. I doubt that we were fully successful in this, at least as far as G2 was concerned. I would be most surprised if the Cuban counter-intelligence service did not have my dual role and that of my predecessors as spies and diplomats clearly pegged. The trick was not to go overboard or give the Cuban government cause for declaring one *persona non grata*, but rather to try to maintain a balance and to conduct business in a positive vein with the various ministries. Of course, the Cuban government was very conscious that in any confrontation it stood to lose much more than we, in that both the Cuban Embassy in Ottawa and their Trade mission in Montreal were riddled with Cuban spies. This imbalance provided us with a certain degree of immunity.

An event in the spring of 1972 nonetheless threatened to blow a hole in the relationship. A bomb went off in the Montreal consulate. The police went in without prior permission, the ostensible reason being to prevent the loss of life and property. The Cuban staff responded by holding off the Canadians with weapons drawn, even if it meant one of their *compañeros* bleeding to death.

Castro responded with great fury. In a wild and at times incoherent speech, he charged the Canadians with breaking international law and carrying out various nefarious activities. In a scarcely veiled threat, he suggested that the Cubans for their part might enter the Canadian Embassy in Havana. This triggered an immediate reaction on our part with the result that key Canadian staff gathered at the

Embassy at midnight to begin the process of disposing of critical documents. In the end, Castro never carried out his threat, obviously determining that the consequences outweighed any benefits.

Repercussions of our unorthodox activities were bound to show themselves sooner or later, and this happened during the final months of our posting. In late 1971, my SIS intelligence contact at the British Embassy, with whom I maintained close liaison, arranged a quiet meeting to let me know that he had had an encounter with G2 at which he had been roughed up, presumably as a warning that they were on to him. The British interpretation was that the screws were being tightened; he passed this on to me as a warning to be on my guard. Shortly thereafter, I spent a night with my family at the secluded resort of Soroa in the mountains of western Cuba. We were the only guests. My wife, small daughter and I were in one cabin, while our boys Scott and Tom were in another next door. Around midnight, a group of four or five persons, including at least one woman, arrived at our door persistently demanding entry. They banged on the door of our cabin, and then on that of our boys next door. The woman in the group, pretending to be in distress, kept yelling "Ay madrina! Dejame entrar! Madrina, madrina! Dejame entrar!" (Please, dear lady, let me come in!) I could only pray that Tom, our oldest, would have the good sense to keep quiet and not open the door. To our enormous relief, they eventually left, having failed to elicit any response from us, but nonetheless the whole thing made for a restless and menacing night. Given the degree of control exercised over access to resort locations like Soroa, I could scarcely interpret this incident as anything other than deliberate harassment and intimidation, and presumably a warning.

The main evidence that I had been picked up on G2's radar came some three months before we were due to move back to Ottawa. I had been asked to fly to Brussels to attend a NATO experts' meeting on Cuba. Just before embarking on the return journey to Havana, I received a message abruptly instructing me to come to Ottawa en route. At headquarters I reported to the head of the intelligence division, where we were joined in the office by two men, identified as members of the CIA, who had come up to Ottawa specifically to meet with me. The information they brought absolutely astounded me. Without providing any specifics, they said that the purpose of their visit was to inform me that the situation had become 'unsafe' and to recommend most strongly that I not return to Havana, but rather remain in Ottawa. They said they could not go into detail but that they were acting on the basis of intelligence available to them. Needless to say, I was caught off guard and rather flabbergasted by this warning that I could only take as serious, since they had made a special trip to pass it on. We had a lengthy discussion during which I pointed out just how awkward it would be, with my wife and three young children still in Havana, not to return. In the end, the gentlemen, while not backing away from their warning, said that if indeed I was determined to go back, then their urgent warning was that I keep my head down and desist from all further activities related to intelligence gathering. This in fact was the course, in consultation with our own people, that I followed for my remaining three months, and we duly departed Havana in the summer of 1972 without any unforeseen complications.

Quite frankly, I never was able to decide conclusively whether to take the CIA men's explanation, that there was a Cuban threat against me, at face value. Perhaps they were trying to get me out of the way, for instance because I was in contact with one or more persons they considered "sensitive" sources, who might be compromised through their relationship with me. Knowing what we know now, perhaps the situation was indeed unsafe. Perhaps the CIA was about to undertake yet another of its literally dozens of assassination attempts against Castro. Had such an attempt succeeded, the Cubans almost certainly would have struck back brutally, with serious consequences for any of us identified as connected to the Agency. The CIA in those days was not known for having much 'heart' when it came to protecting their 'assets' abroad. But nonetheless I was grateful for the warning delivered so forcefully.[7]

I do not have a full picture of any other such arrangements the Department might have made with the CIA. Obviously, at the time of our membership on the International Control Commission during the war in Vietnam, when we were fronting for the West just as Poland was fronting for the Soviet Bloc, a lot of information must

---

7   According to the Cuba Archive, a French national and contract employee at the French Embassy in Havana disappeared and was assumed assassinated by the G2 in 1972. It is said that he was arrested and taken for interrogation to the State Security headquarters. He was never seen again. http://cubaarchive.org/home/images/stories/truth%20and%20memory/ foreign__nationals.pdf

have been funnelled to the State Department and the CIA. Our close ties with the CIA during the period surrounding the expatriation in 1980 of six U.S. diplomats from Tehran, clandestinely housed by the Canadian Embassy, is now well known. Were there other such 'arrangements'? I strongly doubt it. Cuba and Iran were very special cases, and Canadian behaviour was a reflection of the close ties maintained between Ottawa and Washington during the Cold War. Did those of us designated to carry out this activity consider ourselves CIA agents or part of the CIA network? Of course not. We were simply Foreign Service Officers doing our part to counteract a threat not only to the U.S., but equally to Canada.

The Havana posting certainly brought its share of excitement. One morning in 1971, I was sitting quietly in my office taking an hour's instruction with my French tutor, when we suddenly heard screams coming up the central staircase. I picked up my phone and after a few moments got the receptionist, who was in a high state of excitement. She said that two men, who looked like they might have been military, had just burst into the front hall carrying the Canadian flag, which somehow they had managed to remove from the flagpole in the front garden. They were reportedly carrying a gun and a knife under the flag, and had taken two members of the staff hostage. The group of four was now locked in the sunroom on the side of the building. Unfortunately, a member of the staff had immediately called Protocol at the Foreign Ministry and within minutes the place was surrounded by Cuban police, who showed every sign of wanting to enter the building at once. I say 'unfortunately' because, having faced several similar situations in Moscow, I would very much have preferred initially to have kept the authorities out of it, and to have had the chance to negotiate the people out of the building quietly. I was under little illusion as to what would happen to them once captured, and I guess my political sympathies were showing because I would strongly have preferred simply to explain to them the error of their ways and the fate that lay ahead of them if they persisted. In any event, that option was removed. I gather that one reason for the rapid appeal to Protocol was the fear by the Canadian staff member that the assailants might have had something to do with the *Front pour la Liberation du Quebec* (FLQ), some of whose members were by then resident in the city.

We were able to establish telephone contact with the hostage takers in the sunroom. I spoke to them a number of times, asking them what they wanted. Their goal was asylum in Canada. Over the course of the next three hours the chat went back and forth. I offered them coffee, which they eventually accepted, and which I left on the floor outside their door. The captive staff members, with whom they allowed me to speak, said that the weapons were kept largely concealed under the flag, and that they appeared to be authentic. Outside, we debated as to what might be done. In those days, immediate contact with Ottawa was extremely difficult, and instructions could not be obtained, so we were left on our own. We thought about lacing the coffee with a heavy dose of sleeping pills, but wisely concluded that that would probably only have the effect of enraging them. My constant line in communicating with them was that we could not even talk about the future unless and until they gave up their weapons. After a standoff of several hours, they finally agreed to hand over the knife and gun. I took these from them. The gun turned out to be a fake, while the large knife was real enough. The discussion was brief. I explained to them, after discussion with the Ambassador, the long-standing Canadian policy not to accept asylees in the Embassy in Havana, and that they had no choice but to walk out on their own, or for us to have the Cuban police come in and collect them. Indeed there is no question but that such persons, had they been granted refuge in the Embassy, would have remained there for years. Moreover, such a precedent, once established, would have tempted a steady stream of others to follow the example, which in turn would have led the Cuban authorities to clamp a strict quarantine zone around the Embassy. After agonised consideration, the two men said they would leave on their own. I explained to them as carefully as I could that they should under no circumstances attempt to flee or otherwise evade the police, since I was convinced that they would be shot on the spot. It might seem strange but it was with a very heavy heart that I opened the entrance door and conducted them down the front walk, into the welcoming arms of the police and Roberto Melendez, the chief of protocol with the personality of Al Capone. We never heard of them again and I would be most surprised if they were not executed in short order. The thought of having been the instrument in turning over the two young men, whose only apparent aim was to seek freedom, haunts me to this day.

Some time later, a similar case occurred in the French Embassy. This time the Cuban police were not to be denied. If my memory serves me correctly, they shot dead at least one person through the window from the street outside.

Ongoing drama was provided throughout our time in Cuba by the frequent hijackings of airliners from the U.S. to Cuba by various disgruntled types, ranging from criminals to Black Panthers to the mentally deranged. Given our own challenges in moving to and from Canada, it became something of a sick joke to us to wonder if we might book seats on Air Hijacker. If an Air Canada flight should appear at the airport, why should we not be able to take advantage of the direct flight home? Included in the list of the dozens seized was a 747 enroute from New York to Puerto Rico in 1971. The 747's were in their infancy at that point and Fidel, with his ever-inquisitive mind, made a point of personally going on board this behemoth of the skies to check it out. The situation was serious enough that at the beginning of 1970 the Canadian government proposed to Cuba the negotiation of an anti-hijacking agreement.

The Cuban authorities were quite sophisticated in dealing with the hijacking phenomenon. An aircraft, once on Cuban soil, was invariably detained for two or three days for 'administrative' processing prior to being allowed to return to the U.S. During this period, the mostly American passengers were lodged in a Havana hotel, given tours, fed and treated to a sort of vacation break. Of course the Cubans, always looking for hard currency, charged the airlines an exorbitant amount for the socialist hospitality. Given the influx, certain buildings around the city became known as 'hijacker houses', where the hijackers were placed. Most of these people seemed to have the run of the place; some took classes, while others engaged in various forms of labour. Interestingly, quite a number of them tired rather quickly of their new surroundings and sought ways to return home to face the music rather than face the prospect of a lifetime in socialist Cuba. More than one of them showed up at the Embassy to enquire about the possibility of moving to Canada. Such hopes, of course, were categorically discouraged.

The major event of our posting was by far the Quebec October Crisis of 1970. Earlier in the year we had watched with fascination and overwhelming awe the grainy figures on TV from Key West of the first landing on the moon. While Fidel apparently had the equipment to get good reception from American TV stations, we normally could barely capture a signal. Our great good fortune, however, was on that particular night to at least be able to distinguish what was happening, and to see those historic first steps. As for the domestic situation, 1970 was the *Año de los Diez Milliones*, Year of the Ten Millions, when Cubans had been challenged by their leader to produce a record crop of sugar. Everything else was subordinated to this goal. The masses were mobilised and sent into the fields to plant cane, cultivate it and later to harvest the crop. No institution was spared from doing its part. Even those of us who were foreigners, living in our isolated island world, were caught up in the frenzy and we carefully checked the harvest statistics every day. One part of us wanted the campaign to fail, since the whole thing seemed such a ludicrous waste of resources and since victory would signify a resounding triumph for Cuban Communism. But there was another part that empathised with the average people who were deprived of so many basic necessities of life, and we wanted to see them come away with pride. Indeed, at the Embassy, all the staff on New Year's Day devoted a day of labour to the cane harvest, when we took up *machetes*. It was more like a picnic, but we felt some satisfaction at making the symbolic effort. The campaign failed to reach its goals, and Cubans were duly disappointed, but the intent, as is common in authoritarian countries, was to come up with a steady flow of gimmicks calculated to exercise control over the masses. Fidel took great satisfaction in devoting several longer-than-usual speeches to analysing the reasons for failure, but praising the heroic effort.

Then suddenly in the autumn of 1970, the shock of the Quebec crisis fell heavily upon us. From the Embassy we watched with grim fascination as the British Trade Commissioner, James Cross, was kidnapped on October 3 in Montreal and conditions for his release were set; as the War Measures Act was invoked on October 16; and as the Quebec Minister of Labour, Pierre Laporte, was murdered in retaliation and his body discovered in the trunk of a car on October 18. The imposition of the War Measures Act was not without direct impact on our Embassy community. We had to appeal to headquarters to intervene with the *Sûreté du Québec* and ask them to stop seizing the correspondence between a Québécois member of the Embassy and his wife, and their parents, and to desist from harassing them.

Early on, the Government of Canada offered safe conduct out of the country for the kidnappers in return for the release of Cross.

No destination was identified. At the time of the October Crisis, I was in charge of the mission as Chargé d'Affaires, since the former ambassador, Leon Mayrand, had left Cuba definitively, and his successor, Ken Brown, had not yet arrived.

The first meeting took place in October when I was asked by Ottawa, on a highly confidential basis, to approach the Cuban government to sound them out on their willingness to accept the hijackers, should this turn out to be one of the highjackers' demands. Accordingly, I met urgently with Raul Roa, the Cuban Foreign Minister. He was obviously fully aware of the situation, having been kept briefed by the Cuban Embassy and Trade Mission in Montreal. A major concern of Canada at the time was that the Cubans were providing support and encouragement to dissident elements in Quebec, even though the Cubans vociferously denied the charge whenever it was brought up. Roa obviously took smug satisfaction out of having the Canadians come to request assistance in getting them out of a tough spot. Roa said that he would 'consult the Government', by which he meant Fidel, and get back to me.

Two days later, I was summoned to meet with him again. He said that the 'Government' had taken a decision on the matter, which he wished to communicate to me. We were speaking in Spanish and at this point, he departed from his normally rapid-fire Cuban style, to speak very slowly. He also asked that I repeat precisely, word for word, what he was telling me. Roa said that as an act of friendship for Canada, Cuba would accept the kidnappers. However, he wished to make absolutely clear that if this act were to be in any way interpreted as anything other than an act of friendship, then the offer would be retracted. He asked me for explicit assurances on this point, and these I provided on the spot. At no time, either then or later, was the issue of paying costs for the kidnappers ever raised by Cuba, even though there was considerable speculation about this later on in the Canadian media. Nor did the Cuban government ever ask for any other kind of reward. I met with Roa again several times after that.

Towards the middle of November, I was hosting a dinner at home attended among others by Carlos Neira, my chief contact at the Foreign Ministry. Just as we were hitting mid-stride with the main course, I was summoned out of the room to take an emergency telex from Ottawa, telling me that the deal was on and instructing me to inform the Cubans accordingly. Neira and I met at the Foreign Ministry at midnight. I informed him of the new developments, and asked him to ensure the top levels of government were brought up to date. We agreed to stay in close contact.

On November 13, Ken Brown, the new ambassador, took charge of the mission. Towards the end of November, concrete negotiations with the kidnappers began. The RCMP had for some time, before the actual release of Cross, identified the location where he was being held, and occupied the apartment above, around November 25. We were informed that negotiations with the kidnappers had been completed and that, barring any last minute hitches, the group would arrive in Havana late on the evening of December 3. Needless to say, the whole period was fraught with tension, an atmosphere impossible to convey in words. Together, Ambassador Brown and I drove to the airport and watched the Canadian Forces Yukon land.

It was agreed that I would board the aircraft, meet the kidnappers, explain briefly to them the process, then escort them off the aircraft and turn them over to the Cuban authorities.

I was anxious to see for myself Marc Carbonneau, Jacques Cossette-Trudel and wife Louise Lanctot, brother Jacques Lanctot and Pierre Seguin, who had focused the attention of the entire country in such a dramatic way for the past month and a half. Perhaps I expected to encounter a group of aggressive and intimidating characters, but the reality turned out to be something of an anti-climax. All five members of the group were very quiet, anxious, probably a little scared at the prospect of what lay ahead of them, and anything but intimidating. The whole business lasted less than ten minutes. We exited the aircraft where they were loaded into vehicles and driven away to an unknown destination. Thus ended, to all intents and purposes, the saga of the Quebec October Crisis.

Ironically, the kidnappers were lodged for some time in the Hotel Deauville, which happened to be one of the few places where we as foreign diplomats could go out for a meal. Very occasionally, I found myself sitting in the Deauville, with the neighbouring table occupied by one or more of the FLQ group. We exchanged perfunctory greetings, but that was the extent of the contact.

One positive result, from my perspective, emerged from the October Crisis. I had argued for some time, and without success, that we should initiate a modest aid program in Cuba, aimed mainly at expanding people-to-people contacts with the country, as we were doing in the Soviet Union. Following Cuba's reception of the kidnappers, I returned to the charge. To my delight and surprise, and over the vociferous objections of several ambassadors from Washington to Moscow to NATO in Brussels, Ottawa showed its gratitude by eventually setting up such a program under the auspices of the Canadian International Development Agency.

We left Cuba, the gem of the Caribbean, in July 1972, saying goodbye with much sorrow to many Cuban friends. Conditioned as we were by the Cold War mentality, we had little sympathy for the regime and the hardship it had imposed on the population. Equally however, by that time some forty years ago, we were highly critical of what we saw as U.S. complicity by playing, with its sanctions and embargos, into the hands of the Castro government. The main victims were the Cuban people themselves. Had an open, hands-off policy been pursued from the start, there is little doubt in my mind that the nature of government in Cuba would be vastly different today.

I have often reflected in these latter years on my own role as cold warrior in Cuba. I was not focused at the time on the horrendous atrocities committed on the peoples of Chile, Guatemala, Argentina, Brazil and elsewhere, on the subversion of democracy, or on the substantive part played by the CIA. The extent of these activities, the violations of international law and the moral depravity attached to them have only become more fully revealed in recent years. I also was barely aware of the CIA's concerted efforts to assassinate Fidel. Why they were not part of my focus I simply don't know and have no excuse for this. Had I been fully briefed on them, would I have acted differently? Would I have assisted the Agency so enthusiastically? In all truthfulness, I have to admit that it would probably not have changed things much. While a moral issue for me these many years later, it was not at the time. In those days, I, like many of my colleagues, was so caught up in the whole Cold War mindset that I was prepared do almost anything for the cause. An example of this was that in response to an occasional request from Ottawa, I agreed to open, copy and re-seal letters to known Canadian leftists resident in Cuba to whom the Department had agreed to transmit letters from home via diplomatic bag – probably as a means to get hold of their correspondence. At the time I thought that this was probably questionable in legal and ethical terms, but nonetheless agreed to do it.

Our four years in Cuba, from 1968 to 1972, had been a 'double' posting, two years longer than normal for what was deemed a "high-level hardship" post. The reality for us was that Cuba had been a marvellous assignment. We said goodbye to our many Cuban friends with much sadness and, as the years passed, were always to look back on our years there as one of the highlights of our time in the Foreign Service.

The Warden family on home leave, summer 1966, Niagara Falls.

Bill, Varadero, Cuba, 1968.

Laine with Tom, Scott and Lisa in Havana.

Tom, Scott and Lisa in Havana with Josefina, the Cuban parrot.

*Sasha, the Russian dog, with Josefina, the Cuban parrot
and Petunia, the Cuban guinea pig, Havana.*

Chapter Five

DESERTION: AN AMERICAN'S FLIGHT TO HAVANA

The story of our assignment to Cuba would not be complete without recounting the bizarre episode of a major in the U.S. army who in 1967 flew to Cuba.

In May of that year, my wife and I were in Knoxville, Tennessee visiting her family, and preparing to leave for Birmingham, Alabama, to see her other relatives. Shortly before 9 in the morning, Laine's cousin in Birmingham called in a panic to say that our trip would have to be cancelled. Her brother-in-law, a major in the U.S. Army and Aide to the General commanding the Southern Army, had disappeared, along with his four-year-old son. All that was known at the time was that he had rented a two-seater Cessna 150 from a fixed-base operator in Florida, taken off and not returned. The assumption when we got the phone call was that the plane had either crashed or made a forced landing somewhere. The family was in crisis.

No word was heard nor was any trace of the aircraft discovered over the next several days, until suddenly contact was made from the most unexpected of locations. Richard Pearce and his young son of the same name were sitting safely in Havana under the 'protection' of the Cuban authorities. The news struck the families on both sides, all solid southern Republicans, like a bolt of lightning. If Major Pearce had set out to administer maximum shock to all concerned, he could not have devised a better scenario. We ourselves received word of this apparent defection, were as shocked as anyone else, and then went back to our daily activities in Ottawa, giving little thought to the matter over the next several months. Little did we realise at the time that in due course our lives would intersect with those of the two Richards and that this would have a determining effect on the future of both.

The summer of 1967 was fraught with uncertainty. At one point, the possibility was raised that we might be posted to Havana the following summer. Our own reaction was positive, indeed enthusiastic, in that Cuba seemed to present a logical sequel to our time in Moscow. The one reservation that was voiced, and strongly at that, by my bosses was that officers exposed to the intelligence liaison business were normally not considered for assignment to communist countries unless and until they had been 'laundered' through at least one other non-sensitive post. In Defence Liaison

(2) Division, I had ongoing access to the highest levels of security clearance. Whereas the public tends to be under the impression that 'Top Secret' is the highest you can go, in fact it is just the beginning, with code words being assigned to various categories of intelligence and intercept material that take you into the stratosphere. For each category one had to go through a process known as 'indoctrination', whereby in effect one swore an oath in blood not to reveal secrets learned. The concern of the authorities was rooted in the fear that a diplomat might defect, might be compromised and turn over to the enemy valuable insights on current intelligence efforts. The concern was not misplaced, given previous instances of high-level defections and the constant offensive efforts by intelligence services on both sides to recruit high-value targets. Whatever the nature of the deliberations in my own case, a decision was taken that I should be permitted to take up a posting in Cuba and indeed to fulfill the highly sensitive requirements arising out of the agreement of the Canadian government to undertake certain tasks set by the Central Intelligence Agency.

When we arrived in Havana on that hot, humid, suffocating day in July 1968, we carried with us the telephone number of Major Richard Pearce. In the first month of our assignment, there was far too much on our minds in terms of settling into work and living routines to allow us to give much thought to Pearce. At the same time, eventual contact was very much a priority, partly in terms of pure curiosity but mainly with a view to being able to let the family back in Alabama know how the Major and his son were getting on. Moreover, not knowing at that stage what kind of relationship Pearce might have established with his Cuban hosts, we were seized with a certain amount of trepidation both over how Pearce would receive our approach, and at the prospect of drawing to ourselves the attention of the Cuban G2, or secret service.

Sometime in the fall of 1968, Laine dialled the number. Pearce answered, his voice readily betraying the suspicion he felt at receiving this unexpected call. Laine patiently explained the circumstances, the family connection, and the reason for our presence in Havana. The fact that we were with the Embassy tended to heighten rather than allay his concerns. Nonetheless, ever the southern gentleman, Richard Pearce responded graciously to the suggestion that we get together at some point.

Thus it was that shortly thereafter the two Richards appeared on our doorstep one Sunday afternoon. This was the beginning of an acquaintance and indeed a friendship that germinated and lasted over the succeeding four years. I cannot say that we ever got to the stage where we felt particularly intimate with Richard Sr. He was very reserved, every bit the stereotype of the product one would expect from the Virginia Military Institute, every bit the polite southern military officer. Nonetheless, we did reach the point, and relatively quickly, where we felt quite at ease in each other's presence. Following this first contact, we met thereafter every two or three weeks for the next four years, either at our house or his, or on picnics to the beach.

If Richard felt embarrassed by what he had done, he never revealed this sentiment to us. We were careful not to press him on any subject, but as time went on, he did open up enough to allow some fascinating glimpses into his private world. For example, it was not long before we had a good idea of the anguish and tortured thinking that led to his dramatic flight, and the exchange of a promising career for the infamy of a high-ranking deserter.

Even before coming to Cuba, we had been made aware through discussions with his sister-in-law, Laine's cousin, of the heavy psychological burden that Pearce carried with him. His own mother and father had separated early on. His mother totally dominated her two sons and subjected them to a rigorous upbringing. One got the impression that the lifestyle had been frugal, the expectations high, and the career paths of both Richard and his brother probably as much her decision as theirs.

It seems that Richard's marriage to Sandra Lyday of Port Arthur, Texas, was probably more the result of sudden passion or infatuation rather than a longstanding relationship. The two could hardly have been more dissimilar. In contrast to Pearce's disciplined and dominated early life, Sandra was the indulged daughter of the wealthy owner of a Texas shipyard. There was little that Sandra wanted that Sandra did not get — at least if money could buy it. Thrown into the psychological soup was Adley Lyday, matriarch of the Lyday clan. Strong-willed in a way reminiscent of the elder Pearce's own mother, Adley was thrilled out of her mind at the birth of Richard Jr. and at the prospect of an heir apparent to the family wealth and business. She made it quite clear that she intended to organise the child's upbringing and to cater to every whim of the young lord.

Two or three years into the boy's childhood, Richard and Sandra divorced. They were apparently incompatible from the start, a fact obscured by the passion of the honeymoon period. Richard Jr. remained with his mother, his father having periodic visiting rights. During the months that followed the divorce, anger and resentment festered in the Major's heart to the point of becoming an obsession, a cancer eating away and overwhelming career aspirations and rational considerations. Whatever the murky paths his mind traversed, it is evident that the seeds of anger multiplied, eventually leading Richard Pearce Sr. to explore all possible avenues by which his son could be freed from the clutches of the Lyday clan and transported to a "healthy" environment where the four-year old boy could be raised free from the "corrupting" influence of the surroundings in Port Arthur.

Even today as I think back on the whole episode, I still cannot fully grasp how Major Pearce could, in the political circumstances of 1967, have ever arrived at a decision to spirit his son across the million-mile divide separating the United States from Cuba in those days. A more unlikely figure for such a plot could scarcely be imagined. Decorated Vietnam war veteran; supporter of arch-conservative segregationist Alabama governor George Wallace; all-American boy raised in the unambiguous anti-Communist culture of the 50's and 60's; witness to the Bay of Pigs fiasco and the crisis that came within a hair's breadth of placing nuclear missiles 90 miles from U.S. shores. How on earth could Major Pearce ever have selected

Fidel Castro's Cuba as the target for his flight from what he saw as the destructive influence of the younger Pearce's maternal clan?

Perhaps the best explanation was simply the one that Pearce himself gave. Cuba was the one place in the world that was accessible to him, where he could take his son and be beyond the reach of the judicial authorities and his in-laws. Why he thought an upbringing in the rigid Cuban educational system built around the teachings of Fidel, Lenin and Marx would be preferable to one in Texas he never said. Nor was it ever suggested that revenge against his wife and in-laws was the driving motive.

Or was there perhaps a deeper, more clandestine element to Pearce's 'defection'?

It took some time to build a relationship of confidence with Richard Pearce. He later told us that he had initially suspected our motives in contacting him. Were we acting on behalf of the U.S. authorities, or the grandparents whom he seemed to fear even more than the former? We noticed, for example, that he would not allow his child to be out of his sight for long. Nor would he, during the first year, even consider allowing "Little Richard", as we called Richard Jr., to spend the night with our own three children. As we got to know him better and as he opened up, he told us of his conviction that Joe Lyday would spare no expense in retrieving the child. He was convinced that Lyday was perfectly capable of launching a commando raid across the Straits of Florida to appear in the dead of night and carry off his son.

Eventually Pearce recounted how his flight had been many months in the planning. He had taken flying lessons for the sole purpose of implementing his escape from the U.S. He had researched the various aircraft rental possibilities in south Florida. The one gap in his knowledge was how he would be received in Cuba.

On that fateful morning, the elder Pearce and his young son took off in their Cessna 150 from an airfield near Miami, ostensibly on a local flight, intending to return the same afternoon. Their flight was to be conducted in accordance with Visual Flight Rules, which meant in effect that there was no necessity to file any flight plan with the aviation authorities. Given the hundreds of small aircraft flying in and out of the Miami area on any given day, Pearce was able to blend into the general traffic flow without fear of drawing any attention to himself. Once aloft, Pearce took up a heading of almost 180 degrees due south, destination Havana or as close to the city as his dead reckoning might take him. Cuba's coastline sprawled across the Caribbean for some several hundred kilometres, a target impossible to miss. He estimated a flight time of an hour and a half or less.

The Cessna exited U.S. air space at an altitude of a few hundred feet, intending to stay low enough to avoid identification on radar. Once well offshore, Pearce climbed to several thousand feet to ensure that, in contrast to his surreptitious departure from the States, the Cubans would readily detect his entry into Cuban air space. The last thing he wanted was to be shot down as a stealthy intruder on a subversive mission. Shortly after picking up the smudge of the Cuban shoreline ahead, two MIG fighters materialised on either side of him and, with sign language, made patently clear that he should follow their directions. Shortly after noon on that Saturday in June 1967, Major Richard Pearce and his son, Richard Jr., landed at the military airfield in Havana's western suburbs.

Pearce was taken into custody by astonished Cuban officials. Not surprisingly, they found his story and explanations hard to believe. How long he was held he did not say, but evidently the Cubans, who had seen just about everything in terms of American 'tricks', were not about to accept Pearce's story at face value. They took note of the wire reports about the plane's disappearance and the subsequent fruitless search. Pearce asked the Cubans to inform the U.S. authorities of his safe arrival and, through them, the boy's mother and grandparents. This they eventually did through the medium of the Swiss Embassy, which had been responsible for American interests in Cuba ever since the break in relations in 1961.

The U.S., for its part, lost no time in demanding the immediate return of both the plane and its passengers. In this effort, the Americans, as in so many other aspects of their policy towards Cuba, were their own worst enemies. Cuba was not about to react either quickly or positively to any 'demands' the United States might make. The Cuban response was slow, deliberate and ambiguous. The case would have to be studied. The Swiss ambassador was brought into it, and made repeated representations on the basis of the allegedly unlawful removal of Richard Jr. from his mother's custody, the theft of the aircraft and so on. In the small world of Cuba, it was inevitable that Fidel himself should have become personally involved.

Richard Pearce Sr. recounted to me one day what had happened. He was summoned, together with his son, to an audience with the great man himself. In addition to Castro, the Swiss ambassador was present. It was to be a sort of informal court hearing. The ambassador was asked to state the U.S. case, after which Pearce was told to speak for himself. The hearing over, Fidel decided on the spot that Major Pearce together with his son would be allowed to remain in Cuba indefinitely. Fidel then instructed his erstwhile mistress and close associate who had been with him throughout the revolutionary years, Celia Sanchez, to make whatever arrangements were necessary for Pearce's long-term stay. Pearce told me later that one other factor militating strongly in favour of a positive decision for him was the very aggressive approach taken by both the Texas grandparents and the U.S. authorities. The Lydays had apparently hired the same lawyer who had worked on getting Gary Powers out of the USSR after his reconnaissance aircraft had been shot down by a Soviet missile. A hard-charging approach may have helped in the Powers case, but the Cubans were having none of it.

A modest yet pleasant bungalow was assigned to the Pearces on a quiet avenue not far from the Canadian embassy. An amiable black lady named Marta showed up and introduced herself as their cook and housekeeper. Her duties undoubtedly included that of reporting to the G2. Marta was to remain with Pearce throughout his years in Havana. In due course, a blue Chevrolet Corvair, five or six years old, was made available. I say 'made available' because there was no market in Havana in those days where you could go and buy a vehicle. It came through official channels, or it didn't come at all.

At his request, Pearce was given a job teaching English in a Havana school. From the modest stipend earned, Pearce was able, with Marta's assistance, to purchase foodstuffs from a special shop open only to senior military and government officials. Apart from food, there was no other need for money.

The extraordinary thing about these arrangements was that no cost was attached to them. The house was rent-free as were Marta's services. This might seem unbelievable to outside observers, but it wasn't to those of us who were acquainted with conditions in Cuba in those days. Cuba in the late 60's was still involved in sending subversive groups to other parts of Latin America and Africa, and in maintaining ties to all sorts of liberation movements. This meant that it was not uncommon to run across representatives of these movements from across the globe, to say nothing of the large numbers of Viet Cong students. Because of this, the government had a fully functioning system for accommodating and providing for foreigners coming into the country. All of them were considered guests of the state, and Pearce in his own way was simply yet another to be accommodated.

There was a difference, however, in that Pearce, for whatever reason, was treated much better than most of the other 'guests'. I am not sure why, but it is evident that he made a good impression on Fidel and was regarded thereafter as someone under Fidel's wing. Pearce's bungalow was situated in an area populated mainly by senior army officers, which meant that utilities were always working, even when the rest of us were experiencing extremely long power cuts. His well-being was assured by the monthly visits he received from Celia

Sanchez, herself one of the most influential members of the regime in her own right.

There was the matter of the Cessna 150 in which Pearce had flown to Cuba. He tried to make arrangements to have it returned to Florida, but these efforts foundered on bureaucratic shoals on both sides. The Cuban government eventually decided to purchase the aircraft and somehow made payment to the Florida owners. After all, with the American embargo prohibiting the sale of anything of this sort to Cuba, the Cubans were only too happy to acquire it. I am not sure what the aircraft was used for after that, but on a number of occasions I would see it flying over the city.

The set-up as first explained to me by Major Pearce I initially found hard to accept. What compromises had he made in order not only to obtain permission to stay, but even more to be granted a lifestyle that was far above that of ordinary people? Leaving the Cuban G2 aside, I knew the KGB and Soviet intelligence well enough to understand that they would be salivating over the prospect of getting their hands on someone with Pearce's background. As I got to know the Major better and gain his confidence, I had a number of discussions with him on this very point and was brutally frank in stating my views. Pearce's story was completely consistent every time the subject came up. He said that at no time had the Soviets been permitted to come near him, and that the Cubans had not exploited their power to squeeze intelligence out of him. What he stated very clearly was that he was 'eternally grateful' to Fidel for having left him alone and for ensuring that he was left alone. I believed him.

Major Pearce, as far as we could determine, basically lived the life of a hermit. He had no friends apart from us, and he did not mix with the other teachers at his school or with his neighbours. This was perhaps not as much of a sacrifice for him as it might have been for some others, because our impression was of a very reserved, introverted individual – which was one of the ways in which he and Sandra Lyday were total opposites.

Little Richard, by contrast, while very close to his father, was not cast totally in his father's mold. He mixed readily with other children on the street, which meant that he was rubbing shoulders constantly with the offspring of the powerful. At one point after the German Shepherd pup they had acquired through Celia Sanchez died, young Richard went off to the beach with his neighborhood friends and their father, the Cuban government minister Diocles Torralba. Where should he end up but on a dated, spartan yacht the occupant of which was none other than Fidel himself. On that occasion, they stayed out on the boat for some three days fishing and relaxing, while Castro worked on drafting his speech for the July 26th national holiday. During the course of Little Richard's encounters with Fidel – who insisted on telling him that he looked like a little lizard – the sad story of the recently deceased pet was told. The end result was that at 10 pm on the night of their return home, a jeep pulled up at the bungalow, two officers jumped out and, explaining that they had come on the orders of Fidel, presented Little Richard with a three-month-old German Shepherd pup. The Shepherd grew and thrived and lived his entire life with Little Richard. I tell this story as an interesting reflection of yet another side to the multifaceted personality of the Cuban leader.

Somehow or other, U.S. intelligence was managing to keep an eye on Richard Pearce. Flying was one of my passions and at one point in 1970 I saw a reference in a Cuban newspaper to a gliding club operating near Havana. I applied to the Foreign Ministry for authorisation to do some gliding and to my surprise, permission was granted. Richard Pearce and I went out on a number of Sunday mornings to the so-called club, which turned out in effect to be some kind of affiliate to the military. We were received cordially enough, although not with open arms, and made a number of flights. I went through the usual basic training manoeuvres, including spins, wing-overs, and so on. The method of launch was by tow plane, and there was an interesting sidebar to that. The tow plane pilot, Pepe, was a burly fellow in middle age. He wore a large holster with a pistol. I could see that the pistol had a shiny silver plaque on it and one day asked him to let me see it. Pepe told me proudly that he had served on various occasions with Che Guevara both as a pilot and also with him for a time in Bolivia. The plaque carried an inscription from Che, recognising Pepe's meritorious service. Later on I was only sorry that I did not seize the opportunity to question Pepe at length on his time with Che. I carried on with the gliding for a while, but eventually decided to let it go. To put it frankly, as I became ever more involved in certain intelligence-related activities, I decided that discretion was the better part of valour, and that it would be better to remove the temptation that might have existed for some on the Cuban side to arrange for a wing to fall off, or something similar. Perhaps I was being too cautious, but that was my reasoning.

Sometime in 1971, after I had terminated my gliding lessons, a message was received in the Embassy stating that then U.S. ambassador to the U.N., George H.W. Bush, had approached the Canadian mission to enquire about a certain Canadian from our Embassy they, the Americans, had become aware of, who had spent some time gliding in the company of one American citizen, Richard Pearce. The Americans wanted to know if the Canadian could be identified and, if the story was accurate, whether there would be any possibility of transmitting messages to Pearce. I sent a reply to Ottawa describing briefly my connection with Pearce and agreeing to act as intermediary. I told Pearce of the contact; his response was non-committal. In the event, as I recall, nothing further came of the matter. I was, of course, intrigued by the fact that the U.S. authorities had come upon the knowledge of my gliding and association with Richard Pearce. The only conclusion I could draw was that the information derived from the CIA or the National Security Agency, which undoubtedly was monitoring Cuban communications.

My family and I spent the first two years in Havana without a break. We were therefore looking forward to home leave in the summer of 1970. Imagine our surprise when, on checking into the Holiday Inn in Mexico City to await our onward flight to Canada, we received within the first hour an urgent telephone call from Joe and Adley Lyday in Port Arthur, Texas. They were, they said, aware of our contacts with Richard Pearce and were desperate to spend some time with us. They said they were ready to travel on a moment's notice to Mexico City, Ottawa, or wherever. While taken aback by the suddenness of the proposal and wondering about the source of their information, we did agree to a meeting at my parents' home in Niagara Falls the following week.

The upshot of that meeting was that we were able to reassure the Lydays of the good health and spirits of their grandson. They had, they said, been in ongoing contact with Texas congressman George Bush in an effort to bring pressure on the system to aid in their attempts to retrieve young Richard. They seemed to be on personal terms with the Bush family; they had apparently been to the house on several occasions to discuss their case. The initial thrust of the Lydays' approach to us was to ask that we try to broker some arrangement under which Major Pearce would be persuaded to return his son to the U.S. While no specific offer was made, I was left with little doubt but that active cooperation in securing the boy's return might be handsomely rewarded. After all, from someone who might just as willingly pay to send mercenaries in to snatch the boy, this was not surprising. Once we had made clear that we were not prepared to exert pressure or to advocate, the Lydays then pressed us to do whatever possible to facilitate a visit by them to Havana. They were obviously desperate for any ray of hope. The only action I agreed to undertake was to transmit their message to the Major. As for "Big Richard", as we referred to him, Adley said that her only wish was 'to break his neck'.

We returned to Havana where, in due course, I briefed Major Pearce on what had transpired. To our surprise, several months later after giving the matter much thought, Pearce agreed to take telephone calls from the grandparents and eventually to a visit by the latter. The bureaucratic requirements were arranged through the good offices of Celia Sanchez, and eventually the Lydays arrived and stayed for a couple of weeks. We saw them while they were in Havana. They actually stayed in the same house with the two Richards. Laine and I amused ourselves speculating on what the conversation over the dinner table might have been like.

The visit proved to be a turning point in the whole saga, as well as the beginning of the disintegration of Major Pearce's world. In July of 1972, we ourselves left Cuba. Before leaving, I sat down with "Big Richard" and raised with him the issue of what should happen to his son if some unexpected accident, God forbid, should befall him. It seems he had never really thought of this possibility. Nothing came of the conversation prior to our departure, but several months later I received an envelope from Mary Walters who had been my secretary at the Embassy. In it was a letter addressed to me, duly signed by Major Pearce and witnessed by Ms. Walters, stating that, in the event of his demise or incapacitation, he wished me to arrange for the return of his child to his mother. His covering message stated explicitly that I should hold the letter in total confidence with its contents undisclosed to anyone else. The reason for this was obvious. He feared that if the Lydays were to become aware of this provision, they might well arrange for him to be taken out. Was the fear justified? Personally I don't know, but on the basis of what I knew, I had no difficulty in appreciating his concerns.

The Lydays returned to Havana once more a year after our departure. From what we heard subsequently, this time Grandmother Adley was much less subtle in her approach to her grandson, who was by then eleven years old. In surreptitious conversations with him on the side, she apparently did everything possible to place temptation in front of Little Richard, offering him a grand life in the land of milk and honey. Her blandishments were successful and the boy began to press his father to allow him to go back to the States. The next thing we heard was that he had returned to Texas, together with the German Shepherd gifted to him by Fidel.

The disillusionment of Richard Sr. can only be imagined. He had sacrificed his life, his career, virtually everything, to tear the boy away from what he perceived as the corrupting influence of the Texas connection. The boy had come to Havana, settled in to the life of a young Cuban, attended school in his uniform and spoke Spanish like a native, right down to the husky guttural tone of voice characteristic of Cuban speech. He was now a Cuban — but not totally. Even here, the shadow of Fidel had protected him from the hard-core indoctrination that all Cuban children underwent. Yet at the end of the day, the lure of the affluent life had proved overpowering. I could only imagine Big Richard's anguish and sense of defeat. Now his son was gone. He was alone in Cuba, in a culture he did not particularly appreciate, in a political system for which he had no use.

It was not surprising, therefore, when a year later I received a letter from Big Richard in Havana enquiring as to whether the Canadian authorities might permit him to take up residence in Canada and, barring that, what their treatment of him might be should he land on Canadian shores. I wrote back stating as frankly but with as much sensitivity as possible that I thought the chances of his being permitted to settle in Canada were nil. I indicated further that the most likely action of the Canadians would be to deport him forthwith to the U.S.

The next contact we had was several months later from military counsel stating that Major Richard Pearce was being held in Fort Bragg, North Carolina, awaiting trial. The letter asked if I, as the one person who had been in close contact with him in Cuba, would be prepared to write a character reference. Of course I agreed and immediately sat down and wrote the document. I devoted a great deal of attention to its preparation, mainly out of conviction and respect for Pearce, but also because of certain feelings of guilt at having been the conduit or catalyst which had led to such a dramatic change in the situation. I described in detail the various conversations I had had with Pearce during our four years of contact with him. I related the story of his arrival, of his reception by the Cubans and of my impression of his lifestyle in Cuba. In particular I expressed my belief in his assurances that neither the Cuban G2 nor the Soviet intelligence services had been given a free rein to interrogate him. I hoped that my position as a diplomat in a trusted position of an allied country would carry some weight. In forwarding the document to Pearce's counsel, I made it clear that I was more than ready to appear as a witness at the trial. The offer was never taken up.

From that point on, we were relegated to the position of mere observers in the final chapter of the compelling saga, a story that went right to the pit of our stomachs. The overpowering feeling that pressed down on me was not a sense of relief at having seen the return of the boy to his mother and the good life, but rather one of deep tragedy. We were left with more questions than answers. How would young Richard have fared had he stayed in Castro's Cuba? When he reached the age of maturity and had time to reflect, would he have hated his father for having deprived him of an American childhood and the wealth that would have been his? What sort of emotional baggage would he have carried into adulthood, having been torn away at such a young age from his mother? My own feelings were that in fact the situation in Cuba could not have continued forever, that somehow and sometime the issues in young Richard's life would have had to be resolved. I firmly believed that sooner or later, he was bound to return to his home. It was probably only this belief that helped me resolve my own feelings of guilt in having been an instrument in the tragedy of his father whom I had come to consider a friend.

The story of Major Richard Pearce does not end there. I know that he went on trial, that he was convicted for desertion, and that he scarcely served more than a year before he was released. This is where the mystery deepens. There are simply too many questions left unanswered for the saga to be set aside and forgotten. If Major Pearce was the highest ranking U.S. officer ever to desert from the forces, as appeared to be the case, why did the military not throw the book at him? Why was he not shot or at least sent away for life?

A mere year in military prison? That I found quite unbelievable. Moreover, in spite of searching various sources, I never did find any substantial publicity on the legal case, which in itself was most surprising. The only thing I heard from Little Richard's grandparents at the time was that Richard Sr. had been let off on a minor charge largely due to the intervention of the general who had been his commanding officer prior to his absconding to Havana. This I accepted at face value and let the matter drop.

The questions, however, have not been stilled over the years and if anything have grown larger. I recall whispers at the time by the Lydays who themselves were astonished at the rapidity with which Maj. Pearce emerged from custody. They wondered *sotto voce* if perhaps Pearce had all along been a CIA agent. Their musings were reflected in occasional comments by other members of the family. No one, it seemed, had the answer. I had had some questions in the back of my mind, certainly from 1970 on. In the summers of 1970 and 1971, I travelled to CIA headquarters in Langley for debriefing by both the covert and overt sides of the Agency. No one ever took the initiative in raising the Pearce case with me. On both occasions, I referred explicitly to my contacts with him, but to my surprise there appeared to be no interest in pursuing the subject. Why? After all, my contacts there seemed to have an endless appetite for views on all aspects of the situation in Cuba – except for this one.

The truth of the situation will never, it seems, be known. Pearce came out of Fort Bragg and promptly dropped from sight. Through my wife's cousin in Alabama, we did at one point get his telephone number and were able to have a brief conversation with him. Pearce was cordial, but neither did he give any indication of a desire to maintain the contact. His relationship with his son was put on ice. Little Richard had – and still has – a fervent desire to stay in touch with his father. At one point he found out where he was, and travelled to see him. The meeting did not go well and the Major let it be known that he did not wish to see him again. The last we heard of him was that he was reported to be in a dead-end job somewhere on the Louisiana coast. Since that time, he has been invisible.

In 2004 I met up with Little Richard and the conversation naturally turned to the subject of his father. We talked about his father's motivation in going to Cuba in the first place and the rumours about his possible intelligence contacts. Richard Jr. was, and is, as mystified as anyone else. Certainly he did not dismiss out of hand the spy theory. He said that he has often, in reflecting on the Havana years, examined in minute detail his father's habits and general behaviour. The only suspicious element he can come up with is the fact that his father, not one for casual contact with the neighbours or indeed anyone else in Havana, every once in a while in the dead of night would disappear into the back garden where he could be heard conversing with someone in low tones. Suspicious? Maybe. Definitive? By no means. What on earth could his father's role as a spy have been? Someone as acutely under the spotlight of G2 as Major Pearce undoubtedly could scarcely have been expected to act undercover. Was he somehow an agent in place ready for activation in the event of an American invasion or other project?

I should note as postscript to this story that, contrary to our assumption all along, the Lydays were for many years never aware that we were related, through marriage, to Major Richard Pearce. When we referred to this casually, in meeting the Lydays long after leaving Cuba, they were totally and utterly shocked. As they said, we could have 'knocked them down with a feather'!

And so, at the end of the day, we are left only with questions and no answers to explain this unlikely story. What do I think? I tend to the view that Pearce was not a lone actor in the piece. There are simply too many elements that cannot be explained except in the context of a deeper plot. I continue to this day to try to locate Major Pearce. If I ever find him, and if I am able to meet with him, I will ask him outright for the answers to the questions that still cause me hours of speculation. Not that I really expect him to lay the matter to rest.

Little Richard at home in Havana with his dog Snoopy.
Photo courtesy of Richard Pearce Jr.

The decorated Vietnam War veteran Major Richard Pearce, with Richard Jr., prior to their departure for Cuba. Photo courtesy of Richard Pearce Jr.

Chapter Six

COUNTDOWN TO HANDOVER

On June 30, 1997, I sat transfixed in front of the television at home in Calgary as, promptly at midnight, the gates opened and truckloads of troops of the Chinese People's Liberation Army streamed across the border. Their destination was HMS Tamar, headquarters of the British military in the heart of Hong Kong for the past 100 years. Just prior to their arrival, the last governor, Sir Christopher Patton, British Prime Minister Tony Blair, and their entourage of senior officials boarded the Royal Yacht Britannia for a final departure.

The occasion was marked by deeply emotional ceremonies. On the Chinese side, the nation watched as the last real vestige of colonialism and humiliation was eliminated from its territory. For the British, it was the conclusion to the final chapter of the British

Empire on whose territories, in its grandest days, the sun never set. Tears were shed by the large contingent of British expatriates in the splendid new Convention Centre as the massed bands played the imperial march, 'Rule Britannia', and the British flag was lowered for the last time. In its place, the flag of the People's Republic was proudly raised against a background of dazzling fireworks.

My own emotions were mixed. On the one hand, I had been raised in my earliest years under the Union Jack. In our school assemblies during the Second World War, we raised the roof singing, "There'll Always be an England" and "God Save the Queen". There was indeed a lump in my throat as I watched the flag come down and witnessed Scots in their kilts and the Royal Marines beat the retreat. The notion of empire, even if carefully concealed most of the time, was there under the surface, ready to emerge on occasions such as this.

On the other hand, my politics had become anything but conservative. With my head, if not with my heart, I welcomed the end of the Empire. I find amusing, reading through journals I kept at the time, the number of references to the territory's insufferable colonial society. Even as head of the Canadian mission, I frequently felt insulted by the rudeness and superior airs put on by some of the snobbish Brits with whom we interacted or found ourselves sitting beside at dinner. These were the last vestiges of a colonial mentality and, indeed, totally out of keeping with the grand hospitality I had enjoyed earlier as a student in Glasgow. One could only imagine what the ambiance must have been like during the peak period of British rule in India, Malaya, South Africa and elsewhere in the Empire. During our first year in Hong Kong, my reaction was simply to seethe inwardly and keep it to myself. The solution, I learned, was to preempt the insult by acting a bit overbearing myself and pointedly ignoring those who would be rude. In those days, I felt little remorse over the prospect of the Hong Kong British getting their comeuppance from the Chinese who, in their own way, could be equally insufferable when they chose. As Sir Philip Haddon-Cave, the Finance Secretary, pointed out to me shortly after our arrival, "'Don't be fooled. When you look at a small Chinese boy selling widgets on the street, just remember: when he looks at you, he thanks God he wasn't born a round-eye!'"

The hypocrisy of Britain's last governor, Christopher Patton, in raising the flag of democracy and becoming teary-eyed over the 'abandonment' of the Hong Kong Chinese as he took his departure was something I found unfortunate. The colony existed through most of its colonial history under iron-fisted British rule and with scarcely a shred of political democracy. There was no particular reason to suppose that Beijing, having signalled for decades that it valued Hong Kong as an unfettered economic golden goose, was about to introduce any substantive changes. By contrast, China was still something of an 'enigma wrapped in a mystery', and one never knew; Patten has his apologists, and Lord Wilson, Patten's China-friendly predecessor, his detractors, but my own views were much more closely aligned with Wilson's.

There was far too much going on in Hong Kong in the late 70's to spend one's time dwelling on the perverse spectacle of a fading society having difficulty coming to grips with its fate. The territory, in spite of the trepidation and uncertainty beginning to take hold, was vibrantly alive, twenty-four hours a day. It was 'the' gateway to China. Anyone wanting to do serious business on the Mainland had to start in Hong Kong where the economic expertise resided. Hong Kong was the place to find out what was really happening in China, and for that reason, all the major news organisations maintained bureaus there. The Far Eastern Economic Review under its editor, the fearless Derek Davies, was a beacon of accurate reporting and solid commentary throughout Southeast Asia. In the territory itself, economic activity was superheated. The property market was red hot. The modest Canadian residence, which the Government of Canada purchased in 1978 for Cdn $4 million, attracted offers of $16 million less than four years later. Textiles and manufacturing were booming. Hong Kong hosted the world's largest container port. If one happened upon a gathering of grannies in front of a TV screen on Queen's Road Central, it was surely not to watch the Oprah Winfrey show but rather to catch up on the latest stock market quotes and the price of gold.

The Canadian office, known as the Commission for Canada, was one of the country's largest. It housed large trade and immigration sections, and the position of Commissioner was traditionally the preserve of those two departments. I was the first political type assigned to head up the place, the reason being that with the political relationship with China becoming more and more important, it made good sense to strengthen the office's capacity for political analysis and to make more use of the sources available – at least, so the mandarins in External Affairs thought.

Amusingly, I found myself under fire from two sides. The immigration people were mightily annoyed because I had, in their eyes, usurped their right to hold the office. From another quarter came salvoes fired by our ambassador in Beijing, who took exception to the fact that an upstart Head of Mission in the Hong Kong Commission, by reporting his perspective on developments in China, was encroaching on the Embassy's turf. The immigration people I made peace with quite quickly by, apart from being a nice guy, subtly underscoring the fact that I would be writing the performance appraisals for the senior officers at the mission. The Beijing Embassy, headed up by a thick-skinned and capable old China hand, Arthur Menzies, proved a tougher nut to crack. Far from appreciating the insights that might be provided from another source, he lost no opportunity to contradict and dispute political reports from the Hong Kong office.

His miscalculation lay in the fact that he underestimated my own enthusiasm for a good fight. Menzies' protestations simply led to greater efforts and increased output on our part. We occasionally managed to score big time. On February 18, 1979, for example, China launched an all-out attack on Vietnam along the full length of their common border. Menzies for some time had been predicting with his usual confidence that the Chinese would not react to what they considered Vietnamese provocations. We, based on various sources in Hong Kong, saw things differently. A week before the attack, we sent in a report stating that, in spite of what might appear logical, we considered it probable that China would go to war. This is not in any way to belittle the excellent reports coming from Menzies who, with his knowledge of the language and early years spent in China, had insights that were barred to the rest of us.

And so we sniped at each other throughout the better part of our time from our respective posts. I was occasionally moved to utter descriptions of the ambassador that were not at all diplomatic. I am sure that he reciprocated in kind. We occasionally met face to face, where the facade of camaraderie was maintained. Ottawa was quite aware of the heat in the relationship. Jim McCardle, the Director General, travelled first to Beijing and subsequently to Hong Kong in an effort to make peace. In Beijing he discussed the matter with Menzies, who claimed to know nothing of the issue, protesting vigorously that the relationship between us was just fine. McCardle's frustration knew no bounds when, in Hong Kong, he confronted me only to be assured that Arthur and I were the best of friends. The poor man left the post muttering to himself.

The period of our stay in Hong Kong was notable and politically gripping for several reasons. It marked the final repudiation of the disastrous Cultural Revolution that brought tragedy to so many millions, and the end of the era of Mao Zedong. This was replaced by Deng's 'Beijing Spring', which laid the foundation for China's astonishing development that continues today. It was also in that period that diplomatic relations between the U.S. and the People's Republic were finally formalised. The events then occurring gave us plenty of material for reporting purposes. Our Hong Kong sources we supplemented with journeys, as possible, into China, both further into the interior but also to the border regions of Shenzhen and Guangzhou, where we were occasionally invited by the Mainland's official representatives in Hong Kong to witness China's plans for new cities and strategic economic zones. I was not particularly impressed at the time, thinking that we were just listening to more propaganda. Shenzhen and much of the Pearl River estuary at that time presented a beautiful pastoral scene. How things change! The whole area stretching from the Hong Kong boundary north to Guangzhou today has been transformed into one giant industrial area. One important consequence is that in Hong Kong itself, the appearance of the sun against a background of blue sky is a rare occurrence as all the pollution from the Pearl River Delta drifts south, pushed by the prevailing wind.

Looking back today with the benefit of the repose that retirement confers, I become ever more conscious of the fragility of our social structures. The Cultural Revolution came and went. Those of us on the outside observed and analysed, trying to grasp and interpret what was going on. We never really succeeded until later years when we were able to fathom the enormity of the upheaval by reading accounts of personal experiences and hearing tales of the trauma so many lived through. How a whole nation could be so transformed in such a short time is chilling to contemplate. I suppose the same thing happened in Hitler's Germany of the 30's and Pol Pot's Cambodia in the 70's. There is obviously no room for arrogance on the part of those of us fortunate enough to live in a Western democracy. Had

Al-Qaeda succeeded in delivering two or three more powerful blows hard on the heels of 9/11, I am convinced that we would have witnessed dissolution of much of America's democratic structure, given the authoritarian proclivities of the George W. Bush administration.

Not only on the Chinese mainland was life changing; even though less perceptible on a day-to-day basis, the basic structure of Hong Kong society was mutating from one based on British domination and rule, to one focused on the countdown to '97. Already in the 70's, a certain angst was noticeable among the Chinese population, spurred along by, for example, the difficulty in obtaining mortgages due to the inability to secure financing beyond the turnover date. The direct effect on our work at the Commission were long lines of immigration applicants. Many Chinese had fled the Communist regime to Hong Kong and were beginning an urgent, sometimes desperate, search for safe haven after the takeover. For others, it was simply a matter of taking precautions, and the queue for visas included folks from the top to the bottom end of the social and economic scale. Our policy was liberal and Canada opened its doors to tens of thousands who would ultimately have a significant demographic impact, particularly on Canada's west coast.

The other side of the coin was that British influence during our tenure was visibly waning. This was perhaps most noticeable in the aggressive intrusion by Chinese economic interests into bastions once fiercely guarded by the British. One by one, bits and pieces of the Empire began to fall into Chinese hands, occasioning hand-wringing and foul moods on the part of the old Hong Kong hands. Leading the charge was Hong Kong businessman Li Ka-shing, still relatively modest in the pecking order when we arrived in 1977, but destined eventually to control vast swaths of the stock market and to become a power internationally. KS Li, whose family moved from the Mainland to the colony when he was only ten, was the epitome of a migrant's success story. From plastic flower seller to one of the world's richest men, Li built his empire on rare qualities of extraordinary financial acumen, honesty, political wisdom and a large dose of modesty.

The other signs of looming change were the cracks beginning to appear in Hong Kong's rigid social divide between Chinese and Brit. Hong Kong in the 70's represented the dying gasp of the overt racism that formed an integral part of the Empire. Perhaps the most extreme example was the Hong Kong Club, established in 1846. Cardinal rules, even if unwritten, were no women, no children, and no non-whites including Chinese. The same exclusionary approach was still being observed some 130 years later, in the 1970's, when we arrived.

'The Club' had traditionally been the seat of British power in the colony. It was the unquestioned preserve of the rich and the powerful, that is, the *taipans*, heads of the British companies headquartered there, known as *hongs*, and senior government officials. At the head of the mix, to be found in the ballroom or one of the private dining rooms on important occasions, was the Governor, supported by the Secretaries of Government and senior officers of the military. As I look back over the span of thirty years, I am surprised that my predecessors and I were authorised by our own government to join the Club, given the racial and gender qualifications, but obviously sensitivities on the issues were not as acute as they became a few years later, and the opportunities to rub shoulders with the political and business elite were considered paramount. The Chinese, of course, not to be outdone by the British, had their own exclusive clubs.

Within the bowels of the Hong Kong Club was lodged an invisible little group known as The Tripehounds. Chaired by the Governor, The Tripehounds consisted of about thirty of the most powerful Brits in the colony who, as availability permitted, met each Thursday for lunch. And yes, the menu did indeed include tripe. There was no agenda. It was simply an opportunity for the holders of the levers of power to breathe rarefied air and quietly exchange confidences. By some quirk in the past, the Governor had decided that the heads of mission of the three white Commonwealth countries, Australia, Canada and New Zealand, should be invited to join the group. Not that it was automatic; the portal was guarded by the requirement that one first be admitted to the Club through the normal vetting procedures. These were relied upon to ensure that no undesirable element should penetrate the inner sanctum. Should any of the three Commissioners have been black, yellow or any colour other than white, and the gender other than male, he or she would undoubtedly have been excluded.

At the luncheon table, the pecking order was rigidly maintained. The Governor sat in the middle. Places were not assigned, but in fact everyone by some process of osmosis knew his place. Power resided in the middle and flowed out in ever diminishing doses until the end of the table was reached. Mere Commissioners from the 'colonies' floated around the outer reaches. One's first attendance was marked by an invitation to sit on the Governor's right. Thereafter, to usurp the seat of a superior was at one's peril. The old Brits took malicious delight in encouraging the uninitiated to move up the line, and were equally gratified to witness the ensuing embarrassment of the delinquent. Nothing spoken, of course. Just those small gestures of put-down of which the British upper class are masters. The Australian Commissioner and I, seated near the end of the table, amused ourselves by exchanging rude observations *sotto voce* on the habits and behaviour of our luncheon partners.

The old order was coming to an end, even if the outward framework was still in place. The Club's aura had dimmed somewhat by the 70's, its dominance challenged by other organisations such as the American Club and various Chinese entities. Membership had lost some of its appeal. A move emerged just before I left Hong Kong to break the race barrier and admit some Chinese. Even The Tripehounds group, at which attendance was once considered almost obligatory, was beginning to see a thinning of the ranks. The Club itself was falling ever deeper into debt and in 1980 disaster almost struck as a motion was put forward for its disbanding. The solution eventually adopted was to tear down the grand old building and structure a redevelopment in such a way as to ensure the Club's financial health for years to come. Together with the Club building disappeared one of the most visible symbols of the old order. The field was now clear for the new *taipans,* this time of the Chinese variety, to prepare for the territory's reversion to the Mainland a decade and a half hence.

The position of Club president at the time of writing is occupied by a Chinese businessman.

My journal from those days attests that, after the political rough and tumble of Berlin, Moscow and Havana, I found Hong Kong a drastic and not necessarily welcome change. Perhaps it was that most of the Ministers and government delegations who stopped by were more interested in buying suits and shirts than in political enlightenment. Or perhaps it was the crass mercenary nature of the place where almost anyone and anything could be bought for a price. Excitement derived, not from being pursued by secret agents, but rather from watching one's horse win at the Jockey Club. Discussion at dinner revolved around the price of gold rather than Mrs. Gandhi's declaration of emergency or the latest political upheaval. If the truth were told, I felt that I was in a holding pattern; I longed to get back to the front lines of the Cold War. This appetite was only whetted by occasional political forays across the border into China where my concern was not pursuit by Chinese minders but rather defending my reports against complaints of encroachment from Menzies!

We did have plenty to keep ourselves occupied. The management of a mission that size was demanding. Keeping on top of the various programs – immigration, consular, trade, drugs, crime and so forth – for which I had at least nominal responsibility, was time consuming. Most demanding of all was the constant flow of visitors: business people and official delegations such as veterans for the annual Remembrance Day ceremonies.

The sudden influx of so-called 'boat people' from Vietnam in their thousands shortly after our arrival triggered a crisis in which Canada became intimately involved. Watercraft, large and small, produced a daily influx into the colony. Goodness knows how many lost their lives traversing the oft treacherous waters of the South China Sea. As a frustrated licenced pilot with no plane to fly, I was delighted when given the opportunity to ride co-pilot a couple of times on surveillance flights of the Royal Hong Kong Auxiliary Air Force along the coast towards Vietnam. The objective was to spot incoming vessels and report their position to the Marine Police. Such was my desire to fly that I briefly toyed with the idea of joining the Auxiliary, but was quickly dissuaded by the thought of how my superiors might view things if, by some quirk of Murphy's Law, I happened to suffer engine failure and be forced down, say, on China's Hainan Island.

The exodus quickly turned into a humanitarian crisis of major proportions. The sight of freighters grounded off the Hong Kong coast, overloaded with human cargo, stranded for months, and of small boats loaded with refugees with harrowing tales of encounters with weather and pirates clutched at the heartstrings. The refugee issue became a political football in Canada. I pitched in, strongly supporting Canadian humanitarian intervention. Over a relatively short period, our immigration section was ordered to come up with many thousands of refugees and move them to Canada. This was over and above the already large number of Chinese applicants for normal immigration visas. The task was Herculean, although made lighter by a drastic loosening of the criteria for selection. It came down basically to a question of if you had a head and most of the necessary appendages, you qualified. Our people, with section head John MacLachlan at the helm, did a tremendous job. The main role I played, apart from lobbying my own government, was having my photo occasionally taken for the media kissing babies aboard chartered aircraft about to depart for Vancouver.

The British administration, it should be noted, was not uniformly pleased with Canada's generosity. It was the view of some senior officials that by taking so many refugees, we were providing encouragement to the thousands of other Vietnamese thinking of leaving.

No story of diplomatic life in Hong Kong would be complete without reference to the frantic social whirl. At one level there was the incestuous entertaining among the diplomats themselves. A constant feature for most countries was the 'national day reception' staged by the various embassies to mark their nation's birth, liberation, ruler's birthday or, failing something dramatic, some other nondescript event. Invitees included, naturally, all the representatives of other countries with whom the host had diplomatic relations, and prominent local dignitaries. The guest numbers were limited only by the dollar amount the host ambassador had been allocated for the event by his or her government. Of course the Head of Government was invited and, should he or she happen to appear, the host ambassador scurried about, bursting with pride at having been so honoured, and quite convinced that the favour bestowed was the direct product of the ambassador's personal charm and good looks.

The Canadian government in those days seemed to be in a perpetual state of austerity with the result that few funds were made available for events such as Canada Day. The fortunate outcome was that we had a ready-made excuse for limiting our activity to a modest reception for Canadians and avoiding all the wasteful expenditure associated with the more elaborate celebrations put on by other countries.

Nothing could save us, though, from the massive inflow of invitations we ourselves received from members of the Chinese and Canadian business communities. The net result was that we found ourselves at receptions and dinners most nights of the week. "Ah," many of our friends in Canada would say, when told of the lavish Chinese banquets, gourmet lunches and invitations to the finest restaurants, "How lucky you are!" And indeed we were – except for the fact that when the activity goes on week after week, and month after month, one tends to become rather like a walking, talking, perpetually sleep-deprived robot.

Even if by nature a roast-beef-&-mashed-potatoes-&-gravy kind of a guy, I did thrive on most of the exotic dishes that were served up. Most of them were a culinary delight. Some were not. Snake meat I could handle; chicken feet I couldn't. On one occasion after a succession of particularly challenging offerings, I saw with considerable relief that the dessert delicacy was to be apple pie with whipped cream. I therefore helped myself to a large portion only to discover that the apples were water chestnuts, covered with a layer of salt, and topped off with sour cream. Not quite my mom's home cooking. Completing my misery, our Thai hostess having noted my great enthusiasm in taking the first portion, insisted that I indulge in a second. Not only did I have to finish off the second piece, but had little choice but to pretend that I enjoyed the concoction thoroughly.

Our own entertaining tended to be much less exotic, and restricted to solid Canadian fare such as beef, chops, salmon and so on. Our cook, Mr. Leung, did an excellent job, and we received many compliments. An elderly gentleman, he was a model of propriety and decorum while in the dining room. Once through the door into the kitchen, however, Dr. Jekyll became Mr. Hyde as he directed a stream of invective at the stove, the wall, his ancestors, our dogs Pirate and Freddy, and any other target within range. The ranting could be heard but not deciphered from the confines of the dining room, at least by the non-Chinese speakers, and it was a matter of considerable conjecture among our guests as to what opinions he was expressing — except for the Chinese present who maintained a judicious silence.

Mr. Leung's helper on these occasions was the inimitable A-Mei. She was quite unpredictable, capable of a raging temper in her own right, but also of gestures of affection. On one occasion, Jack Horner, Minister of Agriculture, came to dinner along with several other Canadians and Chinese. For one reason or another, Horner attracted A-Mei's devoted attention. She parked herself at Horner's elbow throughout the meal and insisted on doing everything but putting the fork in his mouth for him. Whenever rolls were passed, she would put one on his plate, butter it and present it to him. Horner for his part looked a bit puzzled, but seemed to accept the attention as a Chinese custom.

Diversions in Hong Kong were many. Workaholism was the norm for much of the community. But as hard as one worked, one also attended to the need for occasional relaxation with the same exuberance. For some, it was getting caught up in the gambling fever in horse racing in Happy Valley, or in the non-stop casino scene in nearby Macau. Others recharged their batteries with a Sunday excursion on the corporate junk, otherwise known as floating gin palaces. We got our fix by buying a small sailing craft and taking any spare opportunity to motor out from the Aberdeen typhoon shelter where it was moored, and having a sail on the South China Sea. Often we would simply sail across to Lamma Island, drop the anchor and indulge ourselves in a seafood meal at one of the waterfront restaurants. Other times, I thrived by taking it out in heavy seas beyond Lamma or in completing a circumnavigation of Hong Kong Island itself, dodging ferries, freighters and fishing vessels with little respect for a sailboat's right of way.

The sailboat also provided us with a medium for entertaining. On one occasion, our guests were the New Zealand Commissioner and his Swedish spouse. Madame professed fear of the sea and it was only with the greatest of difficulty that we were able to persuade her to board the boat, and to disembark for lunch on one of the islands. During the lunch itself, Madame consumed a very considerable amount of spirits with the result that she trotted back to the point of embarkation afterwards, and without waiting for an invitation launched herself with a great leap from the dock onto the deck. It was only with difficulty that we dissuaded her on the return journey from taking a dip in the ocean.

Against the backdrop of our mini-world of ministers in search of nimble tailors, fine dining, processing immigrants and pushing exports, history moved on. Mao had died in 1976. The infamous Gang of Four led by Mao's widow, Jiang Qing, instrumental in powering the Cultural Revolution, was arrested a month later. By the time I took up station in 1977, the reformer Deng Xiaoping was making his presence felt. China was changing rapidly. We could sense it all around us, but could not really get our teeth into it. The mechanisms for change, and the processes within the Communist Party itself, still remained largely impenetrable. The Bank of China, seat of Chinese presence and power in Hong Kong, still stood as a bleak fortress whose inner workings were unseen. What was clear was that a slow-motion earthquake was in progress, but what the eventual outcome would be was still obscure. The breathtaking images cast by the Chinese cities of the new millennia were in the future. The White Swan Hotel in Canton (now Guangzhou), catering to foreigners, was still shabby and uninviting. Travel between Hong Kong and the Mainland remained awkward and frustrating. Would a reaction to Deng set in and stifle hopes for modernisation and a better life? Or would the reformers manage to carry the day? These were the issues that preoccupied us and became the stuff of discussion and speculation as I and a few of my colleagues gathered occasionally over beer and a sandwich.

I was ready to leave Hong Kong when the time came in the early summer of 1981. The feeling was not shared by all the family. Indeed, our oldest son, Tom, still lives there, the territory having been his home in a virtually unbroken line since that time. Our daughter, too, returned and lives there at the time of writing. Laine and I are not surprised by this. Hong Kong was a great place for family. The city was safe, public transport superb. Schooling was excellent. The Canadian community was large and welcoming. It was, however, time to move on for one more attuned to fighting the Cold War than promoting the sale of widgets.

The lump in our throats, which was there every time we completed a posting, was very much in evidence as Mr. Wong, our driver, conveyed us for the last time down the hill from Jardine's Lookout, past the Happy Valley racetrack, through the cross-harbour tunnel and thence the short distance to Kai Tak airport. With the usual courtesies, we were taken in a black limo to the steps of the aircraft for official farewells. I would be lying if I did not admit that my eyes were watering freely as we did our last pass over the world's busiest harbour and the incredible city that had become so much a part of our lives. Memories were overflowing, some consequential, others simply trivial flashbacks: memorial services at Sai Wan honouring Canada's heroes who died in Hong Kong's defence in 1941; presenting a gift of harbour seals from the Vancouver Aquarium to Hong Kong's Ocean Park; setting sail in the harbour below for the strenuous 700-mile China Sea Race to Manila; drawing tears from Hong Kong schoolchildren with a heartfelt account of Terry Fox's heroic walk. The mist-shrouded hills of China faded into the golden haze of the afternoon sun as we headed on our long journey up the coast towards Taiwan and Japan, and back to Canada. The firm conviction of most Westerners was that the future of China lay in becoming like us. Personally I was not so sure. This ancient civilisation, home to one-fifth of the world's population, seemed to me more likely to chart its own path.

Bill sailing with Laine's parents, Buddy and Todd Rowe, Repulse Bay, Hong Kong.

Inspecting the Sea Cadets in Hong Kong.

Trying hard to look entertained at a Christmas function, Hong Kong.

With visiting Candian dignitary, Ontario Premier Bill Davis.

Non-stop diplomatic functions, Hong Kong.

Chapter Seven

SEEDS OF CONFLICT

There was a soft thud in the sand beside us. And then another, and another. It was late Sunday afternoon. We were walking in the parched desert-like scrub about a kilometre behind the Ambassador's residence. Looking around to see where the sound was coming from, we spotted a group of children who had emerged from a small clutch of mud huts. The sound was caused by the stones they were throwing at us. With our faithful Dalmatian, Pirate, dashing in circles after anything that moved, from lizards to the creepy-crawlies in his imagination, we had been keeping a wary eye out for the jackals that howled every night outside the compound, and the poisonous snakes that were common enough in the brush. But rocks? Welcome to Pakistan.

We took the hint and moved off, quickly absorbing the lesson that we were in a different culture, that customs in this colourful and fascinating country were something that needed to be learned and observed. Why were the boys throwing stones? Was it because of the Muslim dislike of dogs? Was it because Laine was walking, head uncovered? Was this an early manifestation of the Clash of Civilizations? Or was it simply villagers reacting, as perhaps they had been taught to do for centuries, with caution to any stranger approaching their territory? I imagine that if the boys had wanted to do damage, they could easily have zeroed in on their targets, since throwing stones was something of a national pastime in the countryside. Instead, they apparently simply wanted to warn us off.

It was during our final six months in Hong Kong that the idea of moving to Islamabad was broached. The place at the time had the reputation among foreign service professionals as being the back of beyond, and assignment there as a step towards oblivion. This opinion was obviously held by some of our political masters as well. Not long after we had accepted the proposal and had begun to look forward with enthusiasm to going there, I was passing through the business lounge at Narita airport in Tokyo, when I ran into Canada's extroverted, shoot-from-the-hip Minister for International Trade, and some colleagues. They were at the bar. I sat down with them and, being a spy by nature, I quickly scanned the papers they had left lying on the coffee table. The first thing that caught my eye was a slip of paper with the following written in bold letters on it: "Warden-No to Pakistan!" Talk about timing. The

Minister had evidently been in the process of discussing upcoming ambassadorial postings with the staff accompanying him when I arrived on the scene. In the inimitable Lumley fashion, he began to berate me for accepting Islamabad, said it would be waste of time and experience for me after Hong Kong, and that he wanted to change my assignment to Malaysia – where the action was... trade action, that is.

What Lumley missed was that, while being involved in Hong Kong in trade matters, among other things, was fine for four years, I was far and away more interested in international politics. The main bait that had drawn me to Hong Kong was not trade, but rather the opportunity to become involved in observing and reporting on political evolution in China. Trade matters were best left to our excellent trade commissioners. Politics was the same pot of honey that drew me inexorably to accept the Pakistan assignment. I left Narita, considerably diminished in Lumley's eyes, but more than ever satisfied that Pakistan was the right choice. After all, neighbouring Afghanistan had recently been invaded by the Soviet Union, the resistance had become ferocious and hundreds of thousands of refugees were pouring across the border. The 'Great Game', which had pitted the British Empire against Russia in the 19th century and which I had been reading about for years, had been revived. The conventional wisdom was that the Soviets were positioning themselves for an eventual thrust through Baluchistan to the warm waters of the Arabian Sea ... a political observer's paradise. Little did we, or anyone else, realise that the mighty Soviet Union was at that point less than a decade from ignominious collapse; or that the events unfolding across the border were to play an important role in the empire's demise, and lay the foundation for the bloody events that continue to this day.

Following service in the Soviet Union and Cuba, Pakistan was made to order – and the more I thought about it, the more I relished the idea of pursuing the Cold War, this time on the Asian subcontinent.

Enamoured as Laine and I were at the prospect of moving to a new part of the world, Pakistan in reality turned out to be a far more fascinating place to live and work than we could have imagined. From the drought-ridden Thar desert in the south, to the moonscape of restive Baluchistan; from the teeming and sometimes menacing port of Karachi, up through the northwest frontier to the picturesque Kingdom of Swat and on to the meeting of five mountain ranges at the top of the world in Gilgit and Hunza; we travelled the length and breadth of the country for the next two years, soaking up the images and the culture. This part of the former British Empire has always been cloaked in mystery, intrigue and risk of violence, but we were there at the best of times when at least most areas were accessible to those with an adventurous bent. This is not to say that we did not sense latent hostility to the West or feel the need to stay aware. Yet, the Pakistan posting was one part of the enormous kaleidoscope that is South Asia, and which we were to experience in spades later on when transferred to India. This was 'diplo-tourism' at its best!

While workaholic tendencies ensured that I at least imagined myself as enjoying all aspects of my work, I recognise in retrospect that this was more illusion than reality. How could mediating all too frequent personnel squabbles, pouring over budget figures, or figuring out inventive ways to thwart Ottawa's maniacal and endless attempts to impose ever more onerous administrative requirements to satisfy petty bureaucratic whims compete with the excitement and colour of the world outside the Embassy walls?

Administration in Islamabad, as I quickly discovered, was much more demanding than in a place such as Geneva or Tokyo or Hong Kong. Living conditions were such that the Canadian government built and maintained housing compounds for all Canadian staff. We provided vehicles, accommodation for domestic staff, appliances, and so forth. This was a fine arrangement on paper, but a horrendous headache for the Ambassador who found her- or himself in the position of landlord, unwilling mayor, interior design expert and chief defender of Ottawa's indefensible housing policies to a flock consisting more often of wolves than sheep.

My wife and I had scarcely removed our coats on arrival at the Ambassador's residence when a senior Embassy administrator requested an audience to protest the fact that another newly arrived staff member had spent the last several hours harassing and "screaming" at him over dissatisfaction with their assigned housing unit. This meeting was followed minutes later by the intrusion of the employee in question who seemed to believe that, even though I still did not even know where the nearest toilet was, I was personally responsible for the outrage perpetrated against her and her husband.

This is where I made a bad decision based on faulty judgment. An Embassy clerk with a family had been assigned an officer's house, while the officer had ended up in less desirable accommodation. In my view, the unit provided was satisfactory, even if not ideal. Moreover, in that era, when financial scandals were more often covered up than revealed, I had the rather quaint conviction that one of my main obligations was to protect the taxpayer's purse and avoid unnecessary expense. How naïve! In retrospect, I recognise that the sane course of action would have been to throw money at the problem, rent a large house off the compound in the city for the disgruntled pair to get them off my back, and to hell with the unnecessary expense. On the other hand, I was assured on a number of occasions by persons closer to the officer than I, that she found the misogynous Pakistani society more than she could stomach, and that much of her latent anger was taken out on me.

As I grew longer in the tooth with the passing of years and saw the incredible wastage incurred on every hand by the bureaucracy, to say nothing of the even greater boondoggles of our political masters without so much as a hiccup in response, I regretted enormously the false sense of stewardship ingrained in me from those years when I had difficulty raising a few cents for a root beer. As it was, the consequences of that housing decision, even though explicitly approved by Ottawa, pursued me for years in petty, indirect ways. My only hope is that on Judgment Day, I will finally be exonerated for my foolishness.

Even housing administration did, however, occasionally have its humorous side. At one point, we were replacing the roof on the staff compound. It was lunchtime and one of the staff members was at home and relaxing on the johnny. Droplets began to fall on him from above and he realised that rain was coming in through the overhead ventilator. On reflection, "curious," he thought. "The sky was blue when I came from the office and, after all, we haven't had rain for months." Prompt investigation revealed that the source of the unlikely precipitation was a worker on the roof peeing down the ventilator shaft. Expletives deleted.

Islamabad turned out to be a welcome respite from social obligations after Hong Kong – just as Havana had been after Moscow. If Cuba figured on no minister's 'places-to-visit' list, Pakistan was even less appealing to the travelling political class. The country in fact was distinctly out of favour. It had violated the terms under which a nuclear reactor had been provided by Canada for peaceful purposes. The duly elected Prime Minister, Zulfikar Ali Bhutto, had been removed by a military coup and eventually hanged. Overlooked in the requiem for democracy that followed his execution were the atrocities – torture and killings – that had been carried out under Bhutto's watch in Baluchistan. His wife, and daughter Benazir, still politically active, were under house arrest in Karachi. Flawed democracy had been replaced by dictatorship, and Pakistan had been expelled from the Commonwealth.

This meant that we were freed from one of the necessary but most burdensome encumbrances of the diplomatic job: the care and feeding of boondoggling ministers and parliamentarians. I freely admit that my vision had undoubtedly been warped by the Hong Kong experience. Custom-tailored suits and shirts and what-have-you were still much cheaper in the colony than at home, and the number of taxpayer-funded visits by our wandering politicians was quite incredible. Two Quebec senators and their spouses, ostensibly on a fact-finding mission, appeared unannounced in my office in Hong Kong one afternoon demanding immediate use of our sole mission vehicle for two days, and various other services including an invitation to the residence. Their wrath knew no bounds when I demurred on purely practical grounds, and I was given clearly to understand that the Prime Minister, a 'personal friend', would hear of the unsatisfactory job we were doing. On another occasion, a high level bureaucrat and his spouse arrived for the mandatory shopping weekend in Hong Kong, pursued by angry accusations from Tokyo that they had 'shoplifted' from their Tokyo hotel room two expensive kimonos, available for the convenience of guests, but not as souvenirs. This time I was smart enough to stay out of things. The intrepid Ambassador in Tokyo, and one of Canada's most senior and capable at the time, met the offending party at the airport on their way back to Canada. Sparks flew. The Ambassador paid for the kimonos out of his own pocket. Retribution for such insubordination was swift. The Ambassador was eventually rewarded for his relentless pursuit of righteousness; he called to tell me that his request to extend his posting in Japan by a year to finish out his career had been denied and that he had been offered reassignment to the tiny Canadian mission in Oslo instead.

In wild and woolly Pakistan, there was none of this. Cheap shirts and suits aplenty, but not quite up to ministerial standard. No bright lights, fine restaurants or girlie shows. Alcohol strictly forbidden except to those with a criminal streak. On the other hand, the lovely green marijuana plant flourished in profusion just outside the Embassy gate, but its existence was known only to a privileged few academic and periodic business visitors, who referred to it as "Embassy gold". Mind you, we did not live a life of total temperance. Although forbidden to serve drinks to Pakistani nationals, this rule was more often honoured in the breach than as the rule. A typical scene went something like this. Perhaps a dozen or so Pakistani businessmen accompanied by two or three government bureaucrats would come to dinner. Dinner over, the bureaucrats would depart soon thereafter, whereupon the remaining guests lost no time in ordering whiskey, martinis, rum and coke, and what have you. So much for the threat of a public flogging.

We ourselves were not above pressing our own luck even further. Occasionally we would dine at a small restaurant tucked away on a side street operated by a Chinese family. It was dry of course, but with a wrinkle. The idea was that the client would take a bottle concealed in an innocuous looking bag, hand it to the proprietor, who would then serve it up in a teapot. We ourselves never experienced any problems, but at one point some low level diplomats doing precisely the same thing at the same restaurant were picked up by the police and unceremoniously dispatched from the country. Lesson learned.

The subject of booze was always a ticklish issue. Inside a diplomat's house, alcohol consumption followed the 'don't see, don't tell' rule. For non-diplomatic foreigners entering Pakistan, all alcoholic beverages were confiscated... if discovered. Good friends Jack and Bob, together with their wives Shirley and Marina, visited us for a couple of weeks. Bob's bottle, which he declared to the zealous customs officer, was immediately seized, although the officer did say Bob could get it back when he eventually exited through Karachi. Jack, whom I came to know as one of the most prodigious consumers of Scotch I have ever encountered, with a look of pure innocence declared himself quite free of the substance. We were surprised therefore when, no sooner had they settled into their rooms, Jack, producing a bottle, asked: "Bob, how about a drink?" "But you told the man at the airport you didn't have anything," said Bob. "Do you know what they would have done to you if they had found out you were telling a lie?" "I wasn't lying," said Jack. "I didn't have a thing." "Where did you get the bottle from then?" To which Jack replied, "Unbeknownst to her, I put it in Marina's bag before we got on the plane."

Bob was a bit of a bulldog himself in such matters. His bottle, of course, was not returned in Karachi. Over a lengthy period, Bob built a thick file of correspondence with various Pakistani entities pursuant to his claim to the return of the bottle. To his enormous surprise, a business colleague, when departing the Port of Karachi many months later, pulled it off. On presentation of a letter authorising him to take charge of the famous bottle, the officer at the desk disappeared into a musty room devoted to holding seized items, eventually reappearing with the 12-year-old Scotch now ripened to a mature fourteen or so years.

The protocol rules in Pakistan were the same as those we encountered earlier in the Soviet Union, and were aimed at discouraging free contact between foreigners and Pakistani nationals. Unlike the Soviet Union, however, their practice varied greatly from region to region. About the only place anyone even paid lip service to the rules was in Islamabad, the capital. In over-populated turbulent Karachi, no one accorded them the slightest attention. Under the auspices of Canada's superbly connected honorary consul there, we mixed freely with all manner of locals, attending receptions and embarking on the occasional *bumboat* fishing expedition. Travelling in Sindh, a province known for its resistance to outside authorities, we called on various dignitaries and feudal lords ("Mirs") without hindrance. We dined one evening in a gloomy, fortress-like compound with the head of the dominant Talpur clan and thirty or so of his kinsmen. The women, including my wife, dined separately, and I never laid eyes on the group. As we were sitting cross-legged around the walls of a large room, the Mir produced several bottles of the finest single-malt whiskey, which was served up in shot glasses to all present. Trying to make conversation, I turned to the Mir and asked him, "So you like whiskey?" "No," he replied. "So why do you drink it then," I persisted? "Because they tell us we can't," was his short and humourless response.

It will come as a surprise to no one acquainted with the romance of the Northwest Frontier to learn that resistance to authority was at its strongest in this wild stretch bordering Afghanistan. Neither the Pakistani authorities nor the British before them had been able to establish control over much of the area, dominated by tribal chiefs, their rule reinforced by the mullahs and their primitive fundamentalism. We were naturally attracted by the mysteriousness of the Frontier, but also had good reason to indulge ourselves because of the directives to follow closely the Soviet invasion of Afghanistan then underway, as well as to report on the movement of refugees across the border. Refugee camps dotted the landscape. Peshawar, the provincial capital, we visited frequently and, in the course of doing so, came to know the Governor, General Fazle Haq, quite well, as well as the leading family of the Frontier presided over by the indomitable and very attractive Begum Saifullah Khan. Both contacts provided us with a fascinating window on various aspects of life in the region.

General Haq had been appointed governor by his friend, Pakistan's dictator-president, Zia ul-Haq, to what was arguably the most interesting — and lucrative — job in the Pakistan government. He was himself a Pashtun and knew his territory intimately. From the former British colonial governor's great white mansion with its manicured lawns he conducted himself in the manner of a warlord, had an iron fist and used it as circumstances required, even if he was well aware of the peculiar limitations imposed on his authority by the agreements between the tribes bordering Afghanistan and the government. Under these agreements, the tribes were a law unto themselves and, as long as they kept inter-tribal conflicts down to a dull roar and avoided causing problems for the government, they governed themselves without outside interference. The General knew everybody who was anybody on both sides of the line, and one had the impression that the details and niceties of the law were unlikely to deter him from getting his way.

General Haq I met frequently and was on a first-name basis with. He was a jolly, good-natured, swashbuckling fellow. In an earlier life he had undoubtedly been a pirate. Haq facilitated visits to various Afghan camps in the province and was helpful in organising forays into the Khyber Pass and other areas. Over the Christmas vacation in 1981, our entire family stayed with him at his invitation at the Governor's residence. The main thing we remember about the visit was that our kids became violently ill after drinking the water at dinner, which my wife and I knew by then to avoid. Although I glared at them from across the formal dining table while they gulped down their glasses, they didn't get the hint. The next day we spent trying our best to conceal their periodic vomiting during our excursion through the Khyber Pass for fear of embarrassing our host.

The General, obviously with strong links to the Pakistani Inter-Services Intelligence (ISI), was in charge of organising Pakistani support to the *mujahideen* in Afghanistan and several times promised to take me out to Parachinar and Miran Shah, towns hard on the Afghan border, from where much of the anti-Soviet activity was organised. However, some complication always intervened at the last minute such as shelling from the Soviet side or other security concerns.

On one occasion, a tearful Canadian lady appeared in my office in Islamabad. She had come to Pakistan to try to recover her child who had been abducted by her estranged husband in contravention of a Canadian court order, and spirited off to the Frontier. She had appealed to the courts and tried personal contacts, but all to no avail. She was at her wit's end. I called General Haq, explained the situation and asked if there was anything he could do. "Just leave it to me," was the terse response. Within the week, the child was delivered to Islamabad and the reunited mother and child quickly flew off to Canada. I thanked the Governor but did not enquire as to the details of the operation.

Even at that time, rumours of the General's involvement in the drug trade were rampant and indeed as early as 1982, during our assignment in Pakistan, Interpol described him as a key player. Peshawar, the regional capital, was known as transit point for much of the opium and heroin that moved out of Afghanistan. Indeed, in Landi Kotal just west of Peshawar at the entrance to the Khyber, everything the junky's heart might have desired was on open display. Interestingly, we at the Embassy did not much pursue the drug problem; at least it wasn't our highest priority for the simple reason that we were so given over to countering the Soviet threat. Whereas in Hong Kong, drugs had been a major preoccupation of the mission, I can recall only one or two instances when drug-related issues were directed to the Islamabad mission throughout our assignment. Rumours abounded alleging direct CIA cooperation with the drug lords as part of the cost of sustaining the *mujahideen* resistance, and this was undoubtedly another reason why the subject did not figure strongly on our radar screen.

The General's personal fortunes flourished, and he was reputed to have stashed away several billion dollars in foreign accounts. His relationship with General Zia deteriorated over time and Pakistan's top police official, Dilshad Nazhmuddin, with whom I had become good friends, once related to me that in a meeting Zia had said to Haq: "I'm told that everyone in your province hates you." To which Haq had replied: "In that case I'm better off than you. At least they only hate me in one province!" Ultimately, both men met violent ends, Zia when his aircraft was brought down by a bomb hidden aboard, and Haq when in 1991 he was killed in an ambush. Whether the assassination was related to drugs, or a product of the Frontier code of vengeance is not known.

The brutal Soviet invasion and equally merciless resistance by the *mujahideen* dominated our world. Literally millions of refugees were streaming across the border and the Afghan presence in Pakistan was incredibly intrusive. Camps covering hundreds of acres were a common sight in both the NWFP and Baluchistan to the south. Brightly adorned trucks piloted by suicidal Afghan drivers added to the general mayhem on the highway between Peshawar and Rawalpindi. Both Peshawar and Quetta, capital of the Baluchis, were filled with the detritus of war: amputees, displaced persons, *mujahideen* taking a break from battle and all manner of shadowy groups, from CIA operatives to the foreign fighters who would eventually give birth to Al Qaeda. It was in fact in 1982 that Osama bin Laden and other fundamentalist groups established a presence in the city. If they ignored the Western presence, it was because they had bigger fish to fry across the border. The city as a nest of intrigue reminded me in some ways of West Berlin in the late 50's/early 60's, or Hong Kong in the 70's, but with the flair and mystery of the souk and the bazaar. Little did we realise at the time that even then the roots of the terrorism and tragedy to come in the first decade of the new millennium were being planted in fertile soil.

Canada, like other Western countries, provided substantial financial assistance for the refugees. This led me on a number of occasions to visit the camps near Peshawar and Quetta. Such visits were illuminating, impressive and rather intimidating, all at the same time. I would normally be given a depressing tour around the bleak tent city by the Pakistani administrator, with its women usually hidden away and masses of children running around, and then invited to meet with a 'group' of refugees. The group usually consisted of some five hundred to a thousand turbaned and bearded males seated on the sandy waste in a large circle, the mountains to the west providing a stunning background. I as the sole pale face, with uncalloused hands, in this sea of tribesmen and warriors, would make an impromptu speech praising the Afghans for their resilience and ferocious resistance to the Soviet occupiers, and encouraging them to even greater efforts. Following my rather insipid discourse, two or three Afghans would rise and in succession deliver themselves of impassioned harangues with all the skill of master orators for which their race is so well known. The assemblage, inert to this point, would suddenly come to life and, with every few sentences uttered, spring to their feet and break into the chant, "God is Great!" The gist of their message always tended to be the same, that is, "Don't send us food! Don't give us sympathy! Don't bother about medicine! Send us guns, guns and more guns!" I was an avid reader of old diaries and books written by British participants in the Afghan Wars of the previous century. Little seemed to have changed. Standing in rather menacing circles of this sort in the shadow of the Khyber Pass, I had visions of 1841 when the British, under siege, negotiated safe passage out of Kabul only to have all sixteen thousand slaughtered in the treacherous badlands and, as legend would have it, with only one soul, the doctor, permitted to survive and carry the news back through the Khyber. My mind would drift across the border and I would begin thanking my stars that I wasn't a Soviet foot soldier separated from his unit, facing this crowd and awaiting the most excruciating of medieval executions. In later years when the debate raged over whether persons detained by Canadian forces and turned over to the Afghan security authorities were being tortured, I could only shake my head in wonderment at the naïveté of anyone who would doubt it for a moment.

I myself felt intimidated – and we were supposedly on the same side. At the time, I felt absolutely nothing in common with the fighters in the circle around me and was under no illusion that our alliance was anything other than one of momentary convenience. Ironically, some twenty-five years later it was much the same band of *mujahideen* we had been exhorting to rise up and annihilate the Soviet occupiers who were engaged in deadly combat once again, this time against the occupying armies of the West. Based on gut instinct and a reading of history, as much as on acute analysis, it was those experiences from the early 80's that led me to believe from the very outset that the NATO Afghan war initiated in 2001 was unwinnable.

Of necessity we Westerners followed the rules of the Frontier very carefully. I never tired of driving out through the historic Khyber Pass as it cut through the towering Hindu Kush mountains – route for Alexander the Great's invasion of the Subcontinent – with its tales of blood and heroism, British regimental badges carved into the stone cliffs and still meticulously tended with coats of fresh paint, storybook forts still occupied to keep a semblance of peace among the warlike tribes; but a sense that violence was never far beneath the surface was palpable, and we trod with care. The houses we observed from the road, each a mini-fortress in itself with turret and gun slits, were ample witness to that. For a good portion of our posting to Pakistan, the Khyber was closed to travel because of tribal conflict, usually over drugs. All this meant that we followed closely the admonition greeting those crossing into Pakistan at Torkam on the Afghan border which stated in effect: "All travellers are warned not to leave the road and to reach Peshawar by sunset." This centuries-old admonition was brought home to us on one occasion when, driving the Pass and in the company of a tribal escort, we stopped at a high point to look down the valley. Our son Tom was taking a picture when a tribesman leapt suddenly out of the brush and jumped on him. We were fortunate to have the escort with us who quickly dealt with the fellow, and not so gently. He was, they explained to us, angry because he said our son was photographing the women. It was interesting, because the nearest group of people we could see was so far away that they were mere dots on the horizon; their gender, of course, was not distinguishable. On another occasion, Alan MacEachen, Canada's foreign minister, was invited to lunch in the officers' mess at the incredibly picturesque Shagai Fort in the heart of the Khyber. As usual, the area was troubled and extra security was laid on. This meant that along the full length of the road from the beginning of tribal territory, some twenty miles, soldiers were stationed at approximately one hundred-metre intervals.

One weekend some well-connected friends drove us out of Peshawar and down through tribal territory to the small town of Darra. This area was out of bounds to foreigners and if we had asked for official permission to make the trip, it would have been denied. Darra's claim to fame lay in its multitude of small gun shops turning out all manner of hand-crafted weapons, from AK 47s to grenades to rocket launchers. 'You show it to us and we'll copy it!' The Soviet invasion had proven a boon to Darra and business was booming as tribesmen and *mujahideen* roamed the main street in search of armament. The normal village sounds were punctuated by gunfire as prospective customers tested their chosen weapons by firing them in the air from the middle of the street. The life expectancy of people inhabiting the hills around Darra could not have been great! Before leaving, my daughter and I were each given a small souvenir in the form of a ballpoint pen. But this was a pen with a difference, although you could certainly use it to write. Unscrew the barrel, insert a bullet and reassemble. Unscrew the nib, pull back the pin at the other end, point at one's target, press the pocket clasp, and voila! Enemy *kaput*. The pens sold for five dollars.

Some of our most memorable times in the Frontier were spent enjoying the wonderful frontier hospitality of Begum Kulsum Saifullah Khan and her family. The Saifullah clan, of the dominant Pashtun ethnic group, was one of the most prominent in the province. Blessed with four sons, the family, through strategic alliances and carefully arranged marriages, constructed a powerful political and economic network that reached into the highest corridors of government.

We were invited to attend the wedding of son, Anwar, to the daughter of then Finance Minister, Ghulam Ishaq Khan. This was no simple run-of-the-mill exercise. Rather, as is common in South Asia, weddings involved days of preparation and endless ceremonial rituals. We were caught up in the excitement as the Begum organised the tailoring of elegant silk *shalwar kamizes* for Laine and our daughter.

The event itself was attended by a cast of hundreds of the Pashtun and government elites, and very colourful it was indeed. On the day of the rituals we, including four visiting friends, drove to Abbotabad, home of the bride. There we males collected in the interior courtyard of the large old feudal manor, while the females were gathered inside. For the crush it was impossible to see exactly the details of the ceremony being performed, but at precisely twelve noon, all hell broke loose. That is the only way I can describe it, for at that moment, most of the men pulled out their weapons, ranging from handguns to larger automatics, and unleashed a thunderous volley into the air. I myself was surprised enough, but one can only imagine the looks on the faces of the Canadian visitors. One of them prompted me to ask the Finance Minister, father of the bride beside whom I was standing, if the ammunition was real. "Oh yes indeed Excellency!" came the reply from the Minister, who looked rather insulted, as if I had somehow impugned Pathan virility. But I was prompted further: "What happens to all the lead in the air?" The Minister seemed equally astonished at my naïveté with a straightforward, "Well, it comes down." Left unanswered was my unspoken query as to how the lead shower might affect the quality of life of the local citizenry outside the compound. Shortly thereafter and while we were still pondering the issue, I asked an army colonel: "Does anyone ever get hurt at these weddings?" "Oh yes," was his nonchalant response, after which he went on to elaborate: "I was at a wedding recently. There was a balcony around the courtyard where all the women were sitting. After all the shooting was over, it was discovered that two of the wives had been shot." He did not specify whether they were dead or alive.

Following the ceremony and wedding lunch, we set off in a long caravan of vehicles late in the afternoon for a reception at the groom's family estate in Peshawar. This was no ordinary convoy of cars, at least not for us Canadians. As we proceeded down the highway and as darkness fell, our progress was marked by frequent volleys of tracer shells fired from the cars into the night, ending up goodness knows where. The most comic aspect of the journey arrived when, on passing through the town of Nowshera, a veritable barrage of tracer fire was unleashed over the roof of the police station. The officers on duty came rushing out to be greeted by this pyrotechnic display, not knowing whether they were under attack or how to respond. By the time they collected their wits, the caravan was well past.

It is not surprising that when, all these years later, I think of the Frontier, I think of guns. They were ever present. On another occasion while driving a back road with the Begum's son Javed at the wheel, we were stuck behind another slow moving vehicle that refused to give way. Very calmly, Javed pulled up inches behind the car in front, pulled a pistol out of his belt, sounded the horn, leaned out of the window and made like he was about to shoot. The driver took one glance in his rearview mirror and in less time than one could say "Fire!" was off the road and into the ditch.

Travel was one of the real joys of a posting to Islamabad. The country possesses some of the most majestic scenery and interesting people that one can find anywhere. As Ambassador with broad responsibility for Canada's various programs, there were always a multitude of reasons for roaming the country far and wide. There were Canadian irrigation and hydroelectric projects to be visited, political consultations to be held, eye camps to be opened, newly drilled village water wells to inaugurate. The only problem with the last of these was that on the Ambassador was invariably bestowed the honour of the first glass of water to sample. Normally I would have looked for some spot where the freshly pumped liquid could surreptitiously be dumped, but with a hundred eyes watching my every move, the ritual could not be avoided. Nor could the price that had to be paid in the form of yet another bout of the 'Karachi Kwik-step' and gut-wrenching explosions. It took about three wells before I smartened up and crossed such events off my calendar.

Firsthand tales from the British *raj* fascinated me. I couldn't get enough of the history and geography of 'the old days'. The blood of Empire was for some strange reason in my veins and the sight of the monument just north of Rawalpindi paying tribute to Brigadier General Sir John Nicholson, who marched his force in record time up the Grand Trunk Road to relieve the siege of Delhi during the Indian Mutiny in 1857, never ceased to thrill. His name was magic even among the locals and a group of disciples emerged to worship him, known as the 'Nikal Seynians', even though all the thanks they got was a beating whenever they knelt in worship at his door. The name of Nicholson was to stay with us when, later in Delhi, we met Nora, an octogenarian, who had never lived outside Delhi and who was reputed to be the General's descendant. Norah lived in a ramshackle hut in an overgrown plot in Old Delhi she called 'God's Garden'. Back in Canada eventually, we received a letter from the vicar of the cathedral Nora attended to let us know that Nora had passed away, the victim of a bite by a cobra in her garden that she had taken to feeding.

It was always with a sense of excitement in the gut that we set out for a trip or even a day-long excursion into the Himalayan foothills rising above Islamabad, or the shimmering plains to the south. We had a small roof garden atop the residence and one of my principal joys was to sit there at dusk in the peculiar golden glow that marks the subcontinental sunset. Drink in hand, I loved to soak up the sights and sounds, all the while contemplating the waves of history that had rolled over this ancient land. As the summer monsoon approached and as the sky darkened into night, the lightning would begin to flash over the old British hill station of Murree, six thousand feet above and a two-hour drive away. Thunder, accompanied by violent storms, would roll out of the hills in an unbroken cacophony of sound that one under other circumstances might have interpreted as an extended artillery assault.

The foothills beyond Islamabad were often the target for weekend jaunts, particularly during the scorching summer heat when thermometers rose to 45 and higher. Sometimes we contented ourselves with a picnic in the refreshing cool air of Murree at six thousand feet. Other times, as a family, we would push farther on, often to our favourite spot of Nathia Gali deep in the pine and maple forests some two thousand feet higher, where we would overnight in the old government rest house or in the remarkable 'Greens Hotel'. I say 'remarkable' because the Greens was like a cameo straight from the *raj*. The waiters were outfitted in uniforms that surely predated independence, splendid in earlier days but now just plain grubby. They still moved at a trot as if some unseen commissioner or imperious member of the governing classes were after them. Cleaning of the rooms in the morning consisted of a sweeper appearing with a large broom, beating clouds of dust out of the carpets which, having reduced visibility and affected one's respiratory capacity, quickly settled back into the original location once the pummelling had stopped. The daily bath was taken in a large portable washtub, filled with steaming pails of hot water brought by the bearers, in which one could unwind and easily propel oneself back in history. Seemingly nothing had changed.

The government guesthouse in Nathia Gali was an oasis of solitude, situated high on a hill with a splendid view over forest and mountain. The British had a talent for selecting the best and most scenic pieces of real estate around the empire for construction of their facilities, and in most cases these were simply taken over intact by the successor governments. We used these houses in a number of places and never ceased to be impressed. Again, it was like capturing a bit of history in that nothing much had changed, from the primitive kitchens to the ceiling fans to the ancient attendants running the facilities.

The guesthouses also served as useful venues for getting together with local officials, but with the occasional hazard. My family more than once accused me of working too much, of diluting precious family time with official business. Their protests were sometimes registered in bizarre ways. On one trip into pine-covered foothills of the high mountains, I was engaged in serious conversation with several local elders who had seated themselves in a row along the guesthouse reception area's outer wall. The wall in typical style was about a foot thick and ten feet high, with a series of glass panes at the top to let light in. Suddenly two faces, noses pressed against the panes shaping them into rather pig-like countenances, heads adorned with misshapen, mock-turban pillows, appeared silently above the elders. Our two sons had somehow managed to scale the outer wall and were now bent on testing my reserves of diplomatic self-control. By rights I should have been furious. Instead, I carried on without missing a beat and in the end, after saying farewell to the guests, had little choice but to join in the pillow-headed hilarity.

Our wanderings across the land meeting provincial officials, visiting projects, and promoting Canadian trade were mostly by car. The key actor in all this was our faithful driver Sa'eed, ex-Pakistan military, a no-nonsense kind of guy. One has to have lived in the country to appreciate the challenges of such an occupation. Personally, I believe that the suicide bombers who blow themselves up in Iraq and Afghanistan must have been recruited straight from the ranks of Pakistani truck and taxi drivers. The psychological training required to move from the one occupation to the other would be minimal. Consider the absolute ecstasy with which two lorry drivers race head on at a closing speed of 200 kilometres an hour, only to veer ever so slightly at the last second, the moment of passage marked by the flashing teeth of a wide smile of contentment straight from the gut.

Sa'eed was cut from the same cloth, although his ability to enter fully into the game had been steadily eroded over the years by varying levels of remonstrance from generations of Canadian ambassadors. ("Whew!"; "God dammit, that was close!"; "Slow down or you're fired!"). Nothing, however, had been able to remove the glint from his eye, and the Canadian flag that fluttered from the front fender of the ambassadorial limo as we moved about on official business simply reinforced his self-image of superiority and indestructibility. Driving north on one occasion from the pre-Christian Buddhist centre of learning, Taxila, up into the Himalayan Kingdom of Swat, we traversed a narrow winding track over the spectacular Malakand Pass with the mountain on one side and a precipitous drop off into the river on the other. I was in the passenger seat. Sa'eed saw it as his personal challenge how close to the drop-off he could force other vehicles to come. I admonished him several times with no results. Suddenly there was a crack and with one stroke both Sa'eed's outside rearview mirror and that of the other driver were knocked cleanly off, but without leaving a scratch on either vehicle. He said nothing, but his eyes betrayed the fact that he saw this as the ultimate achievement. As for me, that was enough. After another kilometre or two (to avoid making him lose face), I declared that he looked exhausted and that I should take over for a while.

On another occasion, again travelling over the mountains into the Swat valley, we encountered a tribe of Gujars (nomads) on their way down from the high country to winter in the sweet pastures of the south. Sa'eed, incensed by the fact that the camels refused to recognise the official status of the black limo racing up to meet them, plowed steadily ahead. This time he had to content himself with having one of the stubborn beasts strike his mirror, but this time merely bending it all the way back without breaking it off. It could have been worse. The Gujars were all well armed and would not have had the slightest compunction about meting out instant justice should one of their precious animals been injured or killed. Sa'eed did not say a word but, as usual, was quite unrepentant.

The journeys we took into the mountains to visit political leaders and erstwhile rulers were so impressive as to be beyond telling. The narrow thread of the Karakorum Highway that runs from near Islamabad for fifteen hundred kilometres up the turbulent waters of the Indus River is a monument to Chinese civil engineering skills and much Pakistani blood and sweat. To call it a highway is to disguise the reality of the rockslides, the breath-taking drop-offs, and the challenge of how to keep open this fragile line of communication. To drive it requires skill and strong nerves. How to describe the vista of towering Nanga Parbat at almost 28 000 feet flanked further north by the almost equally high Rakaposhi. This is the area where the mountains are in motion as the leading edge of the younger subcontinent, with Nanga Parbat as its prow, pushes under the old continent guarded by Rakaposhi. The result is literally earth-shaking – earthquakes and tremors are a way of life. Of more practical significance are the regular rockfalls. It may be one that has temporarily blocked the road, or a matter of a few rocks that come crashing down behind, in front of, or on top of the vehicle. It may be the patch of greenery high up the mountainside marking the location of a village, but with a gash through the middle where a slide suddenly reduced a good portion of the village to rubble and brought tragedy.

Accompanied by the American ambassador and his wife, we drove north one day from the northernmost Hunza town of Karimabad, home in the not-so-distant past to a notorious tribe of brigands, possibly remnants of Alexander's invading forces, who earned their living by raiding caravans up and down the fabled Silk Road that linked China and the khanates of Central Asia with the riches of India. With us was the Rani (queen) of Hunza, wife of the Mir, successor to the former rulers of Hunza (the kingdom, originally semi-independent and part of the princely kingdom of Kashmir, and formally annexed by Pakistan some seven years before our arrival). I was driving. As we were bouncing precariously along the lip of the Hunza River, the Rani turned to me and said: "Oh Excellency, you really must drive faster, otherwise we will be hit by some of these falling rocks!" I obliged but never did figure out why it made much difference whether we were going fast or slow. A rock is a rock at any speed.

We stayed with the Mir and the Rani, in their pleasant palace – even if modest when one thinks of princes and princesses. The Mir, Ghanzafar Ali Khan, regaled us with stories of his childhood when, before the road was extended up to Hunza, it would take three days for the caravan carrying him to school in Gilgit to navigate the treacherous ledges and bridges down the river. His boyhood home was Baltit Fort, perched high on a spur above the village bearing the same name. The Fort, built in the eighth century, was occupied till 1945 and then fell into disrepair. A magnificent example of Himalayan architecture of the time, the Prince climbed with us through the crumbling nooks and crannies of his erstwhile abode, at the same time pleading for financial help to fund restoration. Unfortunately, pride and culture counted for little in the Canadian scheme of things and a proposal for making a lasting contribution was nipped in the bud. But the story had a happy ending: in the 90's the Aga Khan, spiritual father of the Ismaili community inhabiting the valley, provided the necessary funds, and the site was in time declared a UNESCO heritage site.

Hunza I found particularly interesting because of its historic role, still unfolding, as lynchpin or fulcrum in the so-called Great Game that for centuries pitted the Russian empire to the north against the British in the Subcontinent. And the game continued. Even as we sat in Baltit Fort at the point where five great mountain ranges meet, the Soviets were just across the Afghan border, making threatening gestures in the direction of the Arabian Sea. To the east lay India, still claiming sovereignty over this princely kingdom as part of the state of Jammu and Kashmir. To the north, over the high Khunjerab Pass, were the Chinese, whose support of Pakistan and whose interest in keeping out both the Soviets and the Indians from this wild area had motivated them to provide the brain and much brawn in the building of the road from Chinese Kashgar to Islamabad. And here we sat in the company of the American ambassador and his wife, whose nation at the time was so intent on putting its foot solidly into the quicksand of the region, little realising that thirty years later that foot would have been sucked in much more deeply. As for the Mir, his loyalties were, first to his people and, second to Pakistan.

The incredible entity that is Pakistan is no less awe inspiring in its southern extremes than in the towering mountains of the north, not so much in the magnificence of the scenery as in the mix of tribes and ancient civilisations and tradition merging into the modern. In some areas life seemed not to have changed much in a thousand years. The highway south follows the spine of the country, the mighty Indus, and it is with a sense of excitement that grips me to this day when I recall the experience of setting out from Islamabad to meet with local officials, to visit some aid projects and to follow the river to its southernmost reaches. The Indus rises far away in Tibet, from where it winds through the world's mightiest mountains, sometimes through chasms thousands of feet deep, finally breaking out onto the broad plain and joining the Kabul River between Rawalpindi and Peshawar.

We travelled far into the south, even if we never did reach the Indus delta where the combined waters of seven rivers and twenty tributaries meander through an enormous estuary to merge with the Arabian Sea. We did, however, see enough of the river to appreciate its tremendous importance to the economy of the country in terms of power generation and water for irrigation canals.

The further we penetrated the interior south of Islamabad, the more conservative the country became, the more frequently Laine's headscarf came out, and the more of her hair and face it covered. It is hard to imagine a culture farther removed from that of main street Canada. An example of this was Jhang, a most conservative Pakistani town where local women dared not appear on the street except fully covered by a burqa, and where the sight of a man's bare arms was somehow considered unbearably erotic. There we spent time with an influential politician, Syeda Abida Hussein. Perhaps as a reaction to the environment in which she had been raised, Abida was one of the more ardent spokespersons for women's rights, and extremely active in various women's projects. She went on to serve as federal minister in several portfolios and later as ambassador to the U.S.

This was a land where feudal lords had held sway since time immemorial. In Nasirabad, we stopped at an estate ruled by four brothers who amused themselves with the sport of tent-pegging, hunting with falcons and training dancing horses. The brothers were surprised when I asked them what would happen if one of 'their' peasants should choose to leave. "Simple enough," said the brothers. "We would send out a posse to bring him back. If anyone makes too much trouble, he simply disappears."

What a curious mixture. The economy was feudal, the literacy rate abysmally low. We were told that it was still common in those parts for females to be abducted by landlords or raiding parties, and for landlords to have the 'right of the first night' following one of his villager's weddings. Yet if the peasants couldn't read, they were certainly literate in a political sense. Almost without exception these folks listened on a transistor to BBC's Urdu broadcasts. If asked, they were quick to say that they wanted 'democracy'... "Now!" If pressed to elaborate, they said they wanted 'Islamic democracy', but no one could quite explain what that meant. Imagine my surprise when I was asked on three occasions in different small villages, "Why is Canada no longer selling uranium to Pakistan?"

The hospitality of the locals was amazing. Time and again we were invited by the humble folk to take tea and even to spend the night. One bold ten-year-old insisted on taking us to his mud-walled hut to show us his cow. Once the boy's mother got over the shock of seeing us (the Urdu equivalent of: "Where the hell did you find these people?"), she summoned her husband who organised tea.

During the trip we stopped at several village projects funded by Canada, from newly drilled tube wells to schools to promotion of handicraft production by women. The climax of the journey, however, was eight unforgettable days meandering through the Thar Desert that stretches through the eastern part of Sind province up to the Indian border, where it merges with the Rajasthan Desert — and incidentally, the only area of the country with a majority Hindu population. The landscape was incredible: unbroken vistas of undulating sand. There were no paved roads, only the occasional endless track seemingly leading to nowhere; no signposts, only sand and sky. A forgotten memory is that of the wind and sand, the former stirring up raging dust devils and the latter providing a fine coating on everything including our teeth. When the rains fail to come, as they had for the three years preceding our trip, the already abysmally low living standard falls to the barest subsistence level.

The line between the desert and the barrage, or irrigated, land was so finely drawn that one could literally stand with one foot in the sand and the other in lush green grass. Once in the sand, we were fortunate to make fifteen miles per hour. The effect was one of driving through deep snow and, much to Sa'eed's relief, I put my Canadian background to good use and took the wheel myself for the next eight days.

Our good fortune was to be accompanied on the journey by our Pakistani friends, Ross and Sorraiya Hussein. Ross as a young public servant had been posted as Commissioner to the Desert several decades earlier, and he retained many good contacts there. Ross arranged for an excellent guide, Alim Shah, a grizzled desert fox who knew the area like the back of his hand. He led us unerringly for hundreds of miles across the land in our faithful four-wheel drive Yukon, which often strained to avoid being mired in the soft sand. How to describe the timeless sight we encountered two or three times a day of one or more camels with riders silhouetted against the far horizon? Where had they come from? Where were they bound?

Villages were few and far between and more often than not populated by a few scores of inhabitants. They were marked by a watering hole, a few trees, some primitive vegetable gardens, goats and cows. Invariably some of the older inhabitants would emerge to greet Ross like a long-lost brother. We were not allowed to pass without sitting and partaking of tea made from questionable ingredients. But this is where our consciences got the better of us. The desert region had been suffering severe drought for some seasons. Starvation was abroad in this corner of the land, perhaps purposely forgotten because of its largely Hindu people. A common experience as we passed any lowly collection of houses was for women and children to approach the vehicle begging for food. This was a dire situation I hadn't heard of in advance and one for which we had not prepared. There was almost nothing we could do by way of positive response. This is why we felt guilty even drinking their tea, but Ross assured us that it would be a grave violation of the rules of hospitality for us to refuse. Just as embarrassing was the 'overhang' of Empire. The supplicants who came out to plead with us usually directed their requests to me, the pale face, instead of to Ross. When we finally returned to Islamabad, I did my best to interest CIDA in the desert dwellers' plight, but attention was so focused on large projects and Afghan refugee aid that it proved virtually impossible to generate relief for these forgotten souls.

The Thar Desert was a collection of conflicting images. The contrasts were startling from one area to another, between the many tribes, and between villages and open sandy wastes. One bountiful rain, we were told, can cloak the barren gray dunes in a lovely green mantle. Yet in this trackless waste, how to explain the town of Diplo, some three thousand souls strong, hard by the Indian border? A Muslim centre, the town at that point had contributed to the nation some eighty-three female and one hundred and sixty-five male doctors, as well as a justice of the Supreme Court. The town also boasted cobbled streets and an underground sewage system, making it virtually unique among Pakistani villages.

The journey left us with an array of lasting impressions: dinner with a Rajput prince; camel training in the cool of the twilight; three labourers in a desert town reading "Revolutions of the World"; tea with Indus Rangers in the absolute isolation of the Rann of Kutch; ubiquitous chicken curry in smudged bowls best downed quickly than lingered over; and gritty sand in every nook and cranny, stretching to the horizon in every direction.

The end point of the safari we reached in Nagar Parkar, a tiny bubble of land extending into India and surrounded on three sides by the area known in India as the Rann of Kutch. How on earth the boundary line was established here I have no idea. There was virtually no civilian population in the bubble and we bedded down for the night hard on the border with an army unit. The sky was cloudless with a bright moon lighting the desert landscape. As we sat in the silence drinking in the peace and quiet in this area over which the winds of war had blown from time immemorial, from somewhere close by we suddenly heard the plaintive notes of a flute. The moment was magical and we would have given anything to be able to hold onto it. All too soon the music faded and we were dropped back into the real world of conflicting armies facing off only a few hundred metres apart.

Life in the capital of Islamabad brought with it the usual endless round of diplomatic functions. For many ambassadors it seemed that there was little else to focus on and a dim view was taken of those who did not observe the accepted protocol. But for some of us, the diplomatic dinners, national day receptions, calls on and by newly arrived colleagues were a real millstone. In retrospect some years down the road, I shake my head at those of our friends who still revel in being invited to an Embassy dinner and suggest how lucky we were to have had such an active and splendid social life. It was work pure and simple, and too much of it was a waste of time.

I often felt sleep deprived, ate far too much rich food and paid for it later on with by-pass surgery.

Some of us actually had a job to do. The Americans were heavily involved in all the usual overt and covert activities that Americans occupy themselves with, and particularly with the war in Afghanistan. The Saudi diplomats were busy dispensing funds for mosques, schools and the *mujahideen*, and recruiting menial Pakistani labour for Saudi Arabia, to say nothing of hosting the numerous Saudi royal parties that maintained compounds around the country and flew in with their hunting falcons. We ourselves were fully occupied with our aid program, promoting commercial ventures, processing immigrants and keeping a close eye on political developments. Nonetheless, excuses for absenting oneself from the social whirl could only be concocted within limits, the result being that scarcely a day went by when we did not attend at least one function.

We devoted a good deal of attention to entertaining Pakistani functionaries whose responsibilities impinged on Canadian interests. The most memorable of these events was a dinner we gave one night for the head of the Pakistan Atomic Energy Agency, Munir Ahmed Khan. Relations on nuclear matters were delicate, to put it mildly, the Pakistanis in Canadian eyes having abused the nuclear cooperation we had provided starting in 1972 with the building of a nuclear power station using Canadian technology. Cooperation ended four years later when Pakistan refused to sign the Non-Proliferation Agreement (NPT).

The dinner with Munir Khan progressed quite normally. I had a good relationship with him, our daughters went to the same school and the conversation flowed easily. Time for dessert. We had been giving the cook a good deal of latitude in designing the various courses and that evening was no different. But this was one dinner when we should have checked the menu carefully in advance. What a *pièce de résistance*! In marched Rehman from the kitchen in a crisply pressed *shalwar kamiz*, his bright red henna-dyed hair setting him off from everyone else in the room. In his hands he proudly held a tray on which was perched a large cake covered with white icing from which sprouted enormous meringue mushrooms. What could have been more suitable to set before a guest to whom we had on several occasions been directed to express our concern over Pakistan's perceived capability for generating mushroom clouds? Where on earth Rehman got the inspiration for his mushrooms, and how he arrived at the idea that mushrooms were a suitable topping for a cake, we never did determine. We had never seen the concoction before, nor did we ever see it again. But for the moment, all conversation ceased as, with mouths agape, all around the table stared in disbelief and the Pakistanis around the table wondered if this was the Canadian idea of a subtle message. The tension was suddenly broken as we all simply cracked up. From her confines in the kitchen, Josefina joined in the general hilarity with several loud shrieks. It lasted only an instant. With all eyes averted from the monstrosity, the banalities of diplomatic conversation quickly resumed. I don't recall if it was the Chairman who received the largest mushroom with his serving.

The nuclear irritant occupied a good deal of our time, as reflected in ministerial and official visits and numerous other interventions. Our objective was to persuade Pakistan to sign the Non-Proliferation Treaty (NPT) and to dissuade them from developing reprocessing and uranium enrichment facilities. This was an exercise in futility and frustration. Dr. Ahmad Khan at no time either affirmed or denied the existence of the facilities. The bottom line, he always made clear, was that as long as India was working on its nuclear capability, Pakistan would march in lock-step. The Chairman made his position very clear. "If you or the U.S. or anyone else will guarantee our security, the matter will be resolved immediately." He then added that if we wanted to pressure anyone, we should pressure India because Pakistan was ready to agree "tomorrow" to open up everything on the basis of mutual arrangements, or to adhere to a pact for a nuclear-free zone. And there was the Catch-22. I was under no illusion that this whole effort was going anywhere, for the simple reason that getting both countries on board the same train was an impossibility. And so we Canadians, who so 'altruistically' had started both nations off on their nuclear program, were at the end of the day left only with needlessly guilty consciences, needless because nuclear capability would eventually have come to both countries with or without Canadian assistance. Were the Pakistanis working on weapons of mass destruction? Of that I had no doubt.

The one major diplomatic exchange between our two countries came in December of 1982 with an official visit to Canada by Zia ul-Haq. The President had been agitating for a visit for some time, partly to press for more aid, but more importantly to shore up his international image. In spite of serious reservations over Zia's dismal human rights record, I supported the proposal mainly because, strategically, I felt Pakistan needed political support at that juncture in facing the Soviet threat. Prime Minister Trudeau eventually agreed and a low-key five-day visit took place. The visit for me was memorable mainly for the impression Zia made on Trudeau. Despite his status as a no-nonsense and sometimes brutal military dictator, Zia at the same time came across as a humble, God-fearing Muslim with a deep family commitment, and this Trudeau was quick to grasp. In a private comment after Zia had left, Trudeau said, "And they always told me he was such a tyrant!" This statement left me a little nonplussed in that Zia without question was an iron-fisted dictator whose opponents were not treated gently. Torture was almost certainly one of the regime's tools. Indeed Zia, with his attempts to introduce *Sharia* law and his use of the state to promote fundamentalism in an attempt to gain legitimacy, must share responsibility for laying the groundwork for much of the Islamic militancy that threatens the country's stability today. It wa also under Zia's direction that the Inter-Services Intelligence agency became so involved with the militant *mujahideen* across the border in Afghanistan, an involvement that played a direct role in the rise of the Taliban. Not that Zia's interest in Afghanistan was primarily motivated by feelings of religious affinity. In reality, his goal was to establish a force amenable to Pakistan's interest in ensuring a pliable neighbouring state.

In retrospect, we lived in Pakistan during the halcyon days for diplomats, especially Canadian diplomats. Canada had always occupied a high pedestal in Pakistan's eyes. Even the severe injury perceived over the termination of nuclear cooperation in 1976 did not dissipate the fundamental resource of good will. We had not been tainted with the super-power ambitions of the United States, the colonial legacy of the British or the commercial opportunism of the Japanese. Our image was rather one of a friendly partner in development, an image that would lead the Pakistani Minister of Finance to say to me one day: "If there is any genuine philanthropist among our partners, it is Canada."

As diplomats, we could move through the countryside with a wary eye but in relative safety. Places like the beautiful Swat valley that later were taken over by the joyless Taliban, were open and welcoming to outsiders. Even the American ambassador often travelled without bodyguards, and he and his wife frequently graced us with the pleasure of their company on our forays outside the capital. 'Terrorism' was a term not yet in the vocabulary, even if the seeds were being sewn and watered. Islamabad, whose construction as capital was begun in the 60's, was still raw at the edges with packs of jackals howling their way through the diplomatic enclave at night. But its cleanliness and order were unique. This is not to say that there was no violence. In many parts of the country one's gun was just as important as an arm or a leg. Just as we arrived in 1981, U.S. Embassy personnel were only then in the process of reoccupying their premises which had been razed by fire during an anti-American demonstration a couple of years earlier when staff had had to be evacuated by Pakistani army helicopters from the roof. Caution was always the watchword. I was personally assigned a bulletproof vehicle. And then there were always the snakes. When visiting the ruins at Taxila, north of the city, Laine had just seated herself on a rock when she noticed a viper sunning itself beside her. Patience Spiers, spouse of the American ambassador, had just entered the residence where she almost stepped on a krait, known as the two-step snake: it bites you and two steps later you're dead.

Peaceful as Pakistan may have been in the early 80's, all the seeds of later turmoil had been planted. Al-Qaeda, the Taliban and the Saudi-supported radical *madrassas* (religious schools), took root during this period. Pakistan in the 80's played a crucial role in the defeat of the Soviet army, just as today it is perhaps the most critical factor affecting the West's war in Afghanistan. What we did not foresee at the time was that the *Law of Unintended Consequences* would within a few short years come back to bite us. Those whom we then supported so enthusiastically and indiscriminately in their struggle against the Soviets would return at the turn of the century in the form of 9/11 terrorists, suicide bombers and militant warriors locked in a life and death battle with our own forces. Western policy, as usual, was extremely shortsighted. If, following the ignominious retreat of the Soviet Union in 1989, the West had filled the Afghan vacuum with a massive aid program, the eventual rule of the Taliban and its domination by al-Qaeda could perhaps have been blunted. Not only did we miss the opportunity once, but inexcusably once again after the Taliban had been thoroughly defeated following the U.S. campaign to avenge the 9/11 disaster.

In the spring of 1983 came the news that we were to be cross-posted to India. We were absolutely delighted, even though our anticipation was much tempered by the fact that shortly thereafter my mother passed away in Niagara. She lived long enough to know that India was next on our agenda and to share in our pleasure.

Direct transfers from Pakistan to India or vice versa, seldom if ever happened. Certainly my own was a first for a Canadian diplomat. Indira Gandhi showed her less than enthusiastic reaction by withholding *agrément* to the nomination much longer than usual. President Zia for his part also played the game by granting me a farewell call only at the very last minute. He did appreciate the humour, however, when I suggested that the posting to India was the result of a demotion. I took away with me considerable gratification, however, out of the fact that, when meeting sometime earlier with Foreign Minister Alan MacEachen, Zia remarked that if relations with Canada were excellent, it was to a large extent due to the hard work of Canada's ambassador.

In September of 1983, we packed our belongings, and with the indestructible Josefina and the unruly Pirate in tow set off up the Grand Trunk road that leads to Lahore, the Indo-Pakistan border and New Delhi. Little did we anticipate the series of tragedies, spawned by political intrigue, that awaited us.

Bill and daughter Lisa in the arms bazaar at Darra, Pakistan, 1982.
An Afghan mujahedeen fighter shows us his identity papers.

A Darra arms merchant poses while Bill and Lisa,
accompanied by Begum Saifullah Khan, examine the wares
on offer at the arms bazaar, Darra, Pakistan, 1982.

Chapter Eight

BAZAAR DIPLOMACY

One of the few times in my diplomatic career that I felt myself at considerable personal risk was in the summer of 1982 when I made two journeys to Tehran. Diplomatic relations between our two countries were in suspense as a result of the so-called 'Canadian Caper' when Ambassador Ken Taylor and his crew had spirited six Americans out of Iran, much to the fury of Ayatollah Khomeini and his fellow revolutionaries. On November 4, 1979 Iranian mobs led by the Revolutionary Guard stormed the U.S. Embassy and took approximately 70 personnel hostage. Six U.S. staff members eventually found sanctuary with the Canadians. On January 27, 1980, posing as Canadians carrying Canadian passports with forged Iranian visas, the six exited Iran via the main airport of the capital. The same day, Ambassador Taylor and the few Canadians remaining with him in Tehran casually left the Embassy. Onlookers might have assumed they were simply going about their normal business. Instead, they headed for the airport, booked on different flights. Taylor and his colleagues were not to return. They left the country and the Canadian Embassy was to remain closed for the next seven years.

Iranian anger knew no bounds.

Not much surprise, therefore, when the Iranian Foreign Ministry in 1981 summarily rejected an overture by Canada to send a senior diplomat to Tehran to try to 'normalize' the relationship. Relations were firmly on ice.

While personal contact between Iranian and Canadian diplomats in other capitals remained frosty, for some reason or other the newly arrived ambassador to Pakistan in early 1982, whom I met at a reception, seemed to take a liking to me. A heavily bearded former commander of the Revolutionary Guard and more recently a commander of the Iranian forces on the Western front in the war with Iraq, Abu Sharif had not a shred of diplomatic experience. Fiercely religious, he reputedly had served as executioner on a number of occasions for some of the regime's enemies. I'm not sure how we struck up the relationship. Perhaps it was because I mentioned to him that I was a regular attendee at the local church, a fact that intrigued him. Or because he saw me as at least a willing interlocutor in the not-so-friendly diplomatic community. In any event, he invited me to his office and, during that and subsequent conversations, we got onto religious themes. I never argued with him, but chose mainly to listen.

In the spring of 1982, Iran's Foreign Minister Ahmed Velayati, who had been appointed six months earlier, made an official visit to Islamabad. Abu Sharif, to whom I had related the story of Canada's attempt to restore the diplomatic relationship, was sympathetic for one reason or another. He invited me to a reception he was hosting for the minister, and arranged a private audience. I was flying by the seat of my pants, but I repeated the story. Velayati rose to the occasion and said he would be prepared to meet a Canadian envoy in Tehran. This news I communicated back to Ottawa who, after chewing it over for a month or so, suggested that I be the one to follow up. This I did with Abu Sharif, with the result that in late June of 1982, I boarded an Iran Air flight from Frankfurt to Tehran.

The flight provided excellent preparation for the chaos of Tehran. Seat assignment had been abolished, resulting in a mad scramble for the best seats. The aisles remained full of people standing, including during take-off and landing. An extra passenger or two would never have been noticed. My three hundred or so fellow passengers seemed to be doing their best to cultivate the unkempt revolutionary look. Two young ladies beside me, returning from college in the U.S., giggled nervously as they donned chadors over their jeans and sweaters in preparation for landing. Landing was an added thrill. With the war with Iraq still on and given the ever-present threat of missiles, the routine was to come in high over the city and spiral down — a new experience in a 747 that seemed to protest by uttering unusual creaks and groans.

Immigration had been alerted by the Danish Embassy to the arrival of a Canadian diplomat. Fortunately. Otherwise I suspect the sight of the first Canadian diplomatic passport to show up since the surreptitious departure of the entire Embassy personnel two years previously might have resulted in complications.

It was made clear to me right from the start that the shots were all going to be called by my Iranian handlers. Contrary to Foreign Minister Velayati's assurances that he would personally receive a Canadian envoy, this was not on. Should I have been surprised? Not at all. We were in the world of bazaar — and bizarre — diplomacy.

At the Foreign Ministry I was ushered past military checkpoints and offices filled with sombre secretaries in black chadors to the Bureau for the Americas and Europe. The whole atmosphere was bleak, like the rest of the city where economic activity seemed to have been frozen by the Revolution. Construction cranes towered over the city — all of them inactive. The Director General, who was to serve as my principal contact throughout, was a young, intense and rather fierce looking man about twenty-five years of age by the name of Sadr. I was given to understand that his main qualification for the job was the fact that he had been one of the student leaders of the Revolutionary Guard in the takeover of the U.S. embassy. In the crazy disturbed world of Iranian politics, this seemed logical enough.

I expected a good dressing down and was not disappointed. I had resolved in advance to listen, but not to react. It was as well that I did because any spontaneous response to the kind of undiplomatic nonsense dished up would not have served the cause. I suspect that some of my colleagues, in my shoes, might have walked out forthwith. I just plugged my ears and let him get on with the rant. I reasoned that it was as well to let the Iranians purge themselves of the venom and vitriol in their spleen. My young interlocutor did a good job of this. He began his diatribe more or less at the beginning of the universe and then, as in a James Michener novel, worked his way through the glorious history of the Persian peoples and their empire, right up to the contemporary, godless perfidy of Canada, the 'little Satan'. With my somewhat warped sense of humour, I found the whole thing a little bit funny and had to restrain myself from smiling on one or two occasions at malevolent descriptions of the Canadian government that even our parliamentary opposition might have found difficult to swallow! We were, Dr. Sadr said, puppets of the U.S., collaborators in counter-revolutionary activity and, what was beyond the pale, purveyors of Zionist influence. The Foreign Ministry, he said, took particular offence at Ambassador Taylor's 'betrayal' since the Ministry had been putting trust in him as an intermediary.

Sadr's statement, needless to say, left me feeling warm and fuzzy!

When it was my turn, I simply explained in factual terms the reason for my visit. I said that we would like to normalize the relationship and at some point in the near future re-assign diplomats to the Embassy. Sadr made it clear that what the Iranians wanted from us, first and foremost, was a profound apology for our scurrilous behaviour.

The dialogue went on for two sessions with other officials, without moving an inch forward. A new national holiday was suddenly declared and I had to delay my departure plans by three days — that is, if I wanted to hang around for a promised third session, even though there seemed little point to it. The apparent breakthrough came during my last meeting with Sadr when the nonsense was stripped away and real intentions emerged. The Iranian bureaucracy was evidently more interested in restoring relations than they had been letting on. This was not so surprising since I had 'improvised' my lines by suggesting that if no progress were made, residual Iranian operations in Ottawa might be shut down. We thus agreed that the most productive approach might be to aim at coming up with a vaguely worded, jointly agreed statement that would have the effect of letting both sides place their own interpretation on it. In other words, the Iranians would, for internal consumption, interpret it as a form of apology while we would simply see it as an expression of regret for the disruption in relations. In fact, Sadr then handed me a fairly innocuous draft that, we agreed, should be submitted to our respective governments. The idea was that we should meet again in three or four months to continue the discussion.

One of the surprising revelations to me during that week was the extent to which a residual Canadian operation in Tehran still existed and carried on. From my briefings in Ottawa I had gained the distinct impression that our own people considered the building closed and gathering dust. Ottawa's only contact was with the Danes representing our interests. I was given a key and the combinations necessary to gaining access to the main building and the secure areas of the mission, the area open only to Canadian staff. To my astonishment, particularly since no one in Ottawa had told me about this – if indeed they were even aware of it – a skeleton staff of three locally engaged employees were still sitting at their desks like shadows out of the past. Apparently the place had been deserted for a period of time following the exfiltration, after which the local staff had come back and resumed taking phone calls and answering queries from the public. They were now the responsibility of the Danish Embassy and were paid by them. I was very touched by their continuing loyalty to Canada in spite of the fact that some of them had been put through difficult times.

Like most others who saw and read the hyped-up accounts of the so-called 'Canadian Caper', I was under the impression that the clandestine presence of the U.S. diplomats under Canadian roofs and their exfiltration had been a matter of the greatest secrecy and super-slick organization. Not so, it appears. I am not a great diarist, but I had kept some daily records, and a nugget occasionally pops out as one reads them. Right after my return to Islamabad, on July 11, 1982 to be exact, I noted in the diary that my discussions in Teheran had "exploded the myth" of the whole thing being totally secret. I confided that two of the locally engaged Iranian employees still at the Embassy volunteered that they had been very much aware of the 'house guests' during the months prior to everyone's 'secret' departure. For one thing, they had seen 'cards' with the names of the U.S. nationals on them. I did not question them closely on the matter since it was of no particular consequence at that juncture, and indeed I was very conscious of the possibility of surveillance. However, I got the impression at the time that these were the kind of cards that one uses for assigning places at dinner. What is known is that the six 'guests' and some Canadians enjoyed Christmas dinner at the home of Zena and John Sheardown in 1979. Whether this or some other dinner occasion is what lay behind the comments about the cards I don't know. The locals were also curious, to begin with, about the "frequent trips upstairs" in the residence by the ambassador and other Canadians, an area placed out of bounds to locals, but they said they eventually put two and two together. The final notation in the diary records my assumption that, if these two informants knew what was going on, then "quite a few others" must have known too. The 'tight security' of which so much was made in later accounts, it would appear, may have left something to be desired. Either the two employees in question were incredibly loyal, or Ambassador Ken Taylor was incredibly lucky. Or a bit of both.

I cannot vouch for the accuracy of the employee observations reported here, but simply report what I wrote at the time.

The security people in Ottawa had given me combinations for various locks, and I was able to use one of them to get into the secure area of the Embassy where the Canadians had worked. The place gave me an eerie feeling. The Ambassador and his staff had purposely left everything in working order: papers on the desks, coffee cups, cocktail invitations waiting for reply. The idea was that no hint was to be given of the pending mass departure. It was as if the biblical rapture had taken place — even if some of the staff members I was personally acquainted with were hardly likely to qualify! Or as if the folks were out to lunch and could return at any moment. In the communications centre, located in yet another locked strongroom, the cipher machines lay smashed with the sledgehammer used in their destruction on the floor nearby. I took a couple of swings myself! The telephones, surprisingly, still had a dial tone, and I called Laine from the Ambassador's office. The one thing I was virtually certain of was that no one had gained entrance to the secure area since it had been locked for the last time by Ambassador Taylor. At least there were no signs whatever of any disturbance of the filing cabinets, papers or other equipment.

Just as interesting was the underground parking garage where several late-model vehicles of departed Canadian staff were still parked. I suppose that some dusty filing cabinet in Ottawa held the documentation, but I had the impression that I could have driven away in one of the Mercedes and no one would have been any the wiser.

Dr. Sadr and I met again in Tehran in September. In political terms, the visit was a complete disaster. The gods, it seemed, were against me. During the summer of 1982, there had been a perceptible hardening in the political atmosphere in Tehran and, reading the entrails, I should have expected a difficult time. A number of Iranian officials had been arrested during the spring and summer, including Sadegh Ghotbzadeh, Khomeini's former revolutionary Foreign Minister, accused of collaborating with the U.S. and plotting the assassination of the Ayatollah. Even more dramatic was the curve ball delivered as I stepped off the aircraft in Tehran, to be greeted by a Danish official with an armful of the day's newspapers denouncing Canada in the most shrill terms over the defection of the leading Iranian wrestler at the world wrestling championships taking place at that moment in Edmonton. To add a bit more spice to the mix was a message I received from Ottawa the day before my departure from Islamabad, reporting the case of a Canadian kidnapped by Iraqi Kurds several months earlier and turned over to the Revolutionary Guard. My instruction was to seek his release. And, oh yes, I should also make representations on behalf of members of the Bahai faith currently mistreated and imprisoned in Iran.

As I sat in my hotel room on the evening of September 14 and contemplated the week ahead of me, it seemed I had a rather large and forbidding mountain to climb.

I was kept waiting for two days for my first meeting with my unsmiling and belligerent young interlocutor, Dr. Sadr. Things did not pick up from where we left off in June, when Sadr had seemed in a relatively benevolent mood. Rather, the meeting consisted largely of an unbroken harangue, ranging from our immoral behaviour in opening the world wrestling championship with so many young maidens flaunting their boobs and bare legs, to our obvious conspiracy with the CIA in organizing the defection of their wrestler. Sadr demanded that we immediately arrange a meeting between the wrestler and Iranian officials. Ottawa in fact responded promptly and affirmatively. However, the face-to-face encounter ended up not happening because the Iranian defector, naturally, was frightened, and absolutely refused to see Iranian officials.

I surprised Sadr by countering with a request for the Iranian authorities to release forthwith Guy Boisvert, the young ATCO employee. Sadr denied any knowledge of the case but undertook to look into it. In actual fact, we knew from intelligence sources precisely where Boisvert was being held, but of course I did not show my hand on this. The purpose for the Iranians holding onto Boisvert was not clear, but we assumed that it had something to do with their anger with Canada and with the possibility that he might at some point serve as a useful bargaining chip.

The overall mood was not enhanced that week by the breaking news that Ghotbzadeh had been executed for alleged contacts with Westerners. This was ironic in that the former foreign minister, who had been the principal Iranian spokesperson while the U.S. Embassy was under siege, had been portrayed in the Western media as a heinous villain.

The three meetings that week went something like this. The first two hours were devoted to a lecture by Sadr who eventually ran out of fresh epithets and was reduced to repeating himself. That over with, I would present the factual Canadian case for restoring normalcy to the situation, following it up with a rehash of the Boisvert case. My concern was that the Iranians would try to use Boisvert as a *quid pro quo* for the return of the wrestler. The line I took was that Boisvert should be released as a humanitarian gesture by the Iranian government and that Canada, for its part, would issue a statement publicly thanking Iran.

My expectations became ever lower as the week progressed. Any hopes of getting anywhere were dashed at the second meeting on September 18 when Sadr, totally ignoring the earlier relatively mild text he had given me, presented an absolutely outrageous press release that he suggested Canada should issue. The draft proposed, among other things, that Canada confess its "vile act" and "wash away the rust of displeasure from the memories of the noble Iranian nation".

At that point I simply closed my briefcase and said it was evident that the problem should be left for "future generations". I saw no common ground and little purpose in examining the respective texts in detail. I said further that I saw no purpose in meeting again except, perhaps, to formalize farewells.

Interestingly, the normally inscrutable Sadr for the first time showed visible signs of pain. He made it quite clear that they indeed did want to meet again.

I opened our third session by saying that a close examination of the Iranian text had simply confirmed my conclusion that my second visit to Tehran had, rather than moving us forward, produced a step backward. I simply said that I hoped the Iranians, at some point in the future, would see their way clear to resuming contacts to our mutual benefit. I added that I hoped the Foreign Ministry would cooperate by authorizing the issuance of visas to one or two Canadian administrative officers to come to Tehran for the purpose of disposing of remaining Canadian property and discharging the locally-engaged staff.

Sadr countered with his own surprise. He announced with some flourish that Boisvert would be released at some point in the foreseeable future to demonstrate Iranian good faith and their interest in expanding relations and resolving difficulties. The commitment on Boisvert was so vague as to leave me with little expectation that anything would happen soon. As in a novel, an intriguing sub-plot regarding Boisvert had been developing during the entire week. At one point, a shadowy individual sidled up to me in the hotel. The gist of his clandestine message was that he could arrange Boisvert's release in exchange for Canadian agreement to supply Iran with missiles. A second Iranian, whom I met for drinks in his home and who had known Ambassador Taylor well, purported to have a good relationship with the head of the Ministry of the Revolutionary Guard, and said that he would make quiet representations on our behalf. He later told me that when he raised the matter, his contact had responded, "What do you mean by asking me to help a Canadian? Do you want to get me hanged?" Whatever the manoeuvres that had taken place behind the scenes, I was deeply gratified that the entire Tehran exercise had not been in vain, and that some progress appeared to have been made, at least on the Boisvert front. However, I fully expected that it would be some weeks or months before Guy Boisvert surfaced again in the West.

I returned to my hotel to prepare for the next day's departure. At 12.30pm, I received a call from the Ministry and to my enormous surprise was given the terse message: "You can come to the Ministry at 5pm to pick up Boisvert." Hurrying to the Danish Embassy, where I had access to enciphered communications, I sent a 'Flash' message informing Ottawa of the latest development. The afternoon was devoted to making arrangements for both of us to fly out the next morning to Rome, and to ensuring that the Embassy there would make appropriate preparations to move Guy Boisvert on to Canada.

So it was that promptly at 5pm I made my appearance at the Ministry. Being Friday afternoon, the Muslim equivalent of Sunday, I was escorted through empty corridors to a small conference room. There I waited in some suspense for what seemed like a long time, but in reality was only a quarter hour. Five unshaven, unsmiling and silent Revolutionary Guards made their appearance, accompanied by a rather short fellow in Kurdish clothing of loose grey pants and long shirt. Boisvert gave the impression of knowing nothing of what was going on and he was very surprised, to put it mildly, when I introduced myself. Sadr, who was in attendance, made a short speech extolling the humanitarian nature of the Revolutionary Government, and I reciprocated with expressions of gratitude. The five Guards, without saying a word, faded away. I explained to Sadr that I had made reservations for Boisvert and myself the next day on the Iranair flight to Rome. Could he please let me have the passport Boisvert said the Iranians had relieved him of when transferred to their custody? Sadr said he had no knowledge of the passport. I then asked, "Can you give me a document of some sort certifying that Boisvert is authorised to leave the country?" Again a blank wall. "That is your problem", is all he said.

So there I was, late on a Friday afternoon, on an empty street in Tehran, ex-hostage in tow — and a Canadian at that — no documents, in a city largely shut down. We wandered the bazaar and eventually found a small photography shop that was open where we were able to get a passport-sized picture. Armed with this, we headed back to the Danish offices where my telephone message to Ottawa was terse and to the point: "I've got him!" I was able to lay my hands on a piece of vellum with the Canadian gold crest on it. I then typed out something along the following: "This is to certify that Guy Boisvert, born on ... in ... , has been released as a humanitarian gesture by the Revolutionary Government of Iran, and is hereby authorised by the Revolutionary Government of Iran to travel on Iranair flight No. ... on September 21, 1982 from Tehran to Rome." I then took the sheet and affixed to it gold seals and red seals and stamps of varying sorts. It was really a grand looking affair such as to impress the most bureaucratic of bureaucrats.

That night Boisvert, still scarcely able to believe his change in fortunes, and I, relaxed in my hotel room, over several generous portions of illegal Scotch, obtained from the Danes, while he told me his story. It was one of those stories interspersed with drama on the one hand and a lot of boredom on the other. The adventure started with his kidnapping by anti-Saddam Kurds who took exception to Western projects in Iraq. To elude Iraqi security forces, over time his kidnappers moved him ever deeper into the mountains, where eventually he was taken by a commando unit across the border into Iran and turned over to the Revolutionary Guard. On two occasions he thought he was going to be shot: first, when initially captured, and second, later on when one of his Kurdish captors, the Peshmerga, 'lost it' and put a machine gun to his head. The treatment in Iran was worse than in the mountains with the Kurds, and he found himself locked up and kept under armed guard. Several times the Guard took him into Tehran where they tried to hand him off to other groups such as the National Police or various jails, but each time were rebuffed. Boisvert was interrogated at length at various times by the Guard, who were particularly interested in trying to identify any CIA connection. Ultimately, on the day of his release, he was simply told to pack up his things. When he arrived at the Foreign Ministry, he assumed it was the Revolutionary Guard building. Before being turned over, he was queried at length by a Ministry official about his treatment. It was only when I arrived at the office that he had any idea that he was about to be released.

Neither of us got much sleep that night — we were too nervous thinking about our prospects for making it through Tehran airport. The flight was due to leave at 9 the next morning. We arrived at 6am to give ourselves plenty of time to face to whatever obstacles lay between the aircraft doorway and us. Boisvert, who had written copious notes during his captivity, gave the bundle to me, which I, foolishly in retrospect, spread around under my shirt. Tehran airport at that point had several checkpoints manned by all sorts of security types: the National Police, the city police, immigration, the Revolutionary Guard, and so on. My diplomatic passport and Boisvert's magnificent departure document in hand, we worked our way through the various barriers only to be brought up short at the checkpoint of the Guard. From there we were quickly hustled into a small interrogation room. And there we waited. Nine o'clock came and went, as did ten, then eleven and twelve. By this time we had begun to sweat a little. I was under no illusion as to the value attached to diplomatic immunity by Khomeini and his people. I was concerned that the next step would be a body search, which would reveal Boisvert's papers that I was carrying, and which would undoubtedly have occasioned a lengthy investigation. Visions of Evin prison appeared before my eyes. From time to time a new bearded face would appear and question each of us in turn about our existence from the beginning of time. Where were you born? What was your mother's name? What kind of work do you do? And on and on.

The flight, we assumed, had left hours ago.

We assumed wrongly. Our predicament was suddenly resolved when a representative of the Office of the President, obviously a person of some authority, appeared, handed me the passport and document, announced, "You can go!" and escorted us past the last checkpoints and out to the plane. To our astonishment, the loaded aircraft had been held for almost four hours. We boarded, and found our seats. The other passengers on board regarded us with some curiosity, but said nothing. The flight took off and some three hours later we landed in Rome. A very happy Boisvert was taken in hand by consular officials from the Embassy who arranged his passage back to Canada.

Happy as I was over Boisvert's release, the episode left a slightly sour taste in my mouth. With Boisvert back in Canada, a press conference was convened by ATCO to celebrate Boisvert's return. Scarcely a mention was made of the crucial role played by the Canadian government. Instead, glory was heaped on the Danes (who had not even heard of Boisvert until I told them about him, and whose only contribution was to provide on-the-ground logistical assistance), and on the security firm hired by ATCO to manage the Boisvert case, but whose substantive role in the actual release had also been virtually nil. Representatives of the firm had met with me in Rome after I turned Boisvert over to the Embassy there and had posed many questions. My distinct impression was that they were looking for some shred of evidence that their activities had had some significant bearing on the release. They seemed rather miffed that the government had managed to pull off what they themselves had not been able to. I don't know why ATCO chose to ignore the Canadian role, but the fact that the company needed to justify the presumably hefty payment made to the security firm may have had something to do with it. If there were other behind-the-scenes manoeuvres, there certainly was no evidence of them in the tough negotiating with Dr. Sadr. As for the Danish connection, this was still the era when some of our fellow citizens preferred to believe the myth that Europeans were much more adept at dealing with such matters than Canadians. Some time later I received a note from Ottawa expressing regret that, in the light of the way the release had been treated in the media, the Department itself had lost an opportunity to spotlight ways in which the Government of Canada provides assistance to Canadians in distress.

As a postscript, the father of one of our Embassy staff in Islamabad worked for ATCO. The latter suggested that we write the company to see if they might acknowledge the Embassy's work on the Boisvert release by sending the small and thirsty Islamabad Canadian Club a couple of cases of Canadian beer. The owner of ATCO was at the time supposedly on the board of a Canadian beer company. I wrote the letter. As it happened, we received nary a word about Boisvert or the beer!

At the end of the day, the main thing that mattered was that Boisvert had been released.

I harboured the hope that in spite of the negative official attitude of the Iranians, we might nonetheless move in an incremental fashion without any formal agreement. My suggestion to Ottawa was that in three or four months we apply for a visa for our Trade Commissioner to go in for a couple of weeks, and later still for an administrative-cum-political officer. There was no substantive response to this proposal and, in any event, our own Trade Commissioner in Islamabad, who would likely have been the one assigned the task, made it clear that he was not prepared to run the risk of travel to Iran.

The net result was that the Embassy in Tehran was not to re-open for another five or six years.

A delighted 23-year-old Guy Boisvert poses in his Kurdish attire following his release from captivity. Photo courtesy of Guy Boisvert.

Chapter Nine

HARVEST OF RAGE

It was the easiest move of our Foreign Service lives. In October 1983, we piled ourselves, our dog Pirate and parrot Josefina into the car and, retracing the steps of conquering armies, drove down the Grand Trunk Road from Islamabad to Delhi. In making the move, I became the first Canadian head of mission to make the transfer directly between the two hostile neighbours. I never ceased to be fascinated by the sights, sounds and smells of any land journey in the Subcontinent, and this trip was no exception. The 'last goodbye' has always been something of a tearjerker for both Laine and myself. Invariably I was embarrassed when taking leave of the local staff in any mission we served in because I always choked up. Islamabad was no different, particularly when it came to saying goodbye to our loyal team members in the residence who had become like family to us. On our last morning, I stood on the roof patio, taking in the familiar sights and sounds: the hill station, Murree, barely visible at the top of the Margalla Hills; incredible teeming and colourful Rawalpindi to the west, shimmering in the early morning heat; the scorched and dusty plains of the Punjab spreading to the south. The memories of two adventure-packed years were re-lived in the space of a few short minutes, the question always in my mind: "Will I ever take in this sight again?"

We overnighted in Lahore, taking the opportunity for one last visit to the fabled Shalimar Gardens, constructed by the Emperor Shah Jahan in the mid 17th century. Here, as elsewhere in the Subcontinent, it was difficult not to be totally overwhelmed by a sense of history. If only the walls could speak, what tales would they tell of the glories of empire and the passage of waves of invaders and traders? We were simply two transient beings, and the only stir we caused was created by the unusual sight of two pale faces accompanied by an unruly black and white dog and a shrieking parrot.

The next day we headed to the border. Our driver, Sa'eed, was to take us all the way to Delhi. There are few borders in the world where mistrust and suspicion reign as absolutely as they do along the Indo-Pakistani frontier. Tales of spies, infiltrators and subversives are legion on both sides. To cross the border was a major undertaking, even for the privileged breed of diplomats, who in those days were the only ones allowed to drive across. On the day we crossed, all was quiet. While sightseers on both sides jostled for a better look across the red-and-white barriers, nothing moved in the treeless no-man's land between the two checkpoints except when honour guards did their daily strut on the two parade squares abutting the border, each attempting to outshine the other. After lengthy checking of papers on the Pakistani side, and the obligatory cup of tea with the Supervisor of Customs, our vehicle moved through. The Indian barrier was raised and suddenly we were in our new home. Although the pet papers were all in order, we nonetheless thought it wise to vacate the automobile quickly and make obeisance to the Indian chief in his office, leaving Sa'eed to do his best to render Pirate and Josefina as invisible as possible. Long experience had taught us not to tempt fate by attracting the attention of lurking inspectors of health, meat, livestock and national virtue.

More tea, and we were on our way again. This time we drove the short distance to the city of Amritsar, long cherished by the Sikhs as the home of the Golden Temple. Although religious unrest was already on the rise in 1983, little did we realise, as we visited the Temple and got a sense of the reverence it evoked for Sikhs, that a national cataclysm soon to transpire on that spot would have a pivotal influence on our entire experience of India. In the meantime, our visit to the city was taken up with more mundane chores such as ensuring the care and feeding of Pirate and Josefina, and soothing Sa'eed's injured self-image after someone in the street, on seeing the car's licence plates, called him a 'Pakistani bastard'. The first major difference from Pakistan that struck me in Amritsar was the fact that women in the street had no hesitation in looking me, a male, straight in the eye. How refreshing!

Whereas Islamabad, Pakistan's artificially constructed capital, had been a relative backwater, Delhi was the exact opposite. Here was a mega-city, the heart of empire, long the home to princes and emperors, target of treasure-seeking invaders. It had been the generator of the highest forms of culture, and the lowest kinds of treachery. Even as we became hopelessly lost in its tangled streets, populated by camels, rickshaws, elephants, wandering sadhus, holy cows and the ubiquitous fume-belching vehicles of the Delhi Transit Corporation, we could only feel a sense of exhilaration at the prospect of making this our abode for the next three years.

If Islamabad had been quiet in terms of visitors, Delhi was the antithesis. Scarcely had we time to find our way from the residence dining room to the kitchen, than Prime Minister Trudeau announced his imminent arrival for the Commonwealth Heads of Government meeting.

This was the era when Canada still played an important and respected, even if diminishing, role on the world stage. The reason the country still batted above its weight largely came down to three factors: Pierre Elliot Trudeau, his cast of well trained, highly respected diplomats, and the halo effect Canada enjoyed, particularly in the developing world. Because of his relatively independent stance and willingness to have Canada take issue on occasion with our American neighbour, our views were valued from Havana to Accra to Moscow to Delhi and Beijing. Regardless of the small minds in Canada denigrating his role to this day, Pierre Elliot Trudeau was seen abroad as a leader to be reckoned with, in spite of, and perhaps because of, his willingness to disagree publicly with Prime Minister Thatcher and President Reagan. This was certainly true in India, where Trudeau's personal relationship with Indira Gandhi was as warm and respectful as such a relationship might be between two leaders.

Trudeau arrived in Delhi in November 1983, with two targets in his sights. The first was to attend the Commonwealth Heads of Government Meeting (CHOGM) scheduled for the last week of the month. The second was, if agreement were forthcoming from the Chinese, to make a quick side-trip to Beijing to press the Chinese to support his recently launched peace initiative. To these two goals was quickly added a third, following the invasion by the United States on October 25, 1983 of the island of Grenada: restoring amity in the Caribbean. We were told to prepare for a luncheon in the residence to be hosted by Trudeau at which he would attempt to bring reconciliation to the bitterly divided Commonwealth Caribbean Prime Ministers. Laine and I, of course, were 'delighted' by this prospect. We had barely unpacked our suitcases, had no idea as to whether the residence staff were up to entertaining ten Prime Ministers, and were to have no opportunity to practise on the resident diplomatic corps before the big event. If ever there would be an opportunity to flame out before we even started, the notoriously fastidious Trudeau provided it.

Trudeau and entourage arrived on November 23 in a Canadian military aircraft. He was already late for the Conference, but this first stop in Delhi was to be short. The Chinese, whom he had been feverishly pressing to discuss his peace plan, suddenly gave the go-ahead, and Trudeau was to leave late that same evening for Beijing.

Once settled in his hotel, Trudeau's two young sons, Justin and Sasha, who had accompanied him, were turned over to the care of his good friends, Hugh Faulkner, Alcan's representative in India, and wife Jane. At the Ashoka, Delhi's government-run host hotel, the lobby decorations included about two dozen gorgeous, sari-clad young women acting as hostesses. Trudeaumania may have been dead in Canada by then, but not so in India, and as the Prime Minister walked in, the young ladies broke ranks and rushed to greet him, asking for a photo. Trudeau, of course, absolutely loved the whole scene.

The first order of business was a quick call on Indira Gandhi to apprise her of his plans. Not much was said at the meeting. In fact, that was why I found it rather fascinating. Trudeau and Gandhi were on some kind of psychic wavelength and seemed to have the ability to communicate without speaking. There was one interlude of approximately three to four minutes in which not a single word was uttered. I later heard that the record for silence between the two in a single meeting was eighteen minutes! I was, in the course of my several calls on her, to observe that Mrs. Gandhi was never a person for small talk. She listened but offered little in return. I once accompanied Foreign Minister Alan MacEachen to see her. The meeting was scheduled to last an hour. We were out of there in twelve minutes.

In his suite and with baggage deposited, thoughts turned to dinner. Trudeau said he wanted to go somewhere really folksy and asked for a suggestion. The only place fitting the description that I could think of right offhand was the Moti Mahal, a somewhat seedy establishment in the middle of Old Delhi specialising in *chicken tikka*, baked in clay ovens. "Good idea," said Trudeau. I trotted over to the protocol office in the hotel and informed them of the plans. After about thirty seconds' deliberation, they came back at me: "No way," they said. "Security reasons." Back I went to Trudeau with the news. "Well," he said, "we're going anyway!" Protocol informed, off we ventured an hour later. Of course, by the time we reached Moti Mahal, the regular diners had all been ejected, replaced by young couples, the men clean shaven, obviously security agents drummed into service to enjoy a meal at government expense and act like your run-of-the-mill Old Delhi diners.

There were probably 10 of us Canadians there and we had a jolly time. Everyone relaxed. We were in no rush since we were to go from the restaurant directly to the airport where Trudeau would embark for Beijing. In the middle of dinner, one of the Prime Minister's aides came up and whispered in his ear: "You know those girls in the hotel lobby who asked for a photo with you? They've all been fired. The Indians say they broke discipline and security rules." Trudeau looked dismayed, said, "Oh no", and carried on. At the airport, we walked to the aircraft. Just before he climbed the steps, he turned to me and said: "Bill, I want you to get those girls re-hired." Tell me why I was not surprised.

Back in the city, it was by now going on 3 am, but I got the Chief of Protocol out of bed. "What were you thinking of," I asked. "The only way you could have improved on the welcome for Trudeau would have been to have fifty girls there instead of twenty! He wants them re-hired. "Impossible," the Chief said. "Well," I said, "I'd like you to reconsider, because I can assure you that the first thing he will ask me when he gets off the plane from Beijing is: 'What about those girls?' And if you don't do something, he'll raise it with Mrs. Gandhi." Towards the end of the next afternoon, I got a call from the Chief. All he said was: "The young ladies have been re-hired."

Trudeau duly arrived back in Delhi. I was waiting for him at the bottom of the steps, where his first question was: "What about those girls?" He was taken in convoy back to the Ashoka. As he entered the lobby, the two lines of young women were there, only this time, it was like walking into Madame Tussaud's museum. No one moved a muscle, all of them looking straight ahead. Trudeau stopped, looked around, and then sidled quietly up to one of the girls and asked: "Hey, how did the photo turn out?"

The only other memorable event about the visit was the prime ministerial luncheon, something of a baptism by fire for us since it was our first shot at entertaining anyone in the Delhi residence. I was always conscious of Trudeau's prickly reputation. The situation was rather delicate since several of the Caribbean leaders were not speaking to each other because of differences over the invasion. We were given advance notice by some of the other High Commissioners that 'their' PM did not want to sit beside this or that PM. In the end, all we could do was follow strict rules of protocol that dictated order of precedence as determined by the length of time a given PM had been in office.

Lunch was set for 1 pm. The dignitaries began arriving on time, but right up to a quarter after the hour, we continued to receive messages that this one or that one would or would not attend. Each call precipitated a mad scramble to rearrange the number of settings and the order of seating. By the time drinks were over, the situation had stabilised and we were able to breathe a sigh of relief. Some ten Prime Ministers showed up. The menu was totally unmemorable, but evidently adequate since Trudeau afterwards expressed his warm appreciation. The luncheon could not eradicate the hurt feelings around the table, but Trudeau was seen by all as the elder statesman and a wise voice, and his intervention certainly exercised a calming effect.

A number of in-house horror stories about dealing with Trudeau preceded his visit. All I can say is that in our own experience he was most gracious and complimentary in the dealings we had with him. He took a personal interest in how we were getting on and in interacting with mission staff, and we engaged on several occasions in light conversation about sailing, canoeing, our earlier life in Cuba and so on. I encountered him several times after that, including during my own retirement, and he always greeted me warmly. The last crossing of paths was in Montreal where, walking down the street in a noonday crowd, I heard this voice, "Hi Bill!" Trudeau it was. I never saw him again.

Following Trudeau's visit, one theme emerged to dominate our time in India: the Sikhs. Social life was frantic, as is normal in any large post. Our immigration and aid programs were among Canada's most active. Business visitors and tourists took up much of the office's time. Yet India was undergoing a national crisis as radical elements in the Punjab raised the standard of revolt, agitating for the creation of a separate Sikh state, to be called Khalistan. For me, the Punjab events were something of a long-term trauma and, as I look back, they eclipse almost everything else. The issue struck at the heart of nationhood, since India itself in 1947 was arbitrarily forged out of a broad conglomeration of princely states, distinctive races and classes, ethnic minorities and linguistic groups, each with their own agenda. Feuding Christians in Kerala, several shades of Communists in teeming Bengal, lamas from Ladakh, sadhus from the Himalayan ashrams, Akalis, Nihangs, tribals, Kashmiris and Sikkimese who still talked of "going to India" when travelling to Delhi or Bombay all formed part of this incredible patchwork. If one part of the mosaic were to crumble, the whole structure could be at risk. The fires of Sikh extremism, already spreading steadily in the Punjab, were stoked by radical Sikh communities abroad, principally those in Britain, the United States and Canada. In the official Indian view, Britain and the U.S. were doing a creditable job of trying to contain the situation in their own countries. Canada was not, and therein lay the reason why the next three years were to prove highly contentious in terms of Indo-Canadian political relations.

Even as we ourselves visited the Golden Temple on our journey to Delhi, tensions were rising over the issue of Sikh grievances, real or imagined. In a classic move designed to divide and conquer her opposition, Mrs. Gandhi had earlier in duplicitous fashion supported the radical Sikh extremist Bhindranwale. He now came back to haunt her. The temperature continued to rise through the rest of 1983 and the early months of 1984. Militants occupied the Temple and fortified it. Matters came to a head in June. On June 5, I met with Rajiv Gandhi, Indira's son, in his mother's compound, which served as the government nerve centre. The purpose of my visit had been to extend an invitation to Rajiv, a former Indian Airlines pilot with whom I had earlier struck up an acquaintanceship based partially on our mutual interest in flying, to visit Canada. The idea of the visit was quickly submerged, as he informed me that at that very moment, Indian troops had initiated an invasion of the Golden Temple to dislodge the 'terrorists'. He wanted me to know since he expected that there would be reverberations in the Sikh community in Canada. He added that if it had been up to him, he would have moved against the militants in the Temple much earlier. This rather surprised me in that my impression up to that point had been that his political instincts were poorly developed, and that he lacked the toughness of his mother.

Operation Blue Star, as it was known, was successful militarily speaking, but at a huge cost. Probably well over a thousand persons were killed and many others injured. The sacred Temple was itself left in ruins. The fundamentalist Sikh leader, Bhindranwale, was killed, but any expectation that the operation would resolve the issue would prove to be in vain. Political assassinations and unrest increased significantly.

Turmoil in the Punjab was directly reflected in increasing agitation in Canada, particularly in the Vancouver area. Radicals were calling the shots and the voices of Sikh moderates had been drowned out or silenced through intimidation and violence. Personally, I was not surprised in the slightest at the growing unrest. If I had been even a moderate Sikh in Canada, I would have been outraged and highly aggrieved at certain of the actions of the Indian government in the homeland. First, Mrs. Gandhi, ever the political animal, was too smart by half as she manipulated Punjabi politicians and in doing so played with fire. Second, having set the house alight, she failed miserably in meeting her responsibilities by failing to nip the problem in the bud and put the fire out. Third, both before and after the Golden Temple episode, the Indian authorities engaged in increasingly aggressive tactics that included everything from torture and large-scale detentions to illegal killings. Human rights abuses were rampant.

The fire thus fuelled itself. Hardliners in the Indian government were matched by the radical voices among the Sikhs both at home and abroad and, in the process, the voices of reason and moderation were drowned out. In Canada, the situation became so acute that moderates in the Sikh community expressed themselves only at serious personal risk. Most saw themselves as caught between a rock and a hard place. Grievances were real and moderates sought to articulate them. On the other hand, to subscribe to anything less than the creation of Khalistan was portrayed by the radicals as betrayal.

Scarcely had we settled in New Delhi than we began to receive summonses to the Foreign Ministry to receive complaints about the activities of Sikhs in Canada. A major complaint was the funding that flowed from Canada to hardliners in the Punjab. Insults to Indian diplomats, desecration of the Indian flag and infringement on Indian premises in Canada were all brought to our attention. In the beginning, the interventions were rather mild. As time went on, officials at the Ministry became increasingly strident, and insisted that we take remedial measures. So serious was the Indian preoccupation that in July of 1984, Mrs. Gandhi herself, in what would be her last communication to a Canadian Prime Minister, personally signed a letter to John Turner in which she went to considerable length to explain the reasoning behind Operation Bluestar. In explicit terms she complained that the Federation of Sikh Societies of Canada was openly advocating the creation of an independent Sikh homeland of Khalistan, and all the while drawing funding from the Canadian Department of Multiculturalism.

In Delhi at the time, our knowledge of abuse of detainees by the Indian authorities was based almost exclusively on hearsay. It was only later that the full extent of violations by the security authorities became known. Torture and mistreatment were widespread. Assassinations were falsely described as accidental deaths that supposedly had occurred during 'armed encounters'. Yet the decibel level of the recriminations between the militants and the government was so high that all else was drowned out. For our part, we tended to look the other way, our own inaction on Sikh militancy in Canada having lost us the moral high ground. Ultimately, from a longer-term historical perspective, 'bleeding heart' voices ended up silenced by the government's hard-line tactics, incarnate in the person of K.P.S. Gill, commander of the Punjab police from 1984 on, who eventually succeeded in throttling the insurgency.

Consuming as the Punjab crisis was, our relationship with India covered a broad range of activities and we were, except for occasional interludes, going full out. A typical day went like this: up at 6 am, in the office by 7:30 am, home by 6:30 pm, followed by evening engagements. Social activity was extreme. Must-attend lunches occurred three or four times a week. After work, there was invariably one – and often two or three – cocktail parties, followed by dinner. In bed by midnight. The weekend provided no let-up.

No sympathy was forthcoming from the uninitiated among our friends back home. "What a wonderful life you lead," was the most common sentiment. "All parties!" In actual fact, for us the cocktail/dinner circuit was by far the most onerous part of the job. We normally received some fifty or sixty invitations each week. Laine and I would sort out the ones we felt we absolutely had to accept – some diplomatic, others from government, most from important contacts in the business and aid communities. The remainder, usually about forty, we would respond to with 'regrets'. The one enormous 'plus' to social activity in India derived from the fact that it almost all involved contact with Indians – unlike our experience in the Soviet Union, Cuba and Pakistan, where contacts with locals were severely limited. Our record for number of events in any one evening was five: three cocktail parties and two dinners. The idea of doing two dinners in one night was not, in the Indian context, so unusual as it might seem. Most Indian dinners involved a cast of dozens, or hundreds. The main idea was to put in an appearance, make one's mark with the host, mingle with the crowd, partake of some of the fancy dishes and, after a reasonable period, offer some contrived excuse for having to leave early.

The scene did provide occasional humour. At a government reception, I was speaking with the relatively new Iranian ambassador, a very conservative type who had already earned the disapproval of many of his colleagues by refusing to shake hands with their wives. Who should appear before us but the even newer Nicaraguan ambassador, a bubbly lady full of Latino charm who was one of Daniel Ortega's Sandinista entourage. I introduced her to the Iranian, whom the Nicaraguan perceived as an anti-American comrade-in-struggle, whereupon she immediately wrapped her arms about him, clasping the bearded gentleman tightly to her ample bosom. All that could be seen of the Iranian were his flapping arms as he struggled to extricate himself. The stuff of great cartoons! Flushed and undoubtedly aroused, he quickly betook himself from the scene.

On another occasion, I went to the Taj Hotel for the wedding reception of the son of a local notable whom I knew only vaguely by sight. Without paying too much attention, I sauntered into the Grand Ballroom off the lobby, where I was greeted like a long-lost friend. In short order I found myself seated on the dais having photos taken with the charming bride and groom. It was only as I was sitting there listening to the chatter around about that something clicked and I realised, "You're at the wrong wedding!" I didn't know the people from Adam, nor they me, but India was like that. With a white face and a business suit, one could have made a career of drifting from wedding to wedding, grand reception to grand reception, and being treated at each one like a VIP.

We ourselves hosted receptions, lunches and dinners for visiting Canadian dignitaries and business people often enough. The Canadian residence was wonderfully set up for offering hospitality. The attractive whitewashed bungalow, set on a couple of acres, was built in colonial times, an exemplary product of the British-administered capital designed by renowned British architect, Edward Lutyens. Four wings enclosed an inner courtyard. All the rooms opened onto airy, private verandas on the outside, and onto the courtyard on the inside. The back of the residence gave out onto a spacious patio and a large green lawn bordered by gardens filled with spectacular flowering shrubs and plants. It was the perfect set-up for hosting everything from intimate dinners to enormous buffets. Four hundred to a buffet dinner was no strain, nor were cocktails for a multitude. The inner courtyard was ideal for concerts by visiting Canadian artists and for sit-down dinners exceeding the formal dining room's capacity of twenty-four. In typical Indian style, a *shamiana*, or brightly coloured canvas marquee, could be erected over the courtyard if weather proved troublesome.

Our permanent staff consisted of a head bearer, his helper, a cook, two 'sweepers', gardeners, a large collection of security personnel who mounted guard on a twenty-four-hour basis, and a tailor who made uniforms for all of them. The whole lot, with their families, were lodged in a compound at the rear of the property, where they presented a remarkable synthesis of Indian life. Hindus, Christians, Muslims, Tamils, Punjabis and more all lived harmoniously together, celebrating each other's festivals and special days. Every Christmas, this extended family, numbering around fifty, would troop over to the main residence for a party consisting of gifts and refreshments. The uncomfortable part for me was that I served, colonial style, as something of a cross between father and feudal lord, arbitrating disputes, but most important of all, holding in effect the power of life and death over each of these souls. To fire one was to condemn that person to lasting shame in his community back home; to deprive the person of the modest home he and his family occupied in the compound was to take away both their abode and means of support. It was not a responsibility I relished.

The set-up might seem a paradise to many Canadians. In fact, a more apt comparison might be to liken it to the role of resident hotel manager. It certainly had its appealing sides and its benefits. But it was also a twenty-four hour job, particularly for Laine, organising the house staff and their activities, and presiding over a bed-and-breakfast for the many Canadian officials and others who lodged with us during their visits. The residence was large, but we ourselves lived almost exclusively in one large bed and sitting room at the rear, viewing the rest of the place as a 'tool of the trade', or hospitality facility. I'm not sure how the system works today, but in those days it was the clear expectation of the Department that one's spouse would share fully, and on an unpaid basis, in the responsibilities of her husband. This was the story of Laine's life and for the twenty-odd years that we were abroad, she performed marvellously and without complaint. If ever a memorial to service were to be set up in the Pearson Building, it should be to those generations of spouses who worked so selflessly to further Canada's interests. To the latter-day feminists who wouldn't think of lifting a finger without getting paid for it, and who regard those earlier generations with scorn mixed with pity, I say: "You have a point. Please see if you can arrange back-pay for those who went before!"

The year 1984 was a difficult one. The constant stream of protests from the Indian government over objectionable Sikh activities in Canada generated an ongoing and uncomfortable level of stress, not only for myself but on a trickle-down basis to other members of the mission. Then came Operation Blue Star in Amritsar and both protests in Canada and the temperature in New Delhi were ratcheted up several degrees. Nasty incidents took place across Canada with incursions into Indian consular missions, threats to diplomats, desecration of the Indian flag and the like. For example, in June, at virtually the same time that I was providing, on instruction from Ottawa, assurances to the Foreign Secretary with regard to the upgraded security being provided at Indian missions in Canada, an armed gunman walked into the Consulate General in Toronto, fired some shots, and then slipped away unimpeded. Through the late spring and summer of that year, I was summoned to the Foreign Ministry to receive strong protests on some eighteen occasions. The situation was so serious that there were even suggestions that India might see itself compelled to withdraw its High Commissioner from Canada in order to emphasise its displeasure and concern. I personally was very understanding of India's anger; indeed this anger differed little from my own at what I perceived as the cavalier treatment these protests were receiving at home. My requests for a firm explanation as to concrete actions being taken largely remained unanswered. My point to the Canadian authorities was: "Simply enforce the law. That is all that is being asked." The Indians knew my feelings. They perceived me as an ally and a valuable spokesman in getting their message across to Ottawa, and I believe this contributed substantially to keeping bilateral relations on a relatively even keel.

As events moved inexorably towards the cataclysm of autumn 1984, Canada was regarded as very much part of the overall problem. How could we, with a straight face, keep on reassuring the Indians of our good intentions when virtually every week seemed to produce yet another outrage? To be fair, I was fully aware that we had the ear and support of those desk officers in the External Affairs unit directly responsible for India, but above them there seemed to be, from the Delhi perspective, only indifference or incompetence. As far as the RCMP and other agencies across the country were concerned, there is no evidence to suggest that they shared our concerns. On more than one occasion, I was informally told to "simmer down"; Canada had lots of experience in dealing with ethnic quarrels as in Latvians, Lithuanians, Croats — so the story went. The Sikh issue was relatively minor, so I was supposed to believe, and the situation merited nothing other than "monitoring".

On the evening of October 30, I attended an outdoor reception at the residence of the local UNICEF representative. As I was schmoozing in the garden, the host called me over to introduce me to the person he was talking to. I didn't catch the person's name, but we chatted for a few minutes after stumbling on the fact that he was of Russian descent and that I had served in Moscow. I excused myself and moved on. Another colleague standing nearby asked me, "Do you know whom you were talking to?" "No," I said, "I missed the name." "Well," he replied, "that was Peter Ustinov!"

The next morning, Ustinov was sitting in an office in the compound at No. 1 Safdarjung Road, where he was to interview Prime Minister Gandhi for Irish television. As Mrs. Gandhi was making her way to the interview, she was suddenly gunned down by her Sikh bodyguards. She died shortly thereafter in the National Hospital. Following Operation Blue Star in June, the Prime Minister had been strongly advised to replace the Sikhs in her guard. Ironically, Mrs. Gandhi, who could be paranoid in so many ways, showed a singularly haughty disregard for her own security, continuing her regular morning meet-the-public sessions even after Operation Blue Star. She refused to replace the Sikh bodyguards, choosing instead to believe in the loyalty of the trusted men around her. She died, a victim of her own error in judgement.

I myself had flown off to Kathmandu that same morning for consultations with King Birendra's inner circle over a contract sought by a Canadian engineering firm. It was from the King's principal secretary that at noon I received the word that Mrs. Gandhi had been assassinated. My first thought was: "Good Lord, let there not be any Canadian connection." My second was: "I've got to get back."

The plane flew over Delhi just as dusk was falling. Fires were lighting up the darkening sky all over the city. I went straight back to the residence. Laine, it turned out, had been driving on her own that morning in the area of the city adjacent to the hospital to which Mrs. Gandhi had been taken. As she drove past the hospital on the way home, a large crowd was gathering, becoming more unruly by the minute. Timing was on Laine's side in that within the next half hour the crowd would turn into a mob on the rampage, taking out their anger on passing vehicles.

For the next several days, law and order collapsed completely in the city. Sikhs everywhere went into hiding. This did not prevent thousands of them being slaughtered, often with the connivance of unscrupulous politicians. Sikh houses were daubed with paint, to serve as a guide for marauding mobs. A Sikh friend of mine, a captain with Indian Airlines, flew a plane back to Delhi from Calcutta on that horrific evening. Although he wore a turban, fortunately he did not sport a beard. Driving from the airport, he saw the cars ahead of him being stopped by a mob and Sikhs being pulled out. He had the presence of mind to stuff the turban under his seat and thereby escaped. We ourselves sheltered a Sikh family for several days, with the firm advice that they remain well within the interior of the building and not let themselves be seen from the windows. The High Commission offices of course were closed and staff, particularly the Sikhs among them, advised to remain closeted in their houses. One staff member called to say that he was barricaded in his house, while seven bodies lay outside on the street. A call to the police elicited no response. At one point, word came that another suburb, where several of our Sikh colleagues lived, was under siege. I decided to drive out to the place with the idea of trying to bring the families into the residence if necessary. What I found in that case was that the men of the quarter, Sikhs and Hindus alike, had joined forces to set up an armed perimeter around the place to repel would-be attackers. What struck me in driving the streets in those critical days was the complete absence of police and military. The security forces, it seemed, were totally paralysed and mobs were left to burn, kill and destroy. Even as I drove to the building where Mrs. Gandhi's remains lay in state to pay my respects, we had to detour several times to avoid rioters ahead of us.

It was amid this chaos, four days after the assassination, that heads of state and government representatives from around the world descended on the Indian capital to attend the cremation ceremonies. Canada was represented by Foreign Affairs Minister Joe Clark, Chief Justice Brian Stevenson and several other politicians. The visit presented a welcome opportunity to brief Clark personally on Indian concerns and the seriousness with which the Indians viewed the situation, and Canada's lack of robust action. He took it all on board, seeming to appreciate my concerns, but after his return to Ottawa, nothing much changed. If attitudes of Canadian authorities toward Sikh militancy were stiffening, it certainly was not evidenced to me in terms of concrete actions.

The cremation took place at dusk in the beautiful park on the banks of the Yamuna River near the same Raj Ghat where the funeral rites of Mahatma Gandhi had years before been held. Foreign dignitaries were mobilised at a designated spot and transported by bus to the cremation site. In true Indian fashion, we were all packed rather chaotically into the transport, with more people standing than sitting. I found myself with the Japanese Prime Minister on one side, and a tiny lady on the other who couldn't reach a strap to hold onto, and so relied on me to keep her on her feet. It was Mother Teresa.

The ceremony itself was full of pathos. As the sun slid lower, the sky gradually turned to that heavy golden yellow so characteristic of the late Indian afternoon. In the Hindu custom, Rajiv dressed in white and, accompanied by his young son Rahul, circled the funeral pyre before setting alight the fuel-soaked wood on which the body rested. As the flames leapt upwards into the golden sky, the grief of the more than million mourners present expressed itself in a collective moan.

The next morning, Joe Clark, together with his entourage and a batch of Canadian reporters set off for the airport. Destiny and a merciless press seemed to have marked Clark out, quite undeservedly, as a man of foibles, and his departure from Delhi was no exception. The military aircraft's captain, we had been assured by the entourage, would obtain the necessary clearances for a flight from Delhi to Addis Ababa where Clark was to announce a CIDA contribution to famine relief in Ethiopia. As it happened, clearance had come through for all but a short essential segment crossing the then communist People's Republic of South Yemen, with which Canada did not have relations. It was expected momentarily. We boarded the aircraft, then waited and waited, the Canadian captain not daring to venture uncleared across the short stretch of remote yet hostile territory. It was scorching on the tarmac and not much better in the cabin. The media were growing restive and jokes began to circulate about 'yet another Clark misstep'. Things were rapidly heading for an absolute disaster when I happened to notice that an aircraft marked "Yemen" had been towed into position beside us. I had no idea whether it was from the 'hostile' south or 'friendly' north. On a sudden whim, I went down the steps and crossed over to the Yemeni plane where I communicated to the guard at the steps that I wanted to speak to the most senior official aboard. In short order I was talking to an aide to the President, explaining our problem. He was, as it turned out, from the Yemen we wanted, and he asked us to give him a few minutes to consult the President who was aboard. Shortly thereafter, the Foreign Minister appeared. Clark deplaned and a brief but amicable meeting ensued on the tarmac between the two aircraft. The Minister from this country with which we had no relations assured Clark that there would be no problem. "Follow us," he said. With much relief, we from the High Commission observed the Yemeni presidential flight depart, with Joe Clark's Boeing 707 tagging along a couple of minutes later. A subsequent article in the Globe and Mail described the event as "Tarmac Diplomacy".

Curiously, and as an anti-climax, the days following Mrs. Gandhi's funeral brought some relief from the high stress we had all been under. The army and police gradually reasserted their control over the city. The 'other shoe' that we had been expecting to fall ever since the tragic days of Operation Blue Star had indeed dropped with dreadful results. But in a macabre sort of way, at least that suspense was over. Mrs. Gandhi's son, Rajiv, quickly assumed the leadership of the party and government. To our great relief, no Canadian connection to the assassination had surfaced. Laine and I decided to indulge ourselves in a few days relaxation out of the city.

And so we found ourselves taking up a previously issued invitation from the Tourism Board of Rajasthan to spend ten days aboard the luxurious Palace on Wheels train. This was a quite extraordinary assemblage of rail cars from the era of the princely states dating back to the beginning of the twentieth century, all drawn by a coal-burning locomotive. The experience was indeed memorable as we boarded in Agra and traversed Rajasthan, state of camels, colourful nomads and limitless deserts, from one end to the other. Our enjoyment was enhanced by having an entire rail car to ourselves, tourism having largely been killed in India as a result of the violence. This consisted of a large bedroom suitable for a prince, complete with several attendants. Meals were taken in the opulent dining car, preceded by drinks in the 'bar car'. 'Bed tea', that venerable Indian custom, was served at first light each morning. I was even offered the possibility of riding for a couple of hours in the locomotive where I was able to fulfil a childhood fantasy, and shovel coal into the firebox. And so we moseyed slowly across the length and breadth of the state from Jaipur and Udaipur, all the way west to the amazing city of Jaisalmer that suddenly rises like a fantasy mirage out of the desert.

The gorgeous days of late autumn and winter of 1984-85 belied the despondency and gloom that gripped the nation. Sikh militants may have wreaked their revenge on Indira Gandhi, but the tragedy of those dark days of October had by no means run its course. Sikh militants were promising more revenge for the October massacres. Others vowed to keep up the struggle against the central government. In November, the British Deputy High Commissioner was assassinated in Bombay, ostensibly for the failure of his government to rein in Sikh militants in Britain. A short time later both I and my British colleague in New Delhi received letters threatening us with a similar fate, prompting the Canadian authorities to send in an armoured car for my use which, given the absence of any provision for easy exit in case of fire or accident or mob assault, I viewed only as marginally less risky than an assassin's gun. Our security force at the residence was supplemented by 24-hour mobile police patrols. Although we did not realise it at the time, Canada's own trauma was yet to come.

The same night of Indira Gandhi's assassination, Rajiv Gandhi, urged on by his closest associates, moved quickly to seize the reins of power. He had never been seen by observers as a 'political animal' or decisive in action. When I called to pay my respects on November 2, Rajiv was clearly still in a state of great shock and apparently incapable of galvanising the security forces. Two or three days were to pass before there was evidence that a firm hand was taking the helm. Stories were making the rounds among the Indian political elite that Rajiv was too weak and could not last as his mother's successor for more than two or three months.

As December gave way to January, some semblance of normalcy returned. The main change for us was in the sudden drying up of visitors of any sort. Unrest is always calculated to stop the flow and so, in a rather perverse way, we were able to benefit from a period of respite from the usual sometimes hectic activity associated with hosting travelling Canadians. Laine and I were able to increase our program of travel in support of Canadian aid and trade activities, as well as to meet regional political leaders. While in Calcutta we were honoured to call on Mother Teresa, who insisted on spending the better part of a day taking us to see her orphanages and Home for Dying Destitutes. A month or two later who should appear at my office in New Delhi than Mother Teresa herself, this time on a mission to seek admittance to Canada of a young boy in her care with a rare disease that could best be treated in Montreal. I said to her, "I'll look after the feds. You pray for the government in Quebec to go along." But even the prayers of this saint could not move the Quebec authorities to agree to an entry permit. To say that I was mightily annoyed would be to an understatement.

The stream of visitors to the residence gradually resumed and included the film director Norman Jewison, Charles Colson of Watergate fame and a host of others. One that sticks in my memory is the visit of the Commissioner of the RCMP — memorable because of the follow-up a month or two later. Our daughter, Lisa, had picked up a puppy with a broken leg in Khan Market, a short distance from the residence, and brought it home. We had the dog, by now named Jehangir, cleared by the vet but had the good sense to keep it isolated from our other dogs. Occasionally, Jehangir would dash out to greet visitors, but contented himself mainly with nipping and springing on Lisa in her bedroom. In time, Jehangir began to show signs of illness and, before long, died suddenly, gasping and shrieking in Lisa's arms. Some tests were run and it was determined that Jehangir had died of the fatal rabies virus. A list was drawn up of the people who had had any contact with the ill-fated puppy. One of them happened to be the RCMP Commissioner, who no doubt was pleased to receive the suggestion that he, like the rest of us, should take himself forthwith to a clinic for a series of rabies injections. It was several weeks before we could rest easily, particularly because Lisa had borne the marks of scratches and puppy bites all over her neck, arms and legs.

Mrs. Gandhi's assassination led to a drastic tightening of India's immigration regulations, one part of which was to expel foreign elements who served no identifiable Indian interest. And so it was that one Saturday evening when Laine and I were uncharacteristically relaxing at home, there was a knock on the door. When opened, there stood a small but radiantly vibrant holy man, surrounded by a throng of some 80 or 90 of his followers, all Canadians as it turned out. In they trooped, led by Swami Shyam, the spiritual leader of an ashram in the beautiful Kullu valley in the foothills of the Himalayas. The group's predicament quickly became evident; they were about to be deported, and had come south looking for help. Any hesitation we might have had about lending our full support was quickly dissipated on learning that one member of the group was none other than Barbara Mulroney, the Prime Minister's sister. I had been made quietly aware previously of her presence at an ashram in Kullu, with the admonition that Mr. Mulroney did not want her membership in the Swami's colony made widely known!

We had a remarkable evening. The furniture was pushed back. Everyone sat in the lotus position on the floor, except for the good Swami, Barbara and myself, who occupied a position of honour on the sofa. All non-alcoholic drinks in the place were quickly consumed, as was any morsel of food that could be found. The next three or four hours resembled nothing so much as a good revival meeting, Hindu style. The jolly Swami dispensed spiritual wisdom, interspersed by what I can only describe as enthusiastic 'testimonies' by his disciples. Intriguing to me was the energy that was generated, and the way in which the worshippers hung on to the Swami's every word with rapt attention. When the Swami laughed in a rather high-pitched voice, which he frequently did, the response was invariably an outburst of mirth in the same tenor. Laine and I, as 'solid Christians', could only hope that the Good Lord and One Saviour would forgive us for allowing some of the three million–odd Hindu deities to take over our household that evening. As the hour approached midnight, the whole crowd decamped as quickly as they had appeared, boarding two rickety buses which, Lord knows, could only have made it all the way from Kullu with His constant attention.

The following week I called on Prime Minister Rajiv Gandhi, whom I knew quite well by this time. He agreed on the spot to intervene. For my efforts, I was immediately admitted to the ranks of the ashram's saints.

I also found more time that winter to pursue Canadian business and aid activities in Nepal and Bhutan. My concurrent accreditation to the Court of Nepal and monitoring responsibility for Bhutan provided ample opportunity to savour the delights of these two Himalayan kingdoms located amidst the most spectacular scenery in the world. On first arrival in a country, a new ambassador presents his credentials. King Birendra of Nepal did not much enjoy the ceremony and his Chief of Protocol was always devising new ways to speed up the system. His solution was to organise new envoys into groups of three or four who would then be run past His Majesty in double-quick time, each ambassador's claim on the imperial presence being less than two minutes. My moment arrived and my colleagues at the presentation event were the new Dutch and Indonesian ambassadors. We jokingly placed bets on which of us could extract the maximum number of seconds from His Majesty. Speed in the interests of efficiency may have its advantages, but it can also have its drawbacks. The Nepali Chief of Protocol evidently shuffled his papers one time too many, with the result that the Dutch was introduced as the Canadian ambassador, I as the Indonesian, and the latter as the Dutch. What amused me most was that the good King did not so much as bat an eye, as he asked me to assure my government of his undying affection.

Canada had substantial trade and development interests in Nepal. Our programs were well meaning, but I was never too sure how beneficial the millions we poured into the place would turn out be. Of course the whole effort was largely self-serving, tied as the aid was to procurement from high-priced Canadian sources. Building health posts and the like was all well and good, but where were the doctors to staff them, and the funds to maintain them to come from once the Canadians had up and left? Providing De Havilland Twin Otters for the national airline was all well and good, but who down the road was to pay for maintenance, spare parts, pilot training and the like? The fact that the government was corrupt, with the Palace insisting on a piece of every pie, and that some of our companies were quite prepared to play the game, hardly set a shining model of development practice. I had to 'act' highly embarrassed on more than one occasion to receive representations from the World Bank representative regarding alleged bribes offered by an unnamed Canadian company which, in effect he told me, set new records of venality.

In the quaint Kingdom of Bhutan, ruled by the most eligible bachelor in the Himalayas, King Sigme Wangchuk, we had some small projects. I managed to travel there twice. The only access to the Kingdom was by a tiny airline, Druk Air, which operated a couple of times a week. On one flight, there were three Canadian friends aboard in addition to Laine and myself and our son Scott, and some Japanese businessmen sitting up front. At one point during the flight the pilot turned around and motioned to us to help ourselves to coffee from the large thermos at the rear. I was closest and so I got up and served coffee to Laine and our guests whereupon the Japanese, who evidently concluded that I was the flight attendant, imperiously summoned me to the front to receive their order. I didn't say a thing and, amid the hilarity of my friends, served coffee and cookies with a flourish. The Japanese were somewhat surprised when, on arrival, the 'flight attendant' was greeted by several officials at the aircraft steps and ushered into a big black limo.

Corruption was a way of life for anyone involved in business or government in that part of the world and had been so since Adam first met Eve. Many Canadians and Americans were wont, both piously and hypocritically, to wring hands and roll eyes in self-righteous disgust at the practice. The reality was that without it, the entire economy would have ground to a halt. The Europeans had few qualms about entering into the game, and the Japanese none at all. With some exceptions, where Canadian firms were showing any degree of success, one could be sure that black money was changing hands. A case study was a concerted Canadian effort to win a contract for a major pipeline that had been put out to tender. Our main competitor as usual was a Japanese consortium. Of course, I, as government representative, was expressly prohibited from providing counsel on the greasing of palms. Both I and the High Commission trade officers did, however, work all possible angles, from meeting with the Prime Minister and every other conceivable senior official, to mustering all our resources to collect intelligence on details of the Japanese bid. I met frequently with top members of the Canadian bidding team. The discussions, frankly, I found frustrating. In this case, the Canadians appeared to be babes-in-the-woods in terms of going head to head with the Japanese. The classic Japanese approach was to bid low, win the contract, and then escalate sharply upwards. This I put to the Canadians: "Cut every possible bit of fat out of the your bid. Propose a system that will function – barely – then jack up your prices later." The standard response to me was: "If they want a 'VW' pipeline, then they should go to the Japanese. If they want a 'Cadillac pipeline' (the CEO's very words), then they should come to us." While I was not privy to the extent to which bribes were changing hands behind the scenes, of one thing I was sure. Whatever the Canadians might be handing out, the Japanese would be trumping them in spades. For Indian officials, this kind of project was a real bonanza, as they played one competitor off against the other with ever escalating demands. And the game was not always crassly reduced to cash. It might involve a fully funded university education for the offspring of one or more key individuals, or any one of a dozen other variants.

Thus armed with our own formula for disaster, we watched as the competition ground its way through the various hoops to its inevitable conclusion. There were some hiccups along the way. When the Indians were on the verge of announcing the winner, we, girded with a letter from Prime Minister Mulroney and accompanied by Foreign Minister Joe Clark, called on Rajiv Gandhi in one last desperate effort to save our bacon. Gandhi did in fact order the competition to be reopened. After a brief interlude, the winner was announced. Surprise, surprise! The Japanese! As is usual in these sorts of situations, scapegoats were sought. Some blamed the company, Others blamed the government. Some went so far as to interpret the loss as a reflection on the lobbying abilities of the High Commission. In the end, it all came down to the question of who was prepared to 'buy' the project. The truth was, burdened by our naïveté, we were never in the game from the start. I knew it and, had it not been so politically inexpedient, I would have told the Canadian company at the start and saved them a lot of money.

I must confess to extreme frustration during the entire winter of 1984-85, leading into the spring that produced the avaition disaster that was to rock both countries. I can only describe the situation from my own perspective in Delhi. Apart from Canadian officials at the lower levels in the Department of External Affairs, it seemed to me that almost everyone else was asleep at the wheel in the matter of Sikh militancy. Perhaps something was churning away in the upper levels of the bureaucracy, but it was not evident to me. Certainly Canadian law enforcement agencies and their counterparts in the local municipalities were, if they paid attention to the issue at all, taking matters far too lightly. A case in point: at the very time I was conveying an apology to the Indian Foreign Ministry for an assault in Canada on the Acting Indian High Commissioner, yet another militant group was clambering up the front of the Consulate in Vancouver to hoist the Khalistan flag. Other irritants involved the insistence of the Multiculturalism Department on continuing its grants to groups pursuing blatantly anti-Indian political aims, and the alleged recruitment activities of National Defence officers at extremist functions.

Serious embarrassment was caused by the fact that the Indian authorities had a much better idea of what was going on in the extremist groups in Canada than did our own security people. For example, a secret intelligence brief made available in 2007 to the Air India Inquiry stated categorically that in 1984 there was "no substantial threat which necessitated vastly increased security precautions." Another document that came to light in the same way described the Sikh situation in Canada as a "relatively minor problem in our inventory of international concerns..." So much for the torrent of paper with which I had been deluging Ottawa both before and after Gandhi's assassination, most of it copied directly to the RCMP security service. So much for the urgent representations I had made to Joe Clark at the Gandhi funeral. And so much for the trauma afflicting India itself. The Keystone Cops could have done better. I had long been aware, primarily from the quality of the information passed to us and occasional remarks by officials, that India's intelligence service had set themselves up in a big way in Canada, using both their High Commission as well as clandestine agents. Normally this would have been a major concern to me, but since we Canadians had dropped the ball almost entirely, I did not pursue the issue with Ottawa.

Indian paranoia if anything increased as 1984 gave way to 1985. Accusations of Canadian laxity vis-à-vis the extremists became a regular feature in the press. It became virtually impossible to hold a conversation in any part of the country without having to parry criticism on the subject of Sikh extremism. As in the period following the assault on the Golden Temple and prior to Mrs. Gandhi's assassination, I began to harbour a sense of foreboding. If there was another shoe to drop, what would it be? And when? The refusal of the Canadian authorities to take the matter seriously created another disaster waiting to happen.

In March, I was handed on an urgent basis a personal letter from Prime Minister Rajiv Gandhi to Prime Minister Mulroney expressing, in the most insistent tones consistent with diplomatic protocol, India's grave concern over the escalating actions of extremist Sikhs in Canada. On May 17, little more than a month before Air India 182 was blown out of the sky with the loss of all three hundred and twenty-nine passengers and crew, Mulroney responded with what I considered a totally inappropriate message. While providing the usual glib and by then less than credible assurances over Canada's commitment to combat illegal anti-Indian activities in Canada, he informed Prime Minister Gandhi in a rather patronising manner that Canadians were watching "with understanding" his efforts to come up with political solutions to India's problems. Having dispensed with the matter in his first paragraph, he then gave equal time to stating his satisfaction over Indian moves that could lead to greater business opportunities for Canadian companies. In interpreting such a letter, of course, one has to take into account that it had been drafted not by Mulroney himself but by some faceless bureaucrat, and that the cavalier tone reflected at least some of the bureaucracy's unreconstructed attitude ("a minor ethnic problem").

In May-June 1985, I returned to Canada for a short period of rest and consultations. During a visit to Ottawa, I was gratified to attend the first formal session of an inter-agency group that had been set up to deal with Sikh extremism. Gratified, yes – yet appalled that it had taken so long to take such a simple and obvious step as to establish a working group bringing all players on the Canadian side under one umbrella.

I landed back in Delhi on Friday, June 21. At noon on Sunday, June 23, Laine and I were sitting beside the pool at the club in the Canadian compound when a member of the staff came up to me with a grim look on his face and said: "An Air India flight has gone down off Ireland." Some time later, news of a suitcase bomb in Tokyo off a flight from Vancouver came through. The other shoe had dropped. I felt sick, nauseous, as the veritable horror of what had just transpired sunk in. A now familiar prayer took over my mind: "Lord, let there be no Canadian hand behind this!", only this time, my prayer would not be answered. Having flown into India from Canada myself so recently, I could relate even more closely to the trauma of the event. Given a few travel adjustments here and there, my wife and I could ourselves easily have been on the ill-fated flight. Two hundred and eighty Canadians, 27 Britons and 22 Indians – the largest mass murder in Canadian history – all snuffed out in an intricately planned act of rage, hatched and designed on Canadian soil.

It should not be difficult to imagine the furious response of the Indian media to news of the event. From the day of the tragedy, there was no doubt left in the minds of the Indian public that Canadian Sikh extremists were behind the downing of the aircraft, and that the Government of Canada, through its negligence, shared in the culpability. According to the Sunday Observer in Bombay on June 30, "Official circles here feel that the disaster may have been avoided if the Canadian authorities had cracked down on Sikh extremists in time as requested by the Indian government repeatedly in the past year." This had been precisely my point all along. It was what I believed then, and it is the position I have taken ever since. It was with a feeling of guilt, laced with some trepidation, that I responded to the summons to the

Indian Foreign Ministry to receive what I expected to be a thorough tongue-lashing. The meeting turned out to be something of an anti-climax, and rather less intense than anticipated. The atmosphere was perhaps best summed up as one of resignation and extreme frustration on both sides. "Hopefully," the Foreign Secretary said, "Canada now appreciates fully the nature of the extremist threat." What more was there to be said?

Several days later, moved as much by feelings of guilt as by sorrow, I went to the airport to attend the arrival of the aircraft carrying the first victims of the disaster. It was not a pleasant experience. My instincts told me to stay in the background, which I did. There was nothing I had to say to the media, and certainly condolences at that point from a Canadian representative would not have been well received by the victims' families.

The lead-up to, and aftermath of, the disaster have been dissected *ad nauseum* in the media and particularly by the official Air India inquiry conducted by Justice Major. I was called in November of 2007 to testify and spent a half-day on the stand. The crux of my testimony was that, in my opinion, the tragedy had been fully preventable. Warnings of potential disaster had been delivered in spades. The failure of the Canadian authorities to act was, consequently, one of the root causes.

Did the Canadian government finally 'get it'? Astonishingly, even by the middle of 1986, when we left India, officials in Canada had still not set up a fully effective, integrated body to deal with

Sikh extremism. A militant minority continued to dominate the Sikh community in Canada, using as weapons of choice beatings of opponents, threats against families and phoney elections to gain control of prominent Sikh temples. Even after the horrific bombing of Air India 182, the courts continued to mete out minor punishment or fines for serious infractions. With few exceptions, the majority of Canadian Sikhs who were decidedly moderate were intimidated into silence.

Our final year in India took its course with no further disasters. In India itself, while significant tensions remained, Rajiv Gandhi moved expeditiously to seek some accommodation with the Sikh community and the Sikh-dominated state of Punjab. Ironically, it was the Sikh extremists in Canada who distinguished themselves as the most vociferous ongoing proponents of an independent Khalistan. Nonetheless, through a combination of heightened awareness, somewhat better police work and good luck, the lid was kept on the pressure cooker.

As the summer of 1985 wore into autumn, some of the bitter taste caused by the Air India tragedy was mitigated by several Canadian initiatives. Prime Minister Mulroney met with Prime Minister Gandhi and established a good personal rapport. In December, Joe Clark led a Canadian delegation to Delhi where he tabled a draft bilateral extradition treaty, something the Indians had long been after.

The Clark visit was the last major ministerial event of my tenure in India and I would be less than frank if I were not to admit that I was delighted. Joe Clark I personally admired and respected greatly as an honest politician in a profession where honesty and integrity did not often stand out. However, I did not always have the same 'admiration' for how the show around him was run. The Delhi delegation included, at my suggestion, a fair number of excellent business people interested in exploring the Indian market. Added to it, however, was a totally unnecessary number of staff from Clark's own office, in addition to the usual bureaucratic gaggle from the Department. Most of the hangers-on had little evident purpose except to enjoy the pleasures of 'delegation tourism' and place undue demands on the limited resources of the High Commission. Over the previous eight or nine years I had organised some fifty ministerial visits to my various posts, and hence had become quite accustomed to the over-staffing of these missions. I once met the New Zealand foreign minister, who had just flown in on a commercial flight accompanied by two aides. Not so for the Canadians. Large aircraft with plenty of supporting resources were the order of the day.

Illustrative of the ministerial attachment to grand scales was the peremptory instruction we received from Ottawa not to book the Canadian delegation on a commercial flight from Ahmedabad to Delhi, as strongly recommended by us, but rather to charter a special Boeing 737 from Indian Airlines. In vain did we warn of the unreliability of an arrangement like this, to say nothing of the cost. The outcome, thoroughly predictable, was that we arrived at the airport in Ahmedabad for the flight, but the aircraft did not. Only several hours later after much badgering and bullying did it show up. Clark of course was not pleased and, as usual, the High Commission took the hit for Ottawa's errant judgement.

Demons seemed to pursue Clark through much of his public life and there was still one waiting for him in Delhi. He was to deliver a major address to a large luncheon gathering of Delhi's business elite. When he got up to give the speech, one thing was missing on the lectern: the speech. For most speech-givers, this would not have been a big deal, if only because the handlers would have had another copy readily at hand. But Clark had his demons, and also the Canadian media ever ready to pounce on something like this. Observing the lack of movement on the part of his staff, I quickly got up and passed him a copy of the speech that had been put out as a press release.

But the demon was not yet through with Clark. It just so happened that in this one copy, among the two or three hundred releases that had been printed, three pages in was followed by a duplicate page three. The Minister unfortunately was halfway through page three for the second time before he noticed that he was repeating himself. Considerable embarrassment and harrumphing ensued. By this time his staff had pretty well gone into hiding under their chairs, trying to disappear, rather than remedy the situation. It thus fell to me once again to approach the lectern and set matters — and pages — right. The crowd all thought it was quite funny but not, of course, Clark himself.

Subsequently, the staff by this time, in typical 'cover-your-posterior' mode, were looking for an excuse – which did not of course countenance the slightest possibility that they themselves may have forgotten to put the speech on the lectern in the first place. Rather, their collective decision was that I must have removed it along with a number of other papers on the lectern after I had introduced Clark. Maybe I did. Maybe I didn't. In the former case, I suppose I could be forgiven, in the absence of any heads-up from the highly paid help, for assuming that like any 'normal' bloke the Minister would carry his own speech to the podium. The mystery will never be resolved. In any event, I could afford to find the mishap rather amusing, in that by that point the idea had begun to germinate that I had had a good run, and should perhaps start looking for ways to remove myself from the 'yes Minister' crowd.

By the spring of 1986, we had begun to take stock and to prepare our departure. Three years, even if short, had enabled us to glimpse many of India's kaleidoscopic images. For example, we saw enough to appreciate that Dominique Lapierre's novel, City of Joy, set in Calcutta, with its eunuchs, lepers, slumlords, overflowing sewer rat infestations and violence, contained not one whit of exaggeration. Its images were one face of the reality to be found in all India's major cities. Yet these same slums, as we ourselves witnessed in traversing the country from Cape Comorin (Kanyakumari) at the southern tip to Leh in the Himalayas could produce children with exquisite beauty, grace and a sense of culture, as they executed intricate dance steps for the occasional visitors. One could only marvel at such dignity amidst absolute poverty.

Where else but in India could one visit a village whose collective pride lay in the ability of one of its number to put a serpent up one nostril and expel it through the other? In Assam we passed through villages stricken with the fear of rampaging elephants demolishing houses in the quest for rice wine fermenting in stills beneath the floorboards. Less than a four-hour drive from Delhi, we used a four-wheel drive vehicle to access a remote valley, an antiquarian's paradise strewn with undisturbed remnants of Jain temples destroyed by invading hordes centuries before. One week after our visit, a woman of the valley was devoured by a tiger.

Yet by 1986, the birth pangs of the 'new India' of the new millennium were already evident. The attachment to 'Nehru socialism', inspired by the Soviet experience, was beginning to weaken. In its international posture and in the context of the Cold War, India remained a source of severe frustration for the West as it continued to profess neutrality but in practice supported Soviet positions. But even here, the policy gulf was narrowing, particularly as the influence of Mrs. Gandhi waned following her assassination, and as Rajiv, much more firmly oriented towards the West, began to make his presence felt.

During our three years in India, traffic had doubled on the roads, with a whole new array of models produced domestically coming onto the market. The private sector had begun to play a much more significant role, and 'liberalisation' had become a catchword.

In our three years we had seen a real surge in the interest of Canadian companies, and in the amount of time devoted by the High Commission to trade promotion. By 1986, a 'made-in-India' satellite was beaming programs to seventy percent of the population, most of whom three years earlier had not even seen TV. The Indian Space Centre was pursuing an active program, while the nuclear industry was pressing ahead with ambitious programs for increasing indigenous capacity.

In the summer of 1986, as always, we left our adopted home with much sadness. We toyed briefly with the idea of retiring on the spot and setting up a more permanent existence in this fascinating nation, the surface of which we had only scratched, but we quickly dismissed the thought. I was at that point only fifty-two. As I wrote in my valedictory dispatch from Delhi, "I leave India with impressions which are on balance reassuring: an immensely rich culture and history; a nation where, given the tremendous variety of languages, ethnic groups and religions, incredible harmony rather than conflict has been the distinguishing trait; a people unmatched in their warmth and hospitality; a society resilient but sorely in need of deep-seated change; a democracy which, even if flawed, is remarkable for its survival and vitality; and finally of a nation with enormous potential and showing signs of renewal."

In July, we packed our belongings and flew to Ottawa.

Bill shakes hands with Indian Prime Minister Indira Gandhi, 1983, New Delhi.

With Queen Elizabeth at the Presidential Palace, New Delhi, on the occasion of her visit to India in 1984. Bill is standing fourth from the right. Next to him is Sir Edmund Hillary, then New Zealand's High Commisssioner to India.

Bill with Mother Teresa, and Laine, below, at the Missionaries of Charity Home for the Dying, Calcutta, mid-1980s.

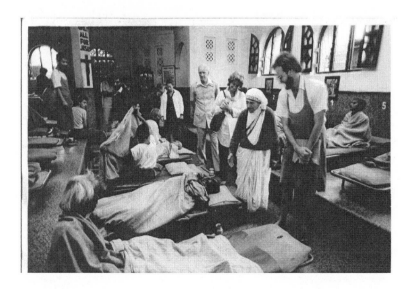

Bill inspecting the Honour Guard at the Presidential Palace, New Delhi, 1983.

Chapter Ten

THE LAST PRESIDENT

"Beel", he said, "Come". The speaker was Mikhail Gorbachev, lately President of the Union of Soviet Socialist Republics. It was past eleven in the evening at the Palliser Hotel in Calgary in March of 1993, the end of the first full day of a ten-day cross-Canada tour. Typical of each day to come, the program had included public appearances, meetings with the media, an official lunch and dinner. Now it was time to relax and recover from the lengthy flight from Moscow via Vancouver. Or so I thought!

Summoned into the presidential suite along with the other nine members of his entourage, all of us expected to say a hasty good night. That was not to be. Without missing a beat the President bade us all sit down at the large dining table, myself at his right hand. He thought for a moment, then said in Russian, "We need whiskey," whereupon I ordered up a couple of jugs of the finest from room service. The party went on till 1:30 a.m. and included a number of folksongs lustily belted out by all, including the President. If the rest of us were droopy-eyed by the time we were released, not so with Gorbachev himself. A man of prodigious energy, he was the life of the party, one moment holding forth on the incredible productivity of Canadian agriculture, the next challenging one or other of his tablemates over criticism that he had been too soft on demonstrators in the last days of the Union.

This was to be the pattern throughout the journey. Indeed, on the flight from Moscow as everyone else was sleeping, he sat wide-eyed and insisted on grilling me on all manner of themes related to Canadian politics and the economy. The schedule each day was full, to the point of being hectic, but this did not alter the midnight routine. "Beel, come!" Then, "Sit." Gorbachev did not speak English except for a few words. And so I ended up at his side each night, surrounded by former members of the Soviet Politburo and senior bureaucracy, listening with the greatest of fascination to the jokes about Brezhnev's daughter, the nastiest of comments about Boris Yeltsin, newly acceded President of the Russian Republic and principal player in engineering an end to the Union, and so on. Yeltsin was due to visit Vancouver in a couple of weeks and to stay in the same presidential accommodation as Gorbachev. Said Gorbachev to me, holding his nose, "Better open the windows wide and air the place out. Very smelly." My Russian, which had been more than passable thirty years earlier, was by now rusty but still good enough to enable me to follow and participate in the conversation. Gorbachev took pleasure out of mimicking my accent.

I had to pinch myself from time to time to confirm that I was living in real time and not some kind of dream. Images from the past kept intruding on my space. I vividly recalled the extreme anxiety of the Cuban Missile Crisis when the world waited with bated breath for the two superpowers to pull the trigger and bring Armageddon, or reach a compromise. Also present in colour were memories of spectacular military parades in Red Square, Soviet leaders atop the Lenin Mausoleum reviewing thousands of goose-stepping troops and the newest weapons in the Soviet arsenal. It was impossible not to experience once again the thrill for a young diplomat of accompanying the ambassador into the Kremlin, the secret and mysterious inner sanctum, the heart of Communism from where Stalin had plotted his empire and consigned millions to the gulags and death in the Siberian wastelands.

Yet how fickle was History. Marxist-Leninist ideology, with its unshakeable conviction that Communism would eventually rule the world, may have assumed the status of religion for inhabitants of the Soviet realm. We ourselves in the so-called Free World had acquiesced in the notion that the Soviet Union was here to stay, at least for the foreseeable future. Yet with unbelievable suddenness, the empire had collapsed and here I was, a mere three decades removed from my Moscow posting, sitting at the right hand of its last ruler, now deposed and himself still suffering from the trauma of eviction from the seat of power.

How Gorbachev came to be in Calgary so soon after his fall from the heights was another story straight from the annals of Cold War oddities. In the late fall of 1991, when Gorbachev and his circle of supporters were facing increasingly heavy sledding in the face of attacks from conservatives on the one hand, and nationalists from the various republics on the other, I was approached by a professor from the University of Calgary, David Whitefield, who had a long history of good relations with Moscow and of moving within the inner circles of the Communist Party of Canada. His membership in the Party, which brought with it surveillance and much harassment from Canadian authorities, had not left him unscarred, and there were many in the University community who questioned his judgements and credibility. It was thus with some incredulity that I listened to his proposal.

According to Whitefield, the circle around Gorbachev was becoming increasingly concerned for his security and had sent out feelers to various contacts around the world for the purpose of identifying a bolthole the President could retire to in case of urgent need. Whitefield wanted to know if the University would, if requested on short notice, bring Gorbachev to Calgary for a temporary period as a distinguished honorary professor. The notion that Gorbachev would want to come to Calgary I considered ridiculous, as did some of my former colleagues in Foreign Affairs in Ottawa off whom I bounced the idea. My scepticism increased as I questioned the professor about his communication with Moscow. According to him, since he was still under surveillance here in Canada, he had to call from a 'safe' phone to a contact in East Germany who would then put him through to Gorbachev's circle in Moscow. Whitefield, when pressed, told me that Gorbachev himself had no idea that these feelers were being circulated. Scepticism notwithstanding, I decided there was nothing to be lost in putting Whitefield's proposal, which I now considered to be more hare-brained than rational, to the President's office. To my surprise, agreement was immediate and I conveyed this to Professor Whitefield just before Christmas, indeed just about the same time that Gorbachev was being pushed out of the Soviet presidency.

Nothing was heard for several weeks, until Whitefield appeared once more in my office to urge that I accompany him to Moscow to meet Gorbachev and discuss the situation. I pondered this for several days and eventually it was decided that Stephen Randall, a colleague of Whitefield in the Department of History, and I would make the trip. Randall and I both considered the exercise little short of preposterous, but decided that nonetheless it would be interesting to have a look around Moscow so shortly after the fall of empire.

We arrived in the capital with the onset of spring, my first visit back to Moscow in twenty-nine years to be precise, where we were received by Yury Krasin, Rector of the Institute of Social Sciences, and a trusted Gorbachev advisor. Randall and I were keen to observe the interaction between Whitefield and Krasin. In this endeavour we acquired little knowledge during the following days beyond confirming that they certainly knew each other. The mystery of the Whitefield connection was never fully resolved. Nonetheless, we met subsequently with several members of the Gorbachev inner circle, such as Vadim Medvedev and Georgy Shakhnazarov, both former members of the Central Committee and among Gorbachev's closest advisors. Curiously, Whitefield's notion of Gorbachev spending an extended period of time in Canada never came up, and the conversations were limited to the idea of a possible short-term visit. We waited and waited. A week passed and both Randall and Whitefield had to return to Canada. I had planned to go with them, but on the last day Whitefield informed me that he had had a middle-of-the-night meeting at which it was stated that if I would remain in Moscow over the weekend, Gorbachev would receive me on the Monday.

I met with the President as promised. Why, I'm not sure, but I was somewhat amused to find him still in possession of most of the trappings of power: large office suitable for a president, bodyguards, advisors and other hangers-on hovering around the fringes. The hour-long meeting went well. We struck up a good rapport. The conversation was general and we covered a lot of ground, but there was nary a mention of Professor Whitefield or of his quixotic proposal. What did come out of the meeting was the germination of the idea of mounting a major Canadian tour. Gorbachev didn't appear much interested, but neither did he exclude the idea entirely. The more I myself thought about it, the more I became hooked.

The next twelve months would see me in Moscow five times. The concept gradually evolved of a tour of five major Canadian cities, the profit to be funnelled into a joint trust fund between the Foundation and the University for the purpose of promoting democratic reforms in the former Soviet Union. It was the hook that caught the President's attention. Gorbachev personally vetted and approved every item on the program. He wanted to see something of Canadian livestock and agricultural operations. And so we arranged for him to spend an evening at Spruce Meadows equestrian facility, to be hosted by its billionaire owners, Marg and Ron Southern. Gorbachev wanted to know if they were 'peasants'. When we allowed as to how the Southerns were not quite your average Canadian peasants, he insisted on our including a visit to a 'typical' farm in the program. At the end of it all, I was profoundly relieved in March of 1993 when the Gorbachev delegation and I boarded the plane and left Moscow. Various political crises were continuously threatening the venture. Indeed, only the day before our departure Gorbachev was still talking about the possible need to cancel. Given the time and treasure that had been invested from the Canadian end, this would have been little short of a disaster.

The tour turned out to be a major success, with a tidy sum going into the newly formed University of Calgary-Gorbachev Foundation Joint Trust Fund. In fact, it produced a good bit more than expected. In all immodesty, I have to say that as I was on the plane to Moscow to collect the Gorbachev team, I came up with the idea of using the visit to tap into Canadian government funding. Right after landing, I called Brenda Kennedy, coordinator for the visit in Canada, and suggested to her that she contact the office of Prime Minister Mulroney and tell them that Gorbachev planned to ask him for a contribution to the Fund. I hadn't consulted the President on this point, but by this time knew him well enough to know that he would appreciate the manoeuvre. Mulroney had always held Gorbachev in high esteem and, in addition to providing us with a government jet for the cross-Canada tour, had also invited him to a private meeting at 24 Sussex Drive, the prime ministerial residence in Ottawa. I was, therefore, delighted when Kennedy called back a few hours later, not to say that the request had been summarily nixed, but simply to report that the Prime Minister wanted to know how much! For want of a better figure, I picked five million off the top of my head. The following day, the reply came that five million would not be possible, but would two million be okay? I suggested to Kennedy that she 'reluctantly' agree that this should be sufficient. On the flight over, I explained the situation to the President. He enthusiastically embraced the idea and, in due course, asked for, and received the commitment. The Fund was off to a good start. It was later to be supplemented by an injection of a further four million dollars.

The Fund continued for ten years. It provided financing for some forty joint Russian-Canadian projects, one condition being that each study come up with practical proposals and/or policy recommendations for government. Every effort was to be made to involve governing bodies in the work of the project. For myself as chair of the Fund for the first several years, it meant travel to Moscow once or twice a year and, on each occasion, the opportunity to sit down for a chat with the President.

Over the years, I did not spend a lot of time on my own with Gorbachev. His entourage was almost always present. Nevertheless, I got to know him well enough to enable me to size him up in terms of personal characteristics. He was very self-confident, but never overbearing. His origins as a tractor driver were a badge of honour that he never tried to cover. His curiosity was legend and knew no bounds. He showed keen regret over the collapse of the Soviet Union, but none whatsoever for the dissolution of the eastern European empire. Gorbachev was very proud of his role in laying the foundation for the transition from empire, but still appeared ambivalent in regard to Western democracy and free markets. He was perhaps at his most resolute in defending his decision not to shed blood in putting down the demonstrations and riots that marked the latter months of his presidency.

The scars of the rightwing *putsch* that could have proven fatal for him and his family were still evident. In our late-night sessions, he referred to the ordeal with anger, mixed with relief that he and his family had come out of it safely. One of the things that struck me most forcefully about Gorbachev was his passionate attachment to his wife, Raisa, and to the rest of his family. Every night without fail, he would call Raisa and have a lengthy chat. I don't know why it should have, but indeed I found it somewhat incongruous that the head of the so-called 'Evil Empire' should exhibit family values much superior to those of many of his detractors in the West. The other element I had difficulty coming to grips with was my impression of a man head and shoulders above most of our political leaders in the West in terms of principle, honesty and invulnerability to corruption. In the course of my career, I had had the opportunity to cross paths with Prime Ministers, Presidents, Kings, many ministers and others in authority. I must in all honesty say that for me Gorbachev was the most impressive of all.

I shouldn't have been surprised after all that had transpired over the previous several years that saw the Cold War come to an abrupt end.

History has a habit of throwing up uniquely inspired individuals to lead the people forward through revolutionary change, for better or for worse. Through his Foundation, Gorbachev has embraced a variety of positive environmental and political causes, and I have always felt him to be someone with the potential to serve on the world stage as a Russian variant of Jimmy Carter, in my opinion the best ex-President of the United States.

My encounter with Gorbachev served as a neat bookend to my journey as a diplomat through the tough and dangerous years of the Cold War. As a young diplomat I thought of Stalin, Khrushchev and their immediate successors as perverse deities dwelling in the dark and mysterious Kremlin from where they exercised the power of life and death over their subjects. The Empire in the end came crashing down, as had all empires that preceded it. Gorbachev, the fallen emperor, somehow made all of us in the West feel good, like we were at the dawn of a new and peaceful era. In our euphoria, we missed the lesson of History. No empire, including the American, will survive forever. Others will arise. New entities will be forged out of the ashes of the old. Whether nations can bring themselves, in a modern world armed with incredible capacity for good and evil, to forego the lust for power and domination over others is still unknown. The answer to this question will almost certainly determine the fate of the human race.

Epilogue

My Foreign Service career effectively ended the day we left India in 1986. Although the tie with the Department was not formally cut until two years later, I had pretty well decided by that time to move on. My years as a diplomat had given me everything I might have hoped for — and much more. Yet at age 52, I felt a need for 'fresh air', and so it was that I leapt at the opportunity, when offered, to spend a year as 'diplomat in residence' at the University of Calgary.

The rest is history. One year turned into two, and then into a second career spanning another dozen years. For me, my goal in the Foreign Service was never to see how high I might climb in anyone's 'pecking order', but rather to push the boundaries and accumulate as many life-enriching experiences as possible. I bridled under the constraints of its occasionally irrational and always power-conscious bureaucracy.

At the same time, I was highly privileged to have served under the same Departmental roof and rubbed shoulders with former greats such as Norman Robertson, Ed and Charles Ritchie, George Ignatieff, John Watkins, Robert Ford and Arthur Menzies. Theirs was a world of vision and commitment. I have nothing but the best of memories of working with so many colleagues who enriched my life and set an example with their wit, wisdom, dedication and incredible work ethic.

By the time we arrived in Calgary, I had earned the title of 'maverick', by reason of my willingness to speak up and out, sometimes in not so diplomatic a manner. Looking back, I don't object to the title; rather, I wear it as a badge of honour. When Departmental management asked for my opinion on this or that issue, I was only too pleased to offer it in unvarnished fashion. At one meeting of Heads of Mission, I was asked to present the 'view from the field' of the Department's administration. I called the shots as I saw them, provocative as ever, to the accolades of my fellow Heads and the consternation of the bosses who immediately began conjuring up various forms of reprisal.

Most diplomats lack guts, I am sorry to say. I suppose it is a trademark of the profession. Work for compromise. Make no waves. Don't upset anyone, particularly those in power. There have, of course, been notable exceptions. Raoul Wallenberg, the Swedish diplomat who during the early years of World War II worked in Hungary where he issued protective passports that saved thousands of Jewish lives, was a pride to the profession. Similarly, Craig Murray, British ambassador to Uzbekistan, 2002-2004, put his career on the line by speaking out publicly against the gathering of intelligence through the use of torture. He was dismissed from the service. More recently, Richard Colvin, a mid-level Canadian foreign service officer who served in Afghanistan in 2006-07, accused the government before a parliamentary committee of knowingly turning detainees over to Afghan security authorities who without question were inflicting torture. For his veracity, he was scurrilously attacked in person by the government, in order to draw attention away from the 'message'. But these were the exceptions.

The University was a generous employer and gave me free rein to pursue my various interests. Human rights, particularly in Latin America, became a passion and I travelled the continent widely as an election observer and in support of various University projects. I became closely involved with the Soviet Union's last President, Mikhail Gorbachev, shortly after he left office, and maintained a close relationship with him and his Foundation for about a dozen years. I had always enjoyed writing and in my post-Department years I derived an admittedly perverse pleasure in pulling the establishment's tail feathers as a frequent contributor to the Calgary Herald and various other publications. The Herald came from a respected liberal tradition, publishing opinions including my own from across a broad spectrum. But all that came to a crashing halt in the early years of the new millennium's first decade when righ-twing interests acquired the paper. The liberal voices were quickly squelched as the publication transformed itself editorially into a Conservative mouthpiece. One of my editor friends, who survived the bloodletting, later told me that it would be 'worth his job' under the new regime to print any of my 'stuff'". Again, on most days I wore this as a badge of honour, but on others had to admit to some frustration at having had my communication channel cut off.

The full extent of my maverick nature revealed itself when, the day after my retirement from the University, I pursued a lifetime fascination and enrolled in a truck-driver training course, eventually running semi-trailers for a short time to Edmonton and then tour buses all across the West. A professor from India once regaled his Calgary hosts with the story of how the driver of his tour bus to Banff had shown up the following week as a principal speaker at an academic conference at the University.

I find it hard to believe that we have now lived in Calgary for a period almost as long as our time in Canada's Foreign Service. If variety is the spice of life, we have certainly been served up the most flavourful of dishes. Mixed in with everything else has been a stint as Associate Chief of Protocol for the Calgary '88 Winter Olympics, and later as Special Envoy for Calgary's bid for the '05 World Expo. Trekking the Rockies, piloting aircraft, canoeing the Yukon River and riding a motorcycle from Dawson City to Victoria to St. John's, Newfoundland, have provided delightful diversion.

All good things must come to an end and the sunset years have truly set in. Genes are not one of my family's strong points and if I can make it through the next five years, I will have lived longer than any of my known forebears. I would dearly love to have another century or two in order to be part of the critical and exciting times to come, but that is not to be. I find it quite amazing to recall my time as a child when our milk and bread were delivered by horse-drawn wagons, and then to fast forward to the present where thoughts turn with anticipation to the prospect of a manned mission to Mars.

I had the good fortune to be a member of the Foreign Service during the halcyon days. The role of diplomat was highly respected and much sought after. When one joined, it was expected to be 'for life", a far cry from the revolving door in the Service today. Ambassadors were regarded by the government of the day not as messenger boys and girls forbidden to speak without explicit approval from the Prime Minister's Office, but rather as valued assets in the formulation, communication and management of foreign policy. Looking back on my own career, I would not change a thing if the year were 1961 and I were faced with the same choices. The changed environment of 2010 is unfortunate but in keeping with the continuing centralisation of power into the hands of one person, the Prime Minister. I am glad I am not part of it.

Perhaps it is trite to say so, but the message I take out of the way the world has unfolded during my lifetime is that just as surely as we have the potential to self-destruct, we also have the capacity to survive and to shape a better future. Canada today suffers from a lamentable dearth of visionary leadership. The great ideas of a Pearson and a Trudeau, and the commitment to human rights of a Mulroney, have given way to a meanness of spirit, an intellectual poverty and negative polarisation of society. History, however, has a habit of throwing up strong leaders when they are most needed and at heart I remain an eternal optimist in looking to the future.

Bill's graduation portrait, Wilfrid Laurier University, 1955.

Bill with his parents and siblings, David and Mary, at the family home in Niagara Falls, 1954.

Bill and Laine at their wedding in Knoxville, Tennesee, September 17, 1959, surrounded by his parents on the left and hers on the right.

A wiser and whiter-haired Bill, 1977.

Bill on one of his election observation missions to Latin America, this one in Nicaragua, 2006. On Bill's right is President Daniel Ortega.

On a rafting trip in Alaska , 2003.

Taking truck driver training, Calgary, 1999.

Resuming the pasttimes of his youth, driving buses, Calgary, 2008.

Appendix

SELECT NEWSPAPER COLUMNS[8]

PART I
THE POST-SOVIET WORLD

SOCIALISM MOVEMENT WAS NOT HISTORICAL ACCIDENT. JANUARY 16, 1992

The Soviet Union has finally come apart. Is Socialism really dead?

Certainly one might be forgiven for thinking so. The chorus of ecstasy from conservatives of all stripes over events of the past two years — from the debunking of Lenin to the ousting from power

---

8 All columns in this chapter appeared in *The Calgary Herald* on the dates indicated.

of Daniel Ortega in Nicaragua to the electoral defeat of the social democrats in Sweden – has been deafening.

The spirit of Joe McCarthy, anti-Communist witch-hunter of the '50s, applauds while Ronald Reagan sees in the triumph of the "free market," vindication for his "Evil-Empire" strategy. George Bush, David Duke, Margaret Thatcher occupy common grounds: the world has been rid of a dangerous plague.

Here at home voices trumpeting the same message have not been lacking. Among these has been that of media king Conrad Black whose writings grace the pages of the Toronto right-wing press and of other papers he himself owns. If one were to believe Black – whose heroes run from Maurice Duplessis who shamelessly trampled democracy in Quebec to Richard Nixon for calling out the National Guard to act as strikebreakers – the only place in the entire democratic world where the "drivelling left" still exercises some appeal is in Canada with its election of social democrats in three provinces.

Black and his right-wing soulmates obviously share a common view: Canada would be in great shape today were it not for the closet-Communists among us who believe in having the rich pay their far share of taxes, the right to strike, unions, health care, unemployment insurance, old age security, and so on.

Hence the euphoria of the Bay Street conservatives in bidding farewell to the "socialist scourge" – and hence the delirious welcome accorded to the new order in which market forces will supposedly reign supreme.

For Black and his millionaire friends, not only has the world turned its back on hard-line communism but equally on Nordic socialism and any other version of the caring society.

The case against socialism is so "open and shut" that these champions of the free market seem incapable even of seeing any real ideological distinction between the murderous "Shining Path" in Peru and Bob Rae's New Democrats in Ontario.

Unfortunately the ecstasy may be premature. Perhaps the applause should be held until the current chaos wrought by the dramatic changes has sorted itself out.

Is communism or socialism really dead?

To this question there are no absolute answers. That the Soviet brand of communism is well and truly buried is certain. That the "Evil Empire" has been dismantled is clear.

In any event, this is not the real issue.

Soviet communism did not materialize out of a mischievous magician's hat. Fidel Castro is not simply a product of his own desire for power. The Khmer Rouge in Cambodia, the rebels in El Salvador, the Communists in West Bengal, Mao Tse-tung and his followers: these were not historical accidents.

On the contrary, communism and the other radical left-wing movements which so disturbed our peace of mind over the past four decades emerged in direct response to intolerable disparities in the distribution of the world's wealth and resources.

The real issue is: Have the conditions which gave rise to communism in the first place — and its perverse mutations — been corrected? Has the enormous gap between the "haves" and the "have-nots" been closed? Can the poor of Brazil and Bangladesh, India and Ethiopia now look forward to a better life?

I think not.

Indeed, there are plenty of indications that the wealth gap if anything is widening.

Consider Nicaragua. The West cheered in 1989 as the Sandinistas were defeated and "democracy" restored. Over the past two years unemployment in that troubled nation has risen from 45 percent to 58 percent. Of the total population some 40 percent are now classified as indigent. The national health and educational systems are little short of disastrous.

And the gap is widening not only in Africa and Asia and Latin America. Even in North America statistics suggest that the real income of the bottom third of the population fell substantially during the '80s — while the health of the thin layer at the top increased. Ask any of the hundreds of thousands of unemployed Canadians.

The short-sighted may applaud the victory of capitalism. For the more thoughtful, however, the most disturbing phenomenon today is the dangerous ideological vacuum which now exists.

The poverty-stricken and the dispossessed can no longer turn to communism for their vision of salvation. Does that mean that they will simply accept their lot quietly? And the hunger and hardship, deprivation and disease that go with it?

Hardly likely.

The more probable scenario is that — unless mammoth efforts are made to deal with the world's glaring inequities — new and more radical ideologies will emerge sooner or later which may make socialism, and even Soviet communism, seem benevolent by comparison.

In Peru, once a relatively tranquil society, peace has been shattered by the emergence of the Shining Path – a vicious guerrilla movement dedicated to the overthrow by the most brutal methods of the established order. The scope of the group's operations has expended over the past year.

According to some, the Shining Path is no more than an isolated remnant of the old radical left. A last gasp.

Others are not so sure. Is the Shining Path indeed the last gasp? Or is it rather a foretaste of a new and more brutal struggle to come?

Perhaps less time should be spent in gloating over the demise of communism – and more in addressing on an urgent basis the basic issues which created it in the first place.

RUSSIA: WEST CAN'T CONTINUE TO IGNORE SLEEPING GIANT. MARCH 30, 1994

March in Moscow is invariably gloomy and grey. The sun scarcely shines. When it does, the ice on the sidewalk from an entire winter's accumulation turns slippery and treacherous underfoot.

The streets are an abomination as snow banks melt leaving behind pools of sludge.

The last days of winter are even more depressing this year as Russia's economic woes continue to deepen and the long-awaited turnaround fails to materialize.

I spent a week in Moscow recently after a year's absence. The casual visitor might be seduced into thinking at first glance that things are not so bad.

The numbers of imported cars on the streets have increased. Over 1,000 GM vehicles were sold into Moscow in 1993 and the rumor is that more top-of-the-line Mercedes were bought last year by Muscovites than dwellers in any other European city. Impressive when you consider the high six-figure price tag.

Supermarkets carrying Western goods have proliferated, as have bars, boutiques, pricey restaurants and casinos.

The biggest nightclub in central Moscow which holds close to 2000 people sold out on New Year's Eve with tickets going at more than $300 a head. And the patrons were mainly Russians.

There is nothing you cannot buy in Moscow — if you have money. But there is the catch.

Some Russians have money — indeed obscene amounts of it.

But reality is that the number of people who share in the new-found wealth is miniscule.

Inflation is rampant — with $1 now fetching 1,600 rubles as opposed to 40 years ago and less than one five years ago.

The average wage is scarcely enough to keep body and soul together.

Social services once taken for granted have either deteriorated or disappeared altogether.

Particularly vulnerable are the poor, the sick, the handicapped and the aged.

But forecasters say the worst is yet to come. The economy has still not bottomed out. It has not faced the crunch of massive downsizing in its outdated and inefficient industrial sector. Billions of dollars flow out of Russia to safe havens in far-off bank accounts instead of being reinvested at home.

Russians themselves are fond of referring to their country as the new Wild West. Russia is, they say, a combination of Chicago of the 1920s and the Klondike Gold Rush.

Indeed, there is gold a-plenty to be made by sharp operators. The scene has been livened up by the emergence of crime and corruption on a massive scale.

The Canadian businessman I stayed with lived in a fortress, was accompanied by bodyguards at all times, and carried a pistol in his belt. Russians talk constantly about their Mafiosi – an ill-defied collection of thugs – who run protection rackets, control widespread prostitution, and generally prey on everyone from wealthy business people to the poor and vulnerable.

Little wonder that there are so many who yearn for a return to the "good old days." And little wonder that Vladimir Zhirinovsky, the populist with his law and order message, has emerged as a potent political force.

With a vast and demoralized armed forces, rampant inflation and a people stripped of their pride and adequate means to live, the situation begs comparison with post-First World War Germany in which Nazism took root.

Educated Russians pooh-pooh the threat from Zhirinovsky. But therein lies one of the real dangers – the danger of not taking him seriously, of treating him like a political clown. The fact is that Zhirinovsky is to Russia in some ways what Ross Perot was to the

U.S. and Preston Manning to Canadians: a lighting rod attracting all the disaffected.

Even his most outspoken detractor would admit that Zhirinovsky in the last election captured the mood of the people and gave expression to their frustrations and their hopes.

Russia today continues to pose an enormous dilemma for the West. It is far too big – and potentially dangerous – to be ignored.

At the same time, it is evident that the usual World Bank prescriptions for downsizing, closing of uneconomic enterprises and general privatization are more likely to trigger political and social firestorm than to produce a healthy, stable society.

For hundreds of years Russia has been pulled in two directions. In the one camp have been those who with fierce pride of country believe that Mother Russia must stand proud and find the answers within herself.

Ranged on the other side have been the so-called "Westernizers" who saw their salvation in Western Europe and America, and in adopting Western ways of doing things.

The battle raged in the early 18th century when Peter the Great tried to drag Russia into the modern age by building St. Petersburg and opening a window to the West.

The battle still rages today. Glitzy new shops spring up daily and American fast food restaurants multiply to cater to the needs of the affluent.

But striking a resonant chord today are not the restaurants – with the food out of reach of most – but rather the strident voice of Zhirinovsky and others striving to rally Russians under a nationalist flag.

The West, so far has done precious little beyond uttering platitudes.

True, there are no magic formulas, and nothing short of a reborn Marshall Plan — with far more money than the West could hope to afford — could effectively reshape the Russian economy.

At the same time, the West's benign neglect of Russia as a friend and partner and in building the peace is nothing short of scandalous — and full of peril — considering the mega-billions poured into preparations for hostilities during the long years of the Cold War.

SHARP WINDS BUFFET CUBA. OCTOBER 22, 1990

It is usually November before the hot humid climate of the Cuban summer relents and the coolness of winter sets in. But a deep chill arrived early this year in the gem of the Antilles.

True, it is not the kind that causes people to don jackets and stay away from the beaches. Rather, the cold wind is more psychological in nature, deriving from sharply increased political and economic adversity.

Anyone who has visited Cuba in recent years, has taken the time to wander the streets of the capital and talk to ordinary Habaneros well know that life is no picnic.

The unravelling of the Soviet Union and disintegration of its empire have left Cuba virtually isolated.

For the first time in its history, the Caribbean island finds itself without the support of a large power.

Up to the turn of the century, the Cuban umbilical reached out to Spain. For the next six decades the United States was the dominant power – replaced in the 1960s by the U.S.S.R.

Even more daunting for the Castro regime is the fact that not only is it alone, but also a prime target for the unremitting hostility of the new-found American obsession with Iraq, Cubans know that they have only a breathing space and that the spotlight will return.

The signs of increasing economic pressure are readily evident. Returning to Cuba recently, for the second time in five months, I could see distinct changes even in that short time. The list, already short, of items available to Cubans in unlimited quantities had been reduced still further. Bread, chicken, cooking oil and matches are harder to get.

Consumption patterns are fast returning to the subsistence levels of the late '60s when lengthy power cuts darkened Havana nightly, and even bread and milk were hard to come by.

As for oil products, Cubans are taking a double hit.

Even before the eruption of the Iraq crisis the Soviets, reflecting sagging ideological ardor and contracting global interests, had begun to reduce the flow.

In particular, the Cubans who had developed the habit of re-selling on world markets a substantial portion of their Soviet imports and have seen a significant source of much needed hard currency begin to dry up.

Then there is the virtually certain prospect, when the current agreement with the Soviets runs out, of having to pay for oil in hard-to-get dollars – and at much higher prices.

Profound fissures in Soviet-Cuban solidarity have appeared.

If Gorbachev was prepared to see his entire empire in Eastern Europe slip away without a struggle, one can understand that his attachment — to faraway Cuba and its costly brand of old-line socialism is very weak indeed.

The deepening energy crisis has initiated a vicious cycle of cause and effect: Lack of oil to fuel power stations has forced a reduction in the work week at many factories; construction activity and the production of cement are down. The newly built oil refinery in Cienfuegos will not be able to open, and work on a new nickel factory has been paralysed.

The impact on daily life in Cuba has been immediate. Cubana, the national airline, has reduced its domestic flights.

Owners of private vehicles will see their gas ration cut by one-third, state organizations by one-half. Bicycles, never popular with Cubans in the torrid heat and humidity, are making their appearance on Havana streets.

Factories, offices and institutions have begun sending employees on a regular basis to the country to cultivate large communal vegetable gardens.

In the circumstances, development of tourism has become a top priority for Cuba.

Large new hotels are under construction and in Varadero, the beautiful beach area east of Havana where 40 percent of the tourists are Canadian, the ambitious plan envisages an increase from 5,000 rooms in 1990 to 30,000 in the year 2000.

So far, the tourist sector has been insulated from the economic crisis — and the government intends to keep it that way.

Cuban tourist enterprises have been given a relatively free hand to use the dollars they earn to import equipment and develop training facilities. A new 500-room hotel under construction on Havana's ocean-front Malecon is a 50-50 Spanish-Cuban joint venture.

Supplies to tourist hotels have not been affected. Tourists can still rent cars, buy gas freely and travel without restriction throughout the island.

The morale of the average Cuban seems to have held up well – perhaps as a result of conditioning from living under austere circumstances for the past three decades.

But there is understandable resentment against the privileged lifestyle of the foreign tourist who has access to special restaurants, hotels and shops.

Meanwhile, the diehard opponents of Fidel Castro in Miami and elsewhere await impatiently the collapse of Cuban socialism. The electoral defeat of the Sandinistas in Nicaragua last April, following on the upheaval in Eastern Europe, generated hope of imminent change.

And indeed, Cuban socialism appears to be facing its severest test in the 30 years since the Revolution swept Castro to power. Just as Saddam Hussein is fighting for his political life in the face of insuperable odds, so Castro faces the prospect of seemingly inevitable economic asphyxiation.

If anything is surprising, it is the resilience the regime has demonstrated. Cubans themselves explain it by saying that Castro was not imposed from the outside as in Eastern Europe.

And there is no denying either the substantial degree of popular support he still appears to enjoy – in spite of the glaring absence of grassroots participation in government decision-making – or the social gains that the Revolution has brought.

Cuba faces two paths into the future. One is that of continued confrontation with the United states, and ongoing economic dislocation. This is certainly what the exile community in the U.S. wants and what the Bush administration is ideologically most attracted to.

The other path is that of normalization and reintegration into the inter-American system. The ending of the U.S. embargo, increased trade, opening of the island to American tourists, would provide a tremendous boost to the Cuban economy.

Ironically, it is probably the latter path – the one which Castro favors and Bush opposes – which over the long run poses the greatest threat to the Cuban government; for the simple reason that with plenty of bread and butter on the table, the strong political controls and siege mentality which have acted as barriers to democratization and political reform lose their justification.

In the same way, a restoration of larger-scale people-to-people contacts through tourism from the United States and family visits would unquestionably prove unsettling to the Cuban people, and particularly with youth.

With Canada's entry into the Organization of American States at the beginning of the year, Cuba has entertained high hopes that Canada would exercise constructive influence on its neighbor. And indeed last spring External Affairs Minister Joe Clark did dispatch an assistant deputy minister to Havana where a lengthy meeting with Castro took place.

The gesture seems to have been hollow and, as one Canadian official explained: "The Cubans think we led them down the garden path – and they're right."

The Canadians lectured Castro on human rights – gaining political points at home – but were unwilling in the last analysis to do anything concrete in the OAS that might ruffle the eagle's feathers.

While Clark has said Canada supports the readmission of Cuba to the OAS "in principle," he has at the same time made it clear that his government will not spearhead any move on the issue.

THE SHAME OF GUANTANAMO. SEPTEMBER 30, 2003

Fidel Castro has come in for a lot of criticism recently for his human rights abuses. The execution of three hijackers and the jailing of dozens of dissidents earlier this year attracted strong condemnation not only from the Cuban leaders, traditional critics, but also from the normally sympathetic European governments and his erstwhile staunch sympathizers.

While the abuses in Cuba pale in comparison to the killings and torture perpetrated in recent decades by dictators such as former Guatemalan leader Rios Montt – now running for president in the coming November elections – the criticism of Castro was nonetheless richly deserved. The detentions and executions reflect an attempt to deflect the winds of change that will inevitably alter the Cuba landscape.

The worst excesses in Cuba these days, however, are not occurring in Havana. Rather, they are taking place at the other end of the island in Guantanamo Bay, where the United States is holding hundreds of faceless prisoners in violation of internationally accepted norms.

In the worst tradition of the repressive dictatorships that were a blight on the Americas for so many years, the Guantanamo detainees are without access to lawyers, their families or the courts. Children as young as 13 are reported by Amnesty International to be among the prisoners.

The choice of Guantanamo was itself a not-so-subtle act of deviant minds. Deviant because the Guantanamo camp was the product of a deliberate decision to flout the standards of law basic to any democracy. Deviant also because the intent was to hide government action from the democratic right of people to know what is going on. Who is there? What are the conditions? Why have there been so many suicide attempts?

A vestige of America's colonial past, Guantanamo is a small enclave wrested from Cuba in the early part of the century and now held in perpetuity. Today, it is America's shame, a legal wilderness where the judge, jury, prosecution and defence will all, in the last analysis, be one and the same person, the president of the United States.

In other words, without any checks or balances, the process will be politically determined from start to finish.

It seems, too, that Castro will not be the only one carrying out executions in Cuba. Recent reports suggest execution chambers are being readied in Guantanamo. I recall walking through Tehran's main cemetery shortly after Ayatollah Khomeini took power and being shocked and appalled by the crude mounds covering the unidentified corpses of victims of the ayatollah's kangaroo courts.

Will Guantanamo's graves at least have names? Will their families be notified, or similarly kept in the dark?

Of 19 executions of child offenders between 1994 and 2002, 12 were carried out in the U.S. — including four in the past 24 months. This does not bode well for any minors held in Guantanamo.

Curious, in the circumstances, that more voices have not been raised against this outrage to the spirit of democracy. Where are the voices of those governments whose nationals, reportedly including a Canadian national, are interned there in violation of international convention? What of the American media who pride themselves on their investigative reporting? Why is it that the protests come only from a few organizations and are little more than voices crying in the wilderness?

What of all those Canadians, including the Canadian Alliance, who continue to justify the Iraq war, citing Saddam Hussein's violation of human rights and the need to bring the rule of law? Are their concerns so patently selective that they apply the presumption of innocence only to Americans and Europeans?

Have the American people themselves become so careless of their fundamental rights and freedoms as to turn a blind eye?

The abuse of power seldom ceases of its own accord. Unbridled power develops its own dynamic. The distinction between democracy and tyranny lies precisely in the existence of effective limits on the power of the state. The erosion of these democratic norms should cause alarm bells to ring for all those in America and the West who treasure their freedoms.

It should cause alarm because a similar erosion of civil rights has been taking place in the U.S. itself since Sept. 11, 2001. Those who dared to express their concerns were labelled "unpatriotic." Only in recent months has the political opposition begun to make its voice heard.

According to the U.S. administration, open trials and access to independent counsel for the Guantanamo detainees would aid and abet the cause of terrorism. This is scarcely believable in all but the most extreme cases. On the other hand, this callous disregard for human and civil rights fits closely with the actions of an administration that has openly demonstrated its contempt for international law, conventions and institutions.

As with Afghanistan and Iraq, no exit strategy appears to be in place for Guantanamo. There remain only questions. Are only those accused of supporting al-Qaeda being held there? Is it possible for Americans to be deprived of their rights and consigned to Guantanamo? Have any trials been held? Is torture being applied?

Will the place eventually close down?

Or, will Guantanamo be maintained in perpetuity as a black hole into which anyone unfortunate enough to be sent there, innocent or guilty, can disappear without a trace?

Castro, at least, will presumably be suitably impressed by this example on his own doorstep of democracy and the rule of law in action.

LATIN AMERICA WARY OF POWER SHIFT. FEBRUARY 2, 1990

The year 1989 left the world breathless as the unravelling of the Soviet empire proceeded at a dizzying pace. In an ironic twist, it was in the latest analysis not the countries of Western Europe which fell like dominoes but rather those of the East.

The shattering of communism's iron-fisted rule was hailed with euphoria in West and East alike. Indeed as the decade ended, the Soviet Union itself showed signs of disintegrating as the two pillars of unity, the Communist party and the Russian nationality came under concerted pressure.

The net result of the political turmoil of the past year has been to tilt the scales of power markedly in favor of the United States. The American right has been quick to claim the credit, pointing to the Reagan-led escalation of the arms race as a key factor in putting the Soviets on ropes economically. And in fact, as the new decade begins one can scarcely argue the contention that the United States has emerged as the world's Number-1 military power by a wide margin.

Beyond Europe and North America, however, the "unbalancing of power" has generated neither satisfaction nor confidence in the future.

On the contrary, the prospect of a United States, its power enhanced and free to act with little constraint in support of its own global interests, has given rise to foreboding. Even within the United States itself, there is considerable uneasiness among those wary earlier of Reagan and now of his like-minded successor.

Concern is rampant first and foremost in Latin America.

Indeed it is ironic that just at the time that the Soviets were loosening their grip on Eastern Europe, the U.S. administration was moving aggressively to consolidate its controlling position in the hemisphere.

All stops were pulled in El Salvador as massive military aid was poured in during November in the name of democracy, to shore up armed forces whose members have participated in the killing of thousands of innocent civilians.

Similarly, in Guatemala, U.S. aid increased in spite of flagrant human rights abuses and an upsurge in the activity of death squads.

Without the defanging of Soviet political resolve, it is at least debatable whether the United States would have ignored Latin American concerns quite so brazenly and launched a full-scale invasion of Panama.

America protestations of concern for democracy might also have been more believable had the same U.S. establishment not earlier greeted with such satisfaction the assassination of the democratically elected president of Chile, Salvador Allende.

Other Latin American countries – particularly Nicaragua and Cuba – see increased vulnerability to American intervention as the price of the new imbalance.

Concern, however, is not limited to Latin America. Countries such as India in Asia and Zimbabwe in Africa, which have traditionally sustained their independence between East and West and derived benefits by being courted by both camps, see themselves as losers as a result of the new power configuration.

A second major consequences of the "unbalancing" will almost certainly be diminished economic assistance to developing countries.

East-West competition at the very least generated something of an "aid race" as both sides attempt to upstage each other and win favor. Not only are traditional recipients of Soviet assistance likely to see their source run dry, but the United States and its allies will also be under less pressure to sustain flows. Candidates for American aid are in the future likely to find more strings attached.

Just as worrisome is the assumption that any massive program for East European reconstruction will come at the expense of development funds for Third World countries. Such an interruption could have a catastrophic effect on poorest nations, already unable to sustain their rapidly increasing populations and saddled with heavy debt load.

At least one final cause for serious concern, primarily to North Americans, resulting from the "unbalancing" is the power vacuum left by the Soviets. While the Soviet military machine still represents a powerful force, its capacity to challenge the U.S. on the international front has been effectively neutralized by the sudden switch of Soviet preoccupations to the domestic scene.

The risk is that a stagnating North American economy will be caught over the next one or two decades in a crunch between an economically vibrant Asia and a reborn and equally dynamic Europe.

Canadian policy makers thus confront formidable challenges as they begin to grapple with the startlingly changed circumstances thrust upon them by the twilight years of the '8os.

Joe Clark's External Affairs Department can expect to face some critical and awkward choices over the next several years — as in responding to the invasion of Panama — which could pit Canada's long-term interests against the more immediate risks of upsetting our American neighbor. On the economic front. Canadians gearing up for the next decade and beyond should presumably be upgrading in dramatic style their efforts to forge new links to Asia and Europe, thereby proportionally deceasing the nation's heavy reliance on the U.S.

BLOODY CAMPUS REVEAL THE TRUTH. MARCH 12, 1990

On a hillside in the gently rolling countryside on the periphery of San Salvador stands the campus of the Jesuit-run University of Central America. Founded about the same time as the University of Calgary, UCA as it is known boasts one of the finest campuses in Latin America.

Imaginative architecture combines with spreading palms, masses of bougainvillaea and the melodious harmony of peacocks and other brightly colored tropical birds. A more idyllic setting would be difficult to imagine.

Appearances, however, are deceiving. In the early morning hours of Nov. 16, 1989 some 30-40 members of El Salvador's elite American trained ATLACATL battalion broke into the Jesuit residence.

The office and small library were subjected to intense fire from automatic weapons; incendiary bombs were thrown.

The perpetrators then dragged the rector of the University, the vice-rector and four other Jesuits into the quiet flower-fringed garden between the residence and the appropriately named Romero Pastoral Centre.

There the fathers were mercilessly cut down in an orgy of bloodletting – their crime the ceaseless struggle to bring justice to the poor of El Salvador.

There were to be no witnesses.

Elba Ramos, the cook in the residence, and her 15-year old daughter Celina were shot in their nearby room. According to the official Jesuit report nothing was left of the face of Elba. The bodies were found, the daughter in the embrace of the mother who was trying to protect her.

The report says that the daughter's expression was one of "peace and tranquil sleep."

The grisly picture was described to me in graphic detail by a Canadian who was one of the first on the scene in the morning.

By the time she arrived, the army cordoned off the area and in a supreme expression of hypocrisy was going through the motions of conducting an investigation.

On March 2 I visited the residence and the garden where the atrocity took place.

Bloodstains in the room of Elba Ramos were still red and flowed literally across the concrete floor.

Bullet holes cut starkly into the humbly decorated walls.

Ten paces away is the entrance through which the Jesuit fathers were pulled in their last moments of courage and terror.

Again the stains.

Blood and guts were still splattered on the wall of the residence. A half burned portrait of Bishop Romero watches silently. A bullet hole bores through Romero's heart.

Bishop Romero was martyred in 1980, cut down by a death squad as he celebrated mass in the cathedral.

The nearby Romero Centre which serves as the university chapel is the picture of tranquillity. Bright and airy, it gives inspiration and hope for the future.

The cross over the altar is in the form of a mural depicting the life of the bishop.

Curving around the black wall is another mural, sketches of men and women in agony, the dead and the tortured reflecting the suffering people of El Salvador.

In this setting of bougainvillaea and the sounds of the tropical garden, the Jesuits, the mother and her daughter have found their final peace.

Across the city in the centre of San Salvador is the country's largest institution, the University of El Salvador. Enrolment is 30,000.

The university also has a reputation for being the country's most highly politicized.

During last November's guerrilla offensive, the university was ferociously attacked by the army. The grounds were seized and have been occupied till this day.

Unwilling to die, the university courageously continued its teaching activity. Classes are conducted in the open, in houses and in rented buildings.

When I called on the rector, our meeting took place in the upstairs room of a small building across from the campus. Approximately 20 people, four or five to a desk, were working in the same office. At the campus itself, all the teaching materials, computers and laboratory equipment have been either destroyed or stolen by the military occupants.

Individual members of UES have suffered, and continue to suffer.

The list of students and faculty currently incarcerated numbers 36. The most recent to be arrested was a young female student of international relations. Elena del Milagro Barahona Ayala was picked up on Feb. 5. She is detained without charges in the women's prison, El Penal Carcel de Mujeres.

According to Rueben Zamoro, General Secretary of the Popular Social Christian Movement with whom I spent a morning, the plight of the people detained is one of horror.

A member of Zamoro's own party was interrogated during February. This person was viciously beaten. The long night of interrogation was punctuated by the screams of both men and women. Zamoro's member estimated that on that particular night some 20-30 people were being beaten and tortured in the centre.

According to Zamoro, torture and killings are still routine.

He himself travels in an armoured car with two guards. AT night he sleeps at home with his wife and five children, a pistol at his elbow. Several years ago, his brother was assassinated by the death squads. More recently a bomb destroyed part of his house.

In the centre of San Salvador stands the American Embassy, a huge sprawling fortress. High walls, rocket deflector and sand-bagged gun emplacements protect the inhabitants.

Power in El Salvador is exercised by the military, the American ambassador, the oligarchy and the government — in that order.

With the country in a virtual state of siege and with the U.S. perceived by many Salvadorans as being the root of their problems, the ambassador needs protecting.

Any illusions one might harbor about the Bush administration's commitment to democracy in Central America quickly dissipate in the harsh light of Salvadoran reality.

Those who planned and executed the crime against the Jesuits were, almost certainly trained in the U.S. El Salvador's interrogators, whose methods range from the highly sophisticated to the most barbarous, are also thought to have developed much of their skills with U.S. help.

Salvadorans widely believe that the U.S. could, if it so desired, put an end to their agony.

The U.S. to date, however, far from using its influence to stop the abuse of human rights has played a role of active complicity.

One example will suffice: The sole witness to the killing of the Jesuit priests, Lucia Barrera, was taken out of the country ostensibly to protect her life. In violation of the U. S. Embassy's agreement to turn her over to Jesuits in Miami, Barrera was held for eight days by U.S. officials in virtual solitary confinement while they tried to get her to change her testimony.

She was, according to the Jesuit report, subjected to abusive interrogations of the sort that would have been considered criminal, had the witness herself been an American.

Barrera was moreover given to believe that if she did not provide the answers her interrogators wanted, she would be returned to El Salvador.

In the circumstances, little wonder that Barrera eventually contradicted herself and denied having seen soldiers. As later revelations showed, her initial testimony was totally accurate.

While the university community struggles to recover from the trauma of November and to rebuild its moral and physical resources, a colonel who led the squad of executioners on the night of Nov. 16 basks in the luxury of one of San Salvador's deluxe military hostels. It was bad enough that only eight out of the 30 or 40 who actively participated in the operations should have come under investigation.

That a colonel and the others should continue to draw full pay and even enjoy occasional visits to the beach, that the investigation is proceeding so slowly and may never reach a conclusion symbolizes the harsh reality of the continuing struggle for justice in El Salvador.

FOR POLITICAL EXPEDIENCY PINOCHET WILL GO FREE. OCTOBER 30, 1998

That Gen. Augusto Pinochet deserves to go to trial is beyond doubt, at least when measured against any international human rights standard.

His dictatorship was bloody. Thousands were taken away in the middle of the night and murdered in brutal fashion by death squads. Many more thousands were tortured by the military and police. The atrocities were perpetrated in the full knowledge of Pinochet and his fellow officers.

The election of Salvador Allende's leftist government in 1970 hit Chile's elites like an earthquake. Rather than serving as a wake-up call to tackle the chronic inequitable distribution of wealth, the victory of the Popular Unity party sounded a call-to-arms to the upper echelons of society that culminated in Pinochet's military coup of 1973. Pinochet quickly moved, not only to reverse the changes introduced by Allende, but to get rid of the democratic process entirely. Human rights were totally disregarded; opponents were simply eliminated.

Confident of his hold on the country, Pinochet in 1988 called a plebiscite for the purpose of legitimizing his rule for another eight years. To the surprise of many, he lost. To the surprise of others, however, 43 per cent of the electorate backed Pinochet. It is worth recalling this factor when interpreting the loud voices in Chile today expressing outrage over the general's detention in Britain. Pinochet continues to command a solid following.

The reaction to Pinochet's arrest is a reminder of how thin the veneer of democracy and respect for human rights is in that country. We should note, however, that virtually no other government, including Canada's, has come out solidly in support of the idea of putting Pinochet on trial.

Interestingly, no such hesitation constrains western governments and leaders from labelling President Slobodan Milosevic of Yugoslavia a war criminal. Similarly, the establishment of a tribunal in The Hague headed by a Canadian judge to try the perpetrators of ethnic cleansing in Bosnia received broad support. Human rights violators from Rwanda have similarly been put on trial.

The comparison raises questions.

Are torture and murder of innocent people, because they happened some 10 years ago and because they were employed in the name of the fight against communism, somehow less heinous than the same thing in Kosovo today?

The reality is that prosecution for "crimes against humanity" is highly selective and generally tends to reflect the political will of the dominant powers. The conviction of Hitler's aides at Nuremberg following the Second World War was an open-and-shut case. However, even today, some half-century later, it is still a matter of heresy to suggest that the droppings of the atomic bomb on Hiroshima and the intentional annihilation of tens of thousands of civilians in German cities toward the end of the war might also have been criminal acts — for the simple reason that the victor calls the tune.

Today it is politically expedient to go after Milosevic but not so Pinochet, even if his crimes were equally as horrendous. It will not suit Britain and Spain, or other countries of Western Europe, to see trade and other relations with Chile disrupted.

Where does one draw the line? If a Pinochet can be prosecuted internationally, why not other political leaders whose actions leave them open to charges of complicity in gross human rights violations? The list might include several Israelis who allegedly had a hand in the massacre of refugees in camps in Lebanon, Chinese leaders for the Tiananmen Square killings, South African politicians who masterminded the outrages of apartheid, British prime ministers who were aware of nasty things being done in Northern Ireland — and even American presidents for actions in Vietnam and the active support of murderous governments in El Salvador, Guatemala and elsewhere. Once one starts down the road to holding heads of state and former heads of state to account, it quickly becomes a slippery slope.

The prosecution of Pinochet almost certainly will not get off the ground. Today's governments are much less committed to the active promotion of human rights than they were 10 or 15 years ago. Trading and financial interests of the powerful countries have long since swept human rights onto the back burner of government agendas.

Pinochet, after some weeks or moths of legal wrangling, will almost certainly be returned to Chile for the reason, if nothing else, that the governments involved do not have the political will to see the prosecution go forward.

While Pinochet may have committed crimes for which a jury might have convicted him in the space of minutes, any eventual judgment against the former dictator will almost certainly have to come from Chileans themselves.

Since Pinochet, before handing over power in 1988, quickly passed laws protecting himself and entrenching the stranglehold of the military over the country's political system, he is likely to get off scot-free.

PART II
THE MIDDLE EAST
GULF WAR I

U.S. WAGING PROPAGANDA WAR. SEPTEMBER 5, 1990

The Iraqi invasion of Kuwait provoked a build-up of propaganda hype scarcely seen throughout the 4½ decades of the Cold War... with the possible exception of the Cuban Missile crisis in 1961.

The United States pulled out all the stops in a massive global effort to portray Saddam Hussein as a budding Hitler and Iraq as a threat to world peace only slightly less formidable than was Germany in 1939.

Consider the facts.

When Iraq launched its attack on Iran and unleashed a bloody decade of war which left a million dead, the United States could scarcely contain its satisfaction at the prospect of its arch nemesis, the Ayatollah Khomeini, being brought to heel.

No threat to world peace was trumpeted.

On the contrary, both the United States and Israel saw benefit in having these sworn enemies of Israel at each other's throats. Arms merchants profited from the carnage.

The more discerning American commentators have been quick to note their government's own distinctive contribution, in tacitly taking Iraqi's side, the emergency of the Iraqi dictator's absolute power — the same way that Panama's Noriega consolidated his power with bountiful American help and a salary from the CIA.

When Saddam Hussein brutally gassed thousands of Iraqi Kurds, the United States was silent.

The discrepancy between today's high rhetoric and bleak reality is stark.

The Khmer Rouge, authors of the horrifying Cambodian massacres portrayed so graphically in The Killing Fields, enjoyed U.S political support because of their capacity to keep the Vietnamese off balance and thereby serve American strategic interests.

The Bush Administration's outrage over Beijing killings lasted only so long as was deemed necessary to placate the initial outburst of public revulsion.

Not so long ago the ultra-conservative Saudi regime was castigated in the United States for beheading women for adultery. Today the American propaganda machine would have us believe that democracy depends on the survival of that government.

If Iraq violated international law in invading Kuwait, so did the United States itself in Grenada and Panama and in mining the harbors of Nicaragua.

If Iraq is to be condemned for harassment of western embassies in Kuwait, why did the international community guard silence over the illegal entry of U.S. troops into the Nicaraguan Embassy in Panama City over similar harassment of the Vatican mission?

On its own doorstep in Central America the U.S. administration has not only ignored the killing by death squads of tens of thousands of innocent persons, but has knowingly supplied weapons and training to the perpetrators.

U.S. authorities this past month refused to release information bearing on the assassination of six Jesuit priests last November in El Salvador on the grounds that it might compromise U.S. interests.

There clearly are double, triple and even quadruple standards in operation – each one custom-designed to the needs of U.S. policy of the moment.

The point is not that one should be surprised to discover that the United States is no paragon of virtue – governments rarely if ever are. Rather, a spade should be called a spade.

Thus, one should recognize that the administration's clamor over the supposed threat to democracy is more than transparent cover for U.S. interests and the Bush agenda.

Canada does not have the global interests of the United States.

Our leaders have not had the same responsibility. Yet our record as a nation also leaves much to be desired.

We have said little about the Kurds or the Khmer Rouge or the undermining of legitimately constituted governments. While making political mileage through the shrill condemnation of South Africa, the government's posture vis-à-vis the death squads in El Salvador and ongoing genocide in Guatemala has been so muted as to have made barely any impact on the Canadian psyche.

Consistency and principle have almost always been dictated by political expedience.

Little wonder that cynicism should dominate the popular view of our politics and political leaders.

While friendship with the United States has been the natural foreign policy cornerstone for all Canadian governments, the present prime minister is the first to have made it the central and totally dominant pillar.

One early morning telephone call sufficed to have Brian Mulroney announce support for the invasion of Panama. In similarly indecent haste and without awaiting a decision by the UN, Mulroney violated long tradition and committed Canada to providing three ill-equipped ships to the dangerous waters of the Middle East.

For what specific Canadian purpose? To help defend, as George Bush put it; "The American way of lie?" Or to make unwilling heroes of the eight hundred Canadians rendered hostage by their government's action? What rash and undiscriminating moves can Canadians expect from the Mulroney vacation in Kennebunkport?

Will we now find ourselves saddled with a "Kuwait tax" to help cover the cost of American forces in Saudi Arabia?

This is not to say that Saddam Hussein should have been taken lightly.

The Iraqi dictator's human rights record and abuse of power rank with the worst. His delusions of grandeur made him a threat to the stability of the Middle East.

But the invasion of Kuwait did not by any stretch of the imagination equate to Hitler's overrunning of Poland in 1939.

Even if the United States determined to move in, surely the appropriate reaction on Canada's part would, as Stephen Lewis said, have been one of "measured response" – and only in concert with a UN mandate. Whose interest does the current crisis serve?

The winners are easy to identify: the Pentagon who will see a lessening in pressure to reduce troop strengths; the armaments industry; those major oil companies who moved with unseemly haste to increase gasoline prices; the consumer society which relies on long-term access to cheap oil; the Bush administration which (at least temporarily) has seen its popularity soar and which has delivered a telling story of American ability to act as the world's policeman; monarchical regimes which exist in crude splendor in a sea of poverty; the Canadian Armed Forces which will surely revive the pressure for new and better equipment.

Just as there are winners, there are also losers. The real victims are the thousands of foreign nationals held hostage and at serious risk; the Palestinians from whose plight attention has been diverted; Canadians who must pay the costs of our naval expedition; the poorest of the world who stood to benefit "peace dividends" flowing from an end to the armaments culture and a diversion of funds to peaceful development.

Even if one concedes the need to draw a "line in the sand," one nonetheless should be clear as to the motives and real issues which underlie the "hype."

WAR BROUGHT DEATH OF
DIPLOMACY. JANUARY 25, 1991

That we are at war with Iraq is the result of the most spectacular failure of diplomacy in the 4½ decades since the end of hostilities in Europe and Japan in 1945. Spectacular in the speed with which the negotiation process was abandoned, and in the resort to arms.

Breathtaking, too, in the seemingly inexorable march to war by the two main protagonists, Saddam Hussein and George Bush. And in the potentially devastating consequences of this modern Crusade.

Diplomacy, it would appear, was never given a chance.

The essence of diplomacy is dialogue between countries and willingness to compromise. In this case, the only dialogue appeared to be that of the deaf.

Saddam Hussein for his part apparently chose not to believe that the United States meant business — or if he did, he seemed nonetheless to renounce from the beginning any idea of withdrawing from Kuwait.

Ruthless and only too ready to sacrifice his people, he called the American bluff.

The Bush administration on the other hand had its own agenda — and diplomacy was not the first item on it. The statements and conditions set out by the U.S. government were not such as to permit the slightest room for manoeuvre. It required, in effect, abject acquiescence by the Iraqi dictator and were put in terms calculated if anything to generate resistance rather than meaningful compromise.

A dynamic of war was, therefore, set in motion from Day 1.

Canada, having become in foreign policy terms over the past year little more than a branch plant of the United States, abandoned its traditional role and readily exchanged its plowshares for swords.

If there was any chance for diplomacy, it came only late in the day when proposals were floated for a comprehensive Middle East conference in exchange for an Iraqi backdown. Saddam showed slight interest; the U.S. none at all.

In the end, the U.S. president pushed the button.

There can be no doubt but that the alternatives to war were not fully exhausted – this in spite of massive government and media propaganda of recent days that would have us believe otherwise.

Sanctions, a key weapon in the diplomatic arsenal, were not given a chance to work. Nor did the Bush administration, from the start, intend to let them work. This is now evident.

Sanctions were effective in Rhodesia; and they worked in South Africa. But they took years.

Why the abdication of diplomacy?

Answering the question is not so easy, primarily because those who make war have always camouflaged their real aims with noble purpose – and with lies. The present war is no different. Fiction takes the place of fact; propaganda replaces truth. This happened in the Crusades of the Middle Ages. It is happening in the modern-day Crusade. And strikingly similar the rhetoric is.

Saddam seized on the time-proven magnet of Palestinian rights to rally the Arab masses – when it was evident all along that ownership of Kuwait's rich oilfields was a prime objective. Along with burning ambition to increase his own power.

As for Bush, cynical American observers saw in the U.S. president's knee-jerk reaction to the invasion last summer a capitalizing on the opportunity to divert attention away from the enormity of the savings and loans scandal – in which his own son was implicated.

Moreover, others pointed to the benefits brought by the war to the massive U.S. armaments industry. The recent cancellation of one single military project, for example, provoked fears that the future of the whole of aerospace giant, McDonnell Douglas, was in jeopardy.

With expenditures running at half a billion dollars a day, who can deny the importance to arms dealers of the war?

Even more striking was the absence from the president's speeches of any mention of oil. On the day he went to war, Bush spoke only of the "liberation of Kuwait" and of "peace".

Clearly no number of killings or rapes or abuse of innocent civilians in Kuwait would have brought U.S. forces into the region had it not been for the presence of some of the world's richest oil deposits.

Consider the fact that in 1982 Syrian President Hafez al-Assad – with whom the United States is now standing "shoulder to shoulder" – dealt with the political opposition in his own country by ordering the destruction of the town of Hama. More than 20,000 defenceless inhabitants died.

Several hundred refugees were slaughtered in the same year in the Sabra and Shatila refugee camps by Lebanese Phalangists while Israeli troops stood guard outside.

Scarcely a word was said in the west.

Little wonder that political leaders have lost their credibility.

There is still today no adequate explanation for the speed with which the United States moved so rapidly from a defensive to an offensive posture. Unless one assumes that meaningful diplomacy was ruled out from the start.

Why did this happen?

The question can be answered only by looking beyond the rhetoric to the dramatic changes in the world's power relationships of the past two years.

With the disintegration of the Soviet empire, the United States has emerged as the single most powerful nation on earth. It has emerged with a profound awareness of its own power and with that peculiar American sense of "what is good for America is good for the world". And with the determination to act decisively where American interests are at stake.

The Gulf, in the eyes of some, presented an irresistible opportunity for the United States to demonstrate its ability to "reach out and touch anyone anywhere" – as U.S. military briefers have been fond of telling visiting foreign delegations for the past several years.

Still smarting from the defeat in Vietnam, it was an opportunity to go in – without its hands "tied behind its back".

The war has taken on symbolic form. It represents in most graphic form the struggle of the affluent high-technology North – incarnated by the United States – versus the impoverished, problem-ridden South embodied in Iraq. Of the Developed World versus the Under-Developed. The "world" against Iraq — as the North American media portrays the conflict.

Yet those in the vanguard of this modern Crusade are by and large the descendants of those same white European crusaders of the 12th century who, covering their voracious economic appetites with good Christian jargon, descended on the same middle East — provoking a legacy of hate and mistrust that has persisted to this day.

Who is doing the actual fighting? The United Sates, Britain, France, Canada, Italy — and very few others. The non-white members of the coalition play little more than a token role.

The war symbolizes the intensifying struggles of the "haves" against the "have-nots".

The discarding of diplomacy in favor of rule imposed by force may signify, it is feared, the emergency of a new Berlin Wall, a new "iron curtain" between the "haves" and the "have-nots". It suggests the intent to use the newly dominant power of the North to impose on the rest of the world a western vision of a new political and economic order.

But it is an attempt to change the world order without addressing the fundamental issues which give rise to the Iraqs and the Saddam Husseins of the real world.

That the immediate war will be won by the new Crusaders is scarcely in doubt.

The old maxim says that: Power corrupts, while absolute power corrupts absolutely.

Its validity has been amply demonstrated in the rise — and imminent fall — of Saddam Hussein.

But what of the new absolute power wielded by the United States and its partners?

Is there any reason to assume that the maxim can now be set aside, since power is in the hands of a democratic government?

Or will this power corrupt absolutely just as it invariably has in the past?

The jettisoning of diplomacy and premature resort to violence on a massive scale — combined with governments' unprecedented masking and distortion of the war's unfolding events — suggest that the process of corruption is already under way.

BUSH CALLED ALL THE SHOTS. MARCH 2, 1991

Judging by opinion polls in the United States, President George Bush might well be justified in interpreting the Gulf War as a huge success. Similarly, Prime Minister Brian Mulroney — disregarding his party's abysmal ratings but taking heart from the increased support of Canadians for the War — might see in the pools justification for Canada's involvement.

The war proceeded according to plan. At least, so the public was assured time and again by the coalition leaders.

Even if we were never at any time informed in advance of exactly what the plan was.

There is even some doubt as to whether any of the leaders — outside the White House — knew precisely what bush ultimately had in mind.

Events of the past several months together with post-victory statements of the generals now make it crystal clear, however, that the U.S. aim from the start was not simply to force Saddam Hussein out of Kuwait. It was to totally destroy the infrastructure of Iraq and its war machine.

From the landing of the first coalition troops in the Gulf in August to the rapid buildup of offensive forces by the U.S. in November, from the firing of the first missile by American forces in January to the eventual setting of conditions for a ceasefire which could not possibly have been met, the strategy, evidently was to show no quarter and to eliminate for years to come Iraq as a power to be reckoned with.

Even if it meant bombardment of astonishing proportions, and the deaths of thousands of innocent civilians.

The war has been hailed by its supporters as a historic victory.

But the critics are equally convinced that the nightmare scenario which they confidently predicted from the outset is also right on track.

That U.S. action in the Gulf should have provoked cynicism and scepticism in spades from a whole host of unlikely bedfellows — ranging from Soviet officials to peaceniks to former U.S. generals to Canadian New Democrats and Liberals — is not surprising.

U.S. foreign policy in recent decades, and indeed for most of this century, has — with few exceptions — never been considered particularly enlightened or far-sighted. Even by friends of the United States.

While espousing freedom and democracy at home, American governments, up till now, seldom paid more than mere lip-service to the same ideals beyond U.S. borders — except where this happened to fit with the pursuit of specific American interests as in Eastern

Europe and the Soviet Union. Liberation movements tended to be seen as the enemy, redistribution of wealth from the rich elites to the poverty-stricken as inimical to U.S. interests.

For its allies the U.S. not infrequently looked – as it still does in Central America today – to dictators and the practitioners of repression. Even though the stories of brutality and human rights abuses matched and even exceeded any of the atrocity accounts coming out of Kuwait.

Did the Gulf War make the opening of a dramatically new chapter for the U.S.? Are we now embarking on a new order in which atrocities and abuse will be condemned wherever they occur? Or was the liberation of Kuwait just another variant on a depressingly familiar theme?

Canada's external affairs minister, Joe Clark, suggests the former. The critics on the other hand find little cause for optimism.

Indeed, there are many who look to the future with a profound sense of gloom and misgiving. For the high-tech western coalition with its missiles and smart bombs and drawing on a base population of several hundred million, the defeat of low-tech Iraq with its mere 17 million people was not so remarkable an achievement.

But there is little reason to believe – on the basis of past performance – that this same coalition has the ability to match its military muscle with the wisdom, foresight and diplomatic skill now needed.

Suffice it to note that Saddam Hussein was in many ways the creation of the members of the coalition – who built his chemical facilities and sold him weapons and overlooked the abuses of his regime for an entire decade. It suited their purposes when Iran and Ayatollah Khomeini were considered the arch-villains.

Was the war a success or a grand debacle?

Consider the results.

The region has been severely destabilized . A power vacuum was created and the scramble to fill it has begun.

Friendly autocratic regimes may have been preserved but their long-term survival is seriously in doubt.

None of the fundamentalist issues which gave rise to the Iraqs and Saddam Husseins of this world were resolved.

The sight of rich westerners mercilessly bombarding less affluent Muslims has given a tremendous boost to Islamic fundamentalism from Indonesia to India to Pakistan, to North Africa. The legacy of hatred will remain for decades and the consequences are unpredictable.

Environmentally, the war was an absolute and predictable disaster.

Contrary to claims of coalition leaders, the UN system was seen by some analysts as having been severely weakened rather than strengthened by the war. All major decisions were taken in the White House. There was no UN command. The secretary general was virtually unseen. The Security Council served as little more than an instrument for validating actions which the United States would have taken whether the council agreed or not.

Perhaps the most serious of all was the complete collapse of international morality – if such morality is based on the assumption that war can be engaged only as a last resort, and that killing can only be justified when no possibility for peace exists.

Iraqi leaders, invoking the name of Allah precipitated the deaths of thousands.

While the White House called on God and held days of prayer, as coalition forces continued the hostilities and killing far longer than necessary to achieve the fundamental goal of removing Iraq from Kuwait.

In the words of Mahatma Gandhi: What greater obscenity than mutual killing in the name of the one God.

For Canadians the war has also left its legacy.

Pressing domestic issues were ignored for several months at one of the most critical periods of the nation's history as the government opportunistically attempted to use the glory of war to bolster its sagging fortunes.

Debate of the war issues was strangled from the start. As with Meech Lake, ordinary Canadians were never given the opportunity to express themselves or even to know in advance what the government's ultimate objectives were.

Control and manipulation of information reached new and alarming heights.

While slashing assistance for the poorer countries, the government had no difficulty in finding a billion dollars to prosecute the war.

In a startling reversal of policy, the only department to receive a real increase to its budget for the coming year was Defence.

Of greatest concern to the critics was Canada's transformation from peacekeeper to partner in war.

This went hand in hand with bitterness over the seeming abdication of sovereignty to U.S. President Bush who called all the shots. It was he, in the view of most, who determined that Canada would go to War and it was he who determined the moment of peace. One looks in vain to find a single major statement or initiative from Ottawa — that was not "made in the United States" — during the entire period of crisis.

In short, the war let many genies out of many bottles.

Was the war a success or a disaster?

The judgment will be for future historians.

GULF WAR II

EX-DIPLOMAT BELIEVES WAR WITH IRAQ A GAME FOR LOSERS. JANUARY 23, 2003

No amount of propaganda can disguise the continuing absence of hard fact in the debate over war in Iraq. For months, the U.S. administration and British Prime Minister Tony Blair have been assuring the world Saddam Hussein has weapons of mass destruction and must be disarmed.

The difference, however, between the propaganda world of the former Soviet Union, of North Korea, or indeed of Iraq and that of the democracies is that if you want people's support, you have to be square with them. You may play on people's fears and appeal to patriotism. That may work for a time in the U.S., but it doesn't wash in the rest of the world.

The reality is that many people in Europe, Canada and elsewhere would readily go along with military action in Iraq if the U.S president were to demonstrate beyond the shadow of a doubt that

Saddam has such weapons and that he intends to use them for more than his own defence.

Instead, all George Bush has done to date has been to cast shadow after shadow on his own credibility. First, the goal was to eliminate weapons of mass destruction. Then, it was to change the regime. After that, the objective became one of liberating the country. The best UN weapons inspectors have been able to come up with are a few empty shell casings. That is not enough.

No wonder people are asking: What is the real agenda? It is not a matter — as some of America's blind supporters would have us believe — of everyone who questions the wisdom of U.S. policies being an America-hater. On the contrary, America has many friends, but friends who prefer fact to propaganda.

If there is evidence of such weapons, let the administration put it on the table. Just as John F. Kennedy did during the Cuban missile crisis in 1962, lay the photographs out in front of the UN Security Council. The world will judge. Let the inspectors do their job. Why the rush?

True, many governments have offered support in the event of an attack on Iraq. It does not require a brain surgeon, however, to determine most of these offers are reluctant and, as in the case of Canada, reflect more a fear of America's big stick if they don't co-operate, rather than enthusiasm for the cause.

As long as the administration fails to deliver conclusive evidence, Bush's detractors must be forgiven for imagining all sorts of alternative motives. Some say it is oil. Others insist the president's hawkish advisers see the situation as a heaven-sent opportunity to establish American muscle and dominance in this most strategic of all regions.

The only thing that that seems certain at this point is that the U.S. firmly intends to invade Iraq, come what may. Security Council resolutions and weapons inspectors increasingly appear as a little more than a charade and cynical genuflection in the direction of world opinion. Unfortunately, there is little evidence the Bush administration has given any meaningful thought to the longer-term consequences.

Many questions remain. What will the world look like in five years? After the American occupation of Iraq, will there be more militants holding aloft Ak-47s? Or fewer? Will America itself be more secure, or less? Will there be fewer weapons of mass destruction? Or will other states conclude the only sure way to ensure security will be to acquire their own doomsday missiles?

There are many friends of America who believe that, by abandoning its commitment to meaningful diplomacy and the rule of international law in favour of the raw exercise of power, the U.S. is setting itself up for future disasters of monstrous proportions. Despite the bravado of Defense Secretary Donald Rumsfeld, the United States is ill equipped militarily, and especially psychologically, to fight a major battle on more than one front.

This weakness becomes even more pronounced if America's allies are half-hearted at best.

Waiting in the wings are many who will be only too delighted to see the U.S. mire itself in quicksand, and to grab a slice of America's power. Other pretenders to global power who stand to gain the most from an American misstep – China and Russia – make supportive sounds about Iraq, but carefully avoid substantive commitments.

The U.S. game today resembles more one of poker than of chess. In chess brainpower and strategy are the features of the champion. In poker, at the end of the day there are mainly losers.

EX-DIPLOMAT FEARS U.S. LEADERS' AGENDA. MARCH 29, 2003

When I was in high school, the Korean War was on. Being young and foolish, I hoped the war would last until I turned 18 and could join the army. In the university, I joined the Canadian Officers' Training Corps to do my part against the Soviet scourge. For the next several decades, as a Canadian diplomat, I served as an enthusiastic cold warrior in hotspots such as Moscow and Havana.

The Soviet invasion of Afghanistan found me in Pakistan. One of my most vivid memories is of travelling to Peshawar in the northwest frontier. There I found myself speaking to an assembly of perhaps 1,000 changing mujahedeen, exhorting them to greater efforts.

Now, I am a peacenik.

How ironic. How did it happen that for most of my life, I was side by side with the Americans against the Soviets, yet now I find myself on the same side as the Russians? Well, I'm not exactly a peacenik. If the inspection process had run for another month or two, and if the Security Council had come to an honest conclusion, without bribery and intimidation, that Saddam Hussein must go, I would have been the first to get on board.

My change in philosophy is not because of any love for Saddam. In the '80s, while the U.S. was assisting Saddam in his war against Iran and turning a blind eye to his atrocities, I was already praying for his demise. Twice on assignment in Tehran in 1982, I saw too much of the devastation he had caused.

There are several reasons why I am against this war. The first is that it quickly became clear that President George W. Bush was determined to invade Iraq, regardless of the inspectors' findings. Otherwise, why the concern over an extra week or two, as Canada proposed?

Secondly, in the '90s, the same group of ultra-hawks who now form the Bush inner circle developed a strategy for American domination of the world. Little noticed initially, the strategy's "Rebuilding America's Defences" includes everything from militarizing space to introducing a new colonialism in the Middle East.

No wonder the Russians, Chinese and French jumped off the bandwagon so quickly. I jumped off too. (Read it: www.ceip.org and click on *War in Iraq*.)

A third reason was a passionate commitment to the rule of law. I don't like the allegations of torture coming out of Afghanistan. I find obscene U.S. accusations of mistreatment of four PoWs while they hold some 700 prisoners in cages in Guantanamo. I don't understand their refusal to approve the International Criminal court, unless they consider themselves above the law.

Finally, I find equally obscene the sight of three white Christian rulers declaring a new "crusade" (Bush's word) on a Muslim country. Taking out Saddam may in the short run save more lives than if he were left in power. Over the long term, the passions inflamed by this war are likely to claim far more.

So, here I am among the peaceniks, so much maligned by the mainstream media in the U.S. and even here in Canada.

Members of the Canadian Alliance, who weep oceans of crocodile tears over Saddam's victims, were nowhere to be found when Saddam was gassing Kurds or abuses were being committed in the Sudan. They said nothing of human rights violations in China, Saudi Arabia and Peru – for fear of affecting their financial interests. No, it was left to the peace activists, the supporters of Amnesty International and others to speak out.

One can only hope this war will be brought quickly to a conclusion and that casualties on all sides will be minimized. Then, as Canadians, we can sit back and await the dire punishment threatened by U.S. ambassador Paul Cellucci. And punished we will be. The ambassador's bullying behaviour accurately reflected the mood of the White House.

As a Canadian, either I reserve the right to make my own decisions, or I surrender to Washington the sovereignty it has not been able to take from us since this country was founded.

MISBEGOTTEN ADVENTURE. SEPTEMBER 8, 2004

If George W. Bush and his disciples are to be believed, the war on Iraq has been a huge success. The Republican National Convention, to the surprise of no one, turned out to be superbly choreographed political theatre. Democracy is at hand. The world is a safer place.

And the reality?

By any measuring stick, the war in Iraq has been a colossal disaster. No matter what innocuous or diplomatically phrased conclusions the commissions and panels of enquiry have been peddling in recent months. Soft talk cannot mask the hard fact that almost all the dire predictions made by critics in early 2003 have come true. No Michael Moore and no Fahrenheit 9/11 were required to reveal the unpalatable face of reality.

Like Moses delivering the Commandments on the mount, Bush and Tony Blair righteously proclaimed the West was in imminent danger from Saddam Hussein's weapons of mass destruction. Any who doubted their word — such as UN weapons inspector Hans Blix — were "irrelevant."

Like a broken record, Vice-President Dick Cheney kept repeating — and does to this day — the fiction that Saddam was involved in 9/11.

The critics in America, Europe and around the world did not have access to a multi-billion-dollar intelligence network, nor to top political analysts. Yet, long before the war even began, many casual observers expressed acute skepticism that WMD existed. In response, they got the inept performance of U.S. Secretary of State Colin Powell with his laughable evidence.

Using common sense, critics warned of the rupture of traditional alliances, of the impetus the invasion would give to terrorist recruitment, of chaos in the Middle East and of the increased danger to western interests. They also warned attempts to impose American-style democracy in Iraq through the barrel of a gun would fail.

The sceptics were given short shrift by the mainstream media in North America. Led by Fox News, the war's cheerleaders included major outlets in the U.S. and Canada. Even today, in the face of incontrovertible evidence, commentators argue Saddam's ouster was worth the thousands of American casualties, to say nothing of the tens of thousands of Iraqi dead and wounded.

That Saddam is gone is fine.

And what has replaced him? A Sunni insurgency that saw hundreds killed in July alone. And Shia unrest fluctuating between mutiny and uneasy truce, creating the constant spectre of all-out civil war.

Much of the country is under no defined control. Prime Minister Iyad Allawi is often described as the "mayor of Baghdad," in reference to the limited extent of his writ. American forces are hunkered down on the outskirts of major towns, making occasional deadly forays.

And what of American interests? Any sense of noble purpose has dissipated.

Meanwhile, the two more dangerous members of the so-called Axis of Evil, Iran and North Korea, pursue their nuclear weapons program virtually unhindered.

There is little doubt but that the large majority of Iraqis yearn for peace and stability. Unfortunately, yearning for peace and a desire for democracy are not necessarily synonymous. In times of turbulence, there is a tendency on the part of those suffering to place their trust in whoever can bring deliverance, whether it be in democratic or dictatorial guise.

The launch of the democratic experiment in Iraq has been anything but auspicious. The blueprint drawn up by former American administrator Paul Bremer was naïve and unworkable.

Since his departure, the administration has been backtracking in its drive to have something positive to show before the November elections.

Its choice of Allawi as prime minister, a man with a chequered record who allegedly shot prisoners in cold blood just days before the handover of sovereignty (denied by Allawi), suggest a note of desperation.

How will it all play out? A fractured nation? A militant theocracy? The outcome remains anything but clear. Senator John McCain, a war supporter, recently estimated U.S. troops will be needed in Iraq for another 10 to 20 years.

Will the macho men of the White House and Pentagon succeed in their attempt to have the war enter the mythology of American victories? More likely, it will be the misbegotten adventure that fanned the flames of Islamic militancy for years to come.

PART III
CANADIAN AFFAIRS

FOREIGN SERVICE ON ROPES. MAY 29, 1990

Vladivostok, 1918: In the frigid Siberian winter young Dana Wilgress accompanies a Canadian military force of 5,000 to Eastern Siberia and takes up his posting as Canada's first trade commissioner to the region, his assignment being the tapping of what was even then seen as a golden market for Canadian exports.

Nanking, 1950: Chester Ronning of Camrose, in charge of Canada's official mission to China during the critical takeover of

Mao Tse-tung's Communists, makes clear his support for immediate recognition of the new regime, but is overruled by Ottawa.

Tehran, 1980: Calgary's Ken Taylor, ambassador to Iran, becomes hero to North Americans when he plays the key role in spiriting six American diplomats out of the country and out of the clutches of the Ayatollah Khomeini.

During the course of almost a Century Canada's Foreign Service carved out for itself a distinguished record.

Largely unheralded and unsung in Canada itself, career service members nonetheless were recognized by their colleagues on the international diplomatic circuit as being among the world's best. They played key roles in keeping the Commonwealth together when the emergence of new colonies to independent status threatened to leave in tatters the fabric of the old British Empire; they were critical actors in the achievement of a Korean armistice at a time when global security was sorely tested.

And Canadian diplomats were the glue sticking together the Middle East peace for which Lester B. Pearson received the Nobel Prize.

Canada in the '50s and '60s became synonymous with "internationalist," "peacekeeper," and "middle power". Canada's diplomats were much of the reason.

All was not glamour.

Canadians lived – and died – in the steamy Vietnamese jungles as they toiled through years of frustrating, thankless service on the UN's International Control Commission.

They manned their embassies through earthquakes and coups, wars and riots: assisting Canadians, sending back reports to their governments, evacuating the sick, playing the role of mediator.

A measure of foreign service calibre was the number of Canadian diplomats, particularly in the decades immediately following the Second World War, who went on to become deputy ministers, heading up major government departments. Even today, several ex-foreign service officers are still to be found within deputy minister ranks.

It came as a shock, therefore, to those Canadians who take more than a passing interest in foreign affairs to learn just last month that Canada's diplomats were themselves sounding the virtual death knell of the service as it existed in the minds and memories of many.

In a no-holds-barred release the Professional Association of Foreign Service Officers let it all hang out. The lengthy statement, prepared by member Daryl Copeland, and purporting to be a contribution to a management study, spoke of a "dizzying fall from grace", of abysmal morale and of a department under siege from without and consumed with ferment within.

PAFSO's main guns were trained directly on departmental management – not so much on External Affairs Minister Joe Clark as on the public service mandarins who run the department.

How is External Affairs supposed to work? The theory is quite simple. Out in the front lines – in the embassies around the world – there are the foreign service officers. Back in Ottawa, the same people who work abroad also staff on a rotating basis the department.

The Pearson Building on Sussex Drive not far from the prime minister's residence is supposed to be the hub, distilling input from diplomats abroad and co-ordinating with other departments at home. The information and ideas flow to External Affairs and a foreign policy is pieced together.

In actual fact, however, External Affairs, so the complaint runs, is increasingly being bypassed. Every department of government, whether Finance or Environment or National Defence, in effect is making its own foreign policy.

Although the paper does not delve into the origins of the issue, it is evident that the dethroning in fact did not begin yesterday or even a decade ago. Rather it was with Pierre Trudeau in the late '60s and early '70s, with his barely concealed cynicism for Pearson's peacemaking and international vision, who began to ignore the foreign service.

Trudeau, during the period of his rule, significantly reduced the role and influence of External Affairs. Indicative of his less than high regard and most traumatic was his action in the late '70s in breaking with tradition and appointing non-career persons into the top jobs of the department. Morale began its long slide.

As if the wresting away of the helm were not enough, External Affairs according to PAFSO has in many ways been its own worst enemy. The paper is anything but diplomatic in its frontal attack on departmental management: managerial skills are seriously lacking; some senior officers are incompetent; good ideas disappear into a "black hole"; boat rockers" perish while "boot lickers" prosper; the appraisal and promotion systems are in shambles.

In such circumstances, successive governments beginning in the '70s in looking to fill ambassadorial jobs increasingly bypassed the foreign service and sought their stars elsewhere.

Mulroney, for example, made more patronage appointments than Trudeau in one-third the time.

The problem with the patronage appointments, however, was that they were just that: in too many cases the appointees were not competent for the job and Canada's image suffered as did the morale of the career people who had to put up with them.

The result of all this is, according to Canada's own diplomats, our foreign policy delivery systems are today in a mess — a conclusion in which a number of outside experts concur.

Canada's action on the international scene is said to have become more like a discordant symphony than a finely tuned composition.

In the corporate world, survival and success can be achieved only when all units in the corporation — finance, marketing, product development and so on — have their act together. By this measuring stick External Affairs which is supposed to be putting Canada's act together on the international stage is, according to its own employees, a dismal failure.

Take, for example, the Panama fiasco at the beginning of this year. Canada had just announced its intention at long last to join the Organization of American States. Now even the most junior diplomat in the service is acutely aware of Latin American sensitivities to the U.S. intervention in the region. So how did Canada react to the U.S. invasion of Panama? Indeed with enthusiastic and immediate support.

How could such a faux pas happen? Simply because neither Clark nor the professionals in External Affairs were even consulted. The decision was taken elsewhere in the government and External Affairs was told after the fact. Their role was – as has become too often the case – not one of making policy or even of having input but rather one of damage control.

Little wonder then that frustration should be intense among Canada's foreign service officers. When the feeling of irrelevance is put together with the alleged lack of leadership from senior officials within the department, the resulting loss of morale should surprise no one.

The main losers according to the diplomats are, however, Canadians themselves.

Given the accelerating pace of change and the transformation of the global environment, the Department of External Affairs and the machinery for making foreign policy and promoting trade – in other words, for keeping the country in the mainstream – are, they say, desperately in need of renewal. Synchronized team effort is needed more than ever. The alternative is for Canada to be left on the sidelines.

ONLY A MIRACLE CAN SAVE CANADA. JULY 5, 1990

Let me put the cards on the table, I am, and always have been a passionate believer in Canada. The romantic version, that is: From Sea to Sea and under one flag and one Parliament.

Through almost three decades as a Canadian Foreign Service officer from the Soviet Union to Hong Kong to India, I never ceased to thrill to the strains of O Canada or to wonder at the marvel of having been born a citizen of the world's most blessed nation.

Somewhere along the way — whether as a result of osmosis or Trudeau propaganda I do not know — I came to view Quebec with its language and distinctness as one of the jewels in Canada's crown. So attracted in fact was I to the sparkle of this jewel that there was virtually no price I personally would not have paid to ensure that Quebec remained as part of "my" country.

The last three decades, however, have been hard on the romantics. Time and again Quebec has upset the national composure and threatened the national dream.

In the centenary year of 1967, for example, our biggest birthday bash of all was marred by French president Charles de Gaulle's mischievous cry of "Vive Le Quebec Libre" to ecstatic throngs from the balcony of Montreal city hall.

The appeal to nationalist fervour came in the aftermath of a triumphant procession from Quebec City to Montreal along the historic "Highway of the King," an experience de Gaulle likened to his entry into Paris following the city's liberation from the Nazi occupation.

Non-Quebecers were outraged. Even more, we were disturbed deep down. De Gaulle's arrogance was bad enough. But how were we to explain to ourselves the fervor and excitement with which ordinary Quebecers greeted this brutal act of interference into Canadian affairs?

Most disconcerting of all, de Gaulle had acquired a reputation for pre-science, vision and a sense of history. He made no secret of his belief that Canada was made up of two tribes — the French and the rest – nor of his expectation that Quebec's role should and would one day change. We asked ourselves: How could the pompous general presume to understand the march of Canadian history better than we ourselves?

English Canadians breathed a deep sigh of relief when de Gaulle prematurely departed Canada in a huff.

The next trauma burst upon English Canada three years later in the form of the so-called October Crisis. The crisis was triggered by the kidnapping of British trade commissioner James Cross and the murder of Quebec labour minister Pierre Laporte by the radical Quebec Liberation Front. English Canada put these events down to the action of a small group of terrorists, to a misguided group on the fringe of society.

The crisis was eventually resolved when the kidnappers gave themselves up in exchange for safe passage to Cuba.

At the time I was serving with the Canadian Embassy in Havana. It fell in fact to me to meet the Armed Forces aircraft which carried the FLQ activists to Cuba.

What a shock it was on boarding the plane to take charge of the passenger and turn them over to the Cuban authorities. Expecting to be confronted by hardened villans, I was thoroughly nonplussed to find myself talking to fresh-faced young Quebecers who, apart from their evident nervousness, seemed quite indistinguishable from any other young Quebecer one might meet on the streets of Montreal.

I found myself wondering to what extent these young people represented – even if an extreme form – the broader aspirations of their generation.

Six years later, the legacy of de Gaulle seemed never more alive than in November 1976, when with the delirious accolades of the young, the idealistic, the artists and the poets, René Lévesque acknowledged the electoral victory of the Parti Québécois. Separation threatened.

By that time my family and I were in Quebec City on a one-year program for federal public servants. The year served its purpose: We left Quebec duly impressed with the distinctness of Quebec society, its relative homogeneity, its richness – and most important of all, with a vision of the wonder that is Canada in all its parts.

Most unforgettable that year was the PQ victory and the deep emotions it unleashed. The lesson learned was that if every French-speaking Quebecer consists of several parts, at least one of those parts is strongly nationalist. What struck – and disturbed – me most in 1976 was the satisfaction all French-speaking Quebecers, whether PQ partisan or federal Liberal or Conservative, took out of the victory.

I began to understand that those who thrilled to de Gaulle's liberation cry in 1967, the radicals who joined the FLQ in 1970, the crowds which saluted Levesque's victory in 1976 were simply different faces of the same Quebec soul – a soul determined to preserve its identity at all costs.

Lulled by the tranquillity of the mid '80s, de Gaulle's memory faded like that of a nightmare. It was only as the national dream came crashing down around us in this year of Meech Lake that we suddenly realized that the general's ghost had never been exorcised.

Why did Meech Lake fail?

One could cite many reasons: the progressive disappearance of national symbols and the unravelling of psychological unity;

privatization and free trade; growing intolerance and inability to compromise; the sabotage of the Meech spirit as interest groups everywhere determined to achieve all their goals at one fell swoop.

But first and foremost the accord failed in my view because certain key leaders in English Canada, egged on by the combined anti-Quebec and anti-Meech forces, failed to comprehend the vision that de Gaulle had no difficulty tapping into more than a quarter-century ago — the vision of a Quebec destined to protect, preserve and promote its distinctness at all costs.

Even now in post-Meech era it is quite amazing how many Canadians — in spite of all the blatant signs to the contrary — still are unable to grasp the fact that the national dream has shattered; a watershed has been reached; distinctness within Canada may be out but Quebec sovereignty in one form or another is as sure as tomorrow's sunrise. Baffling is the continuing assumption on the part of some that we can now simply pick up where we left off on June 22.

Where do we go from here? At the beginning of 1990 there were three possible scenarios. To continue building the national dream on the basis of the Meech compromise; a substantial restructuring of the country around two equal parts; or Quebec and the rest each going their separate ways leaving no more than a vague hope for a future common market.

In the middle of 1990 we have been reduced to two.

The prospects of restructuring within a federal framework preserving one flag, one anthem, one parliament are dismal at best. Simply because this would require vision and statesmanship beyond the apparent ken of any political figure on the horizon today. Witness the tawdry nature of Herb Gray's response on June 23 to the death of Meech. Or the waffling of Jean Chretien. Or the performance of the ultimate publicity-bound in sincerity's clothing, Clyde Wells.

Barring a miracle — and miracles admittedly do happen — the die now appears cast and Quebec sovereignty wants only modest political skill and manipulation on the part of the PQ leader in order that it become reality.

Non-Quebecers will almost certainly have a heavy price to pay. If we were earlier wasting too much national energy on Quebec and its notions of distinctness, just see what the cost of divorce will add up to.

A Canada torn in two and separated by 1,000 kilometres has about as much chance of long-term survival as a nation as the proverbial snowball.

Internationally, Canada's stature and influence will decline drastically.

Contrary to the expression of concern emanating from Washington, those with their hands on the levers of political and economic power can scarcely conceal their delight at the rich regional plums about to fall into the U.S. basket.

De Gaulle and Mordecai Richler were right.

Canada was a nation of tribes. As Richler said, how appropriate that the country should die to the beat of drums on the grounds of the Manitoba legislature.

EXTERNAL AFFAIRS DROPS THE
BALL. SEPTEMBER 10, 1990

Does it strike you as odd that Canada should suddenly decide to send pathetically ill-equipped warships far from its shores to the dangerous waters of the Persian Gulf without the United Nations having sanctioned the effort? And without Canada's direct interests having been spelled out.

Or did you ever wonder why Canada was taken by surprise when the United States invaded Panama? Or when Brian Mulroney heard about what was happening only when George Bush called him on the telephone that same morning?

Consider the shock with which Canadians recently learned of U.S. overtures to Mexico on the subject of free trade. To say nothing of Canada's floundering response to Enterprise America, the Bush Administration's belated but aggressive move to revitalize and entrench the free-market approach in Latin America's 600-milion strong market.

Most Canadians in fact, are not even aware of the new thrust even though its vision, reflecting Bush conservatism is highly political in nature and encompasses the vast continents stretching from the Arctic to Tierra del Fuego. External Affairs did not anticipate Enterprise America, nor has it as yet formulated a comprehensive Canadian response.

A vacuum in Canadian foreign policy making there surely is.

One need not puzzle for long over the reason.

To put it simply, the capacity for analysis and long-range policy making has all but disappeared from Canada's Department of External Affairs.

The causes are twofold.

The first has its roots in the early 1980s when all foreign relations functions – both policy-making and delivery systems – were merged into one giant department. Thus International Trade, Immigration, aid and a host of other activities were all forcibly squeezed, like commuters at rush hour on the Tokyo subway, into the same vehicle.

The trouble was that External Affairs, even if it could boast some of the brightest stars in the public service, had never been known for excellence in management skills. The period following the consolidation of foreign affairs functions in 1982 brought with it an acute case of indigestion and steadily deteriorating quality of performance.

The mandarins in the Pearson Building on Sussex Drive, whether brilliant minds such as Alan Gotlieb or accomplished trench fighters like Derek Burney (now ambassador to Washington), were – to put it bluntly – not up to the management challenge. The ball was thrown to them; they let it drop.

The second cause lay in the progressive so-called downsizing of the Department of External Affairs throughout the 1980s. External along with most other government departments was expected to shed hundreds of jobs.

The problem, however, was that the positions axed were almost invariably those related to policy making. The only secure jobs were those which, if eliminated, would quickly draw the hot breath of the public on to the necks of the politicians. Thus, scarce resources were redirected to processing visas for immigrants and wealthy entrepreneurs, to organizing programs for business travellers, and to helping Canadians who might get into difficulty abroad.

The capacity for policy making was pared to the bone.

Consider the fact that External Affairs has virtually no officer whose sole purpose is to analyse events and develop policy towards Europe or Asia, let alone Latin America, Africa, the Middle East or any other region.

Our embassies even in the major capitals of the world have been largely denuded of their political and economic analysts.

Paramount for bureaucrats in External are the day-to-day demands of ministers, dealing with foreign VIPs, or arranging travel schedules for MPs and members of the cabinet.

Major foreign policy moves today are as likely to derive from Brian Mulroney's responses to telephone calls from the White House as from a studied calculation of Canada's interests.

In too many circumstances, Canadian foreign policy is either non-existent, or lacking in depth, or a mere caricature.

The only ray of light on an otherwise dreary scene has been the minister Joe Clark. Clark by comparison with most of his colleagues on the government benches has become something of a national treasure. He is highly respected by foreign ministers and by Canada's own foreign service. He has an excellent grasp of the issues and constantly seeks new and meaningful initiatives.

The sad thing is that Clark's quest for a dynamic and relevant foreign policy has been largely thwarted by the glaring deficiencies of his own department and by his own leader.

Ministerial speeches, no matter how good they are, are no substitute for in-depth analysis, a capacity to plan for the future and to follow through.

The incredible irony is that never in the post-war period was there more of a burning need for sound policy than there is today.

Our world is rapidly shrinking. Events unfold at a dizzying space.

Europe, Japan and the United States all present formidable challenges, and possess awesome policy-making capacity.

Canada is in grave danger of being left behind.

At the very least, one might expect to find some hint of concern on the part of the government over the country's seeming headlong rush into international oblivion.

Its only formal response to date has been the corporate review undertaken by management. A remarkable exercise in bureaucratic double-speak, the review details the additional personnel cuts to be made and in the same breath describes what marvellous improvements will be wrought in the department's performance.

The ultimate irony is that, far from moving to correct the fundamental problems, the Prime Minister's Office seems intent on accelerating the self-destruct momentum.

Not content with reducing the size of External Affairs, Mulroney continues to foist on the department his friends and freeloaders who, far from contributing anything useful, for the most part simply take up remaining positions and have to be carried on the shoulders of the professionals.

Mulroney has already in less than half the time span made far more patronage appointments to diplomatic posts than Pierre Trudeau – himself no paragon of virtue in this regard.

Anger currently runs deep among foreign service officers over the recent appointment of a Mulroney crony to a second-rate position – in the embassy in Zaire of all places – at a salary some 25 per cent higher than that of the ambassador.

The main fear, however, is that the big heist is yet to come. A shuffle of the cabinet and senior public service in the aftermath of Meech Lake is widely speculated on.

Who will be named to the 20-odd ambassadorial posts to be filled this year?

If past performance is any guide, the Prime Minister's Office will add to the department's woes – and the country's foreign policy crisis – bypassing the professionals and reserving a significant number of slots for friends Mulroney wishes to reward or move aside.

The golf scores of these recipients of patronage may well improve. But the country's international standing will not.

TORIES NOT THE ONLY ONES WORRIED BY REFORM. MARCH 11, 1992

One thing is clear: the Tories of Prime Minister Brian Mulroney are scared of the Reform party. On reading the government's latest budget, Preston Manning should have felt flattered. It was almost as if Don Mazankowski had lifted much of it straight out of Reform's Blue Book.

But if the Tories are concerned, they are not the only ones. Take the members of Canada's visible ethnic minorities. They are just as apprehensive – for different reasons. Talk to these people and you quickly sense an underlying feeling of acute disquiet. For many of them, the Reform party is seen as a threat even if they can't explain why.

Reform leaders are aware of this – and are trying to do something about it. Look at the papers they have published: Does the Reform Party Promote Racism?, Correspondence with Jewish Community Leaders, "The Party's Multiculturalism Policy; and others. The famous Blue Book is full of the "value and dignity of the individual person" and so on.

Why then the concern of non-whites? The only surprising thing in all this is that Reform party leaders are themselves surprised.

Watch the news coverage of Reform party meetings. On the TV screen, non-white faces are few, almost non-existent.

Reform party policy papers reek of white, Anglo-Saxon, middle-class culture. Party Leader Preston Manning may genuinely believe that his policies come from "the people" – but it is clear that they emanate largely from only one stream of Canadians. There is little reflection in them of Canada's rich multicultural heritage. The party's paper on multiculturalism starts off on an offensive note by underlying that the whole subject is "not a major concern."

The paper talks in disparaging tones of "hyphenated Canadians" (the term itself reflects a high degree of insensitivity), overlooking the fact there are in reality many people in this country who are proud to be Indo-Canadians, Chinese-Canadians, Lebanese-Canadians, Scottish-Canadians and so on.

While the Blue Book would not deny the right of individuals or groups to "preserve their cultural heritage," the party nonetheless promotes the incorporation of immigrants into the "mainstream" or "national culture." Just what is this mainstream? Who is to define it?

What of those who prefer to maintain an identity separate from the "mainstream" — or to stay in the creeks and little rivulets, which make this country's social landscape so rich? Do they become second-class citizens? Reading this sort of thing, one does not need to have an overactive imagination to become paranoid.

Or consider this: one of the 56 reasons we are urged to vote Reform is so that we can get rid of the turban from the RCMP — even though the party apparently has no problem accepting the 101 other changes to the uniform which have been made over the past century. What sort of mentality would include this kind of attack on one specific community in a book of policies?

A priority Blue Book target for cutting the budget deficit is "foreign aid." No explanation. No solution. No suggestions as to how to get around the fact that much of the world — regions in which hundreds of thousands of "hyphenated" Canadians have their origins — lives in grinding poverty, or that one-seventh of the world's population consumes seven-eights of the world's resources. Just cut these "handouts" to foreigners and leave them to their own devices.

The Reform party would renege on the agreement reached with Japanese Canadians for the establishment of a Foundation for Race Relations.

And after all this and more, Reform party leaders are surprised that members of minority communities are apprehensive?

Reform's leaders may be good Christians, tolerant, anti-racist, and all that. They may take great pains to protect their opposition to radical fringe groups. But no amount of righteous indignation or propaganda can blot out entirely the sense of unease which the combination of policies — such as the ones described above — is bound to evoke.

Manning he would not deny that the party has attracted the interest of all sorts of unsavoury individuals and groups. Even if the party itself is not racist, why is it then that some racists are attracted to it? Even if the party is not ant-Quebec, why does it attract the enthusiastic support of the anti-Quebec camp? Even if the party itself is not anti-immigrant, why is it that those who are, feel a natural affinity with the party? Why is it that the crowd who at the drop of a hat says: 'If they don't like it here, let them go back' think the Reform party is the answer?

If you were a Canadian with your roots in Salvador or Somalia or Vietnam, would you feel inspired or reassured by the people you see in and around the Reform party?

Perhaps the party instead of protesting its purity and morality so loudly should think about painting its book in more than one single color. Perhaps it should spread its populist wings a little more broadly, expand its idea of who the "common people" are, put itself in the skins of the ethnic minorities, try to understand their feelings and views, and then honestly reflect these in Reform policies.

I got into a discussion recently with some members of a visible minority. Probably not a single member of this community, numbering well over a 100,000 nationally, has yet joined the Reform party. Some of the people I was talking to were attracted to the party's policies on finance and government, but they were worried about allegations of racism.

My advice to them was: Join the party if you are so inclined.

Test the waters. See if the party's definition of the "mainstream" includes you and your culture and your language and your attachment to the country from which you come. Mix with the people. Ask them if they will give up the anti-turban policy if it is shown to be contrary to the Charter of Rights and Freedoms. See how welcome you are.

Express your views as members of a minority community and see if they are listened to.

Only then, I said, can you and the rest of the critics pass fair judgment on the Reform party.

CANADA CAN NO LONGER STAND SILENT. DECEMBER 27, 1993

The Academy-Award winning film, Panama Deception was recently shown on national TV in Canada. The film, based on the 1989 invasion of Panama by the U.S., strips away the official American propaganda surrounding the event and reveals the rape of that country in all its ugliness.

Thousands of deaths, mass graves, concentration camps, are all the stuff of which Panama Deception is made. The film-makers deserve full credit for courage and tenacity in uncovering the facts.

But it comes as no surprise that the film has received very little exposure in the U.S. itself. Nor is it surprising that the Americans have tended simply to shut out this sordid chapter in recent history from their collective psyche.

This is because the majority of Americans cling to the naïve belief that their country's main goal in whatever it does abroad is to promote democracy. Any evidence to the contrary is simply excised from the mind.

And this in spite of the U.S. record in Vietnam and Central America and East Timor – and Iran before Saddam Hussein.

East Timor is a good example. At the same time that the American media were trumpeting the evils of the Khmer Rouge in Cambodia, and Hollywood was producing a film on The Killing Fields, the same media were almost totally silent on the equally genocidal nature of the massacres of East Timorese by Indonesian forces.

For the simple reason that Indonesia was considered an ally and too important to upset by putting it under the international spotlight.

The "Panama Deception" taught Canadians at least two important lessons. The first was how far the Mulroney government went during the past decade in Americanizing Canadian foreign policy.

For example, within hours after the U.S. invasion, Canada declared unconditionally support for the violation of Panamanian sovereignty – all on the basis of a chummy phone call from George Bush to Brian Mulroney. No critical evaluation by Canada's own experts. No measuring of Canada's interests.

As far as Mulroney was concerned, what was good for America was good for Canada. Clearly the goal of the Bush administration was to lay the groundwork for continued U.S. domination of the Panama Canal and to undermine the treaty signed by former president Jimmy Carter. Canada's reaction was to follow along like an obedient puppy dog.

The second lesson of Panama Deception was how far the Liberal government will have to backtrack in order to restore even a semblance of independence and respect to Canada's position on the world scene.

The past decade for Canadians has been little short of humiliating. We blindly followed the American line in Nicaragua, either actively or passively condoning gross violations of international law and of that country's sovereignty. Even when Canadian-sponsored aid projects were destroyed by U.S. — sponsored Contra rebels and workers murdered, Canada kept silent.

Appropriate expressions of horror were uttered when six Jesuit priests were assassinated by government forces in El Salvador in 1989.

But not once did Canada register energetic protests with Washington over the Bush administration's ongoing massive support for murderous regimes in San Salvador and Guatemala City. We politely tut-tutted when the UN Truth Commission published its findings on El Salvador this past year, indentifying American complicity in the ongoing horror.

But Canada's silence was outrageous, considering that the Mulroney government through its diplomatic representatives in those countries knew all along exactly what was going on — just as we now maintain silence on Panama and kid ourselves that the whole U.S. operation was aimed at halting drug-trafficking. Even though statistics suggest that drug traffic through Panama doubled after the invasion.

Canada all along had its own window on Panama. Why the conspiracy of silence?

During the '80s when Saddam Hussein was perpetrating massive human rights abuses on his own people, Canada sat idly by and said nothing as the West equipped the Iraqi army.

But when the Gulf War rolled around and Saddam Hussein overnight became America's leading villain, the Mulroney regime just as quickly jumped on the bandwagon and unquestioningly joined the Crusaders.

Canada has for years known what was going on in Iraq. Why did we wait for an American signal before saying anything? Or was it because by that time 24 Sussex Drive had become little more than an appendage to the White House?

So let us see if Jean Chretien can take the puppet off the string. And restore to Canadians some of their lost pride.

The road back will not be easy. After all it was not the Conservatives who first kept quiet in the late 70s about the atrocities in East Timor.

It was the Liberals.

ONE MAN IS MAKING A DIFFERENCE. APRIL 15, 1994

A well-known Mountie rode into our town recently. His boss, the detachment commander in Quesnel, B.C., suggested that he keep his head down. He had a good reason. The Mountie was Const. Baltej Singh Dhillon, the first and — to date — only member of the RCMP to wear a turban.

His visit was to Alberta and to Calgary. The Alberta where yesterday's red-coated men from Lethbridge collected no less than

$100,000 in the middle of the deep recession to try to run Const. Dhillon out of the force.

The Calgary where apostles of intolerance took the lead in signing up 200,000 people to try to get Parliament to do the same thing.

It is not surprising then that his commander gave him a few words of advice. It doesn't seem to matter that police forces around the world – London, Toronto, Singapore, Hong Kong, Malaysia, and many more – permit the turban.

It doesn't matter that Sikhs and turbans were in Canada long before many of those who, with names and accents betraying their origins are now creating much of the fuss.

Many Calgarians don't care a hoot if Quebec leaves Confederation. On the contrary. Let them go. But a turban on a Mountie? The patriotic juices begin to flow.

Const. Dhillon did appear in public in Calgary. But he was among friends – some 400 of them – at a gala dinner, resplendent in his uniform – *and turban*.

He is an outstanding young man. Regardless of what one thinks of the turban, one cannot help but admire a person who is prepared to stand up quietly but unflinchingly for his beliefs. To challenge prejudice and accept without rancor all the abuse and insults hurled his way.

It takes guts. Const. Dhillon has those in spades.

I had the privilege of spending a couple of hours with Const. Dhillon during his visit. Ironically, he embodies all of the virtues which so many Canadians cherish: family values, honesty, integrity, hard work, compassion. His reason for joining the force, he says, was not because he wanted to cause a commotion, but rather because his dream for as long as he can remember was to help people.

Dhillon's presence in the RCMP has a more pragmatic side to it. After the Air India disaster in the mid-'80s in which hundreds of people perished, the force suddenly realized that it had no one in its ranks who could talk to the Sikh community in its own language, no one who could gain its confidence, no means to carry out a complete investigation.

Shortly thereafter, the top brass decided to correct the situation and recruiters spread out across the country, looking for first-rate young people from the country's minority communities.

Dhillon was one of those who answered the call.

Not surprisingly, Dhillon and his kin have had to take a lot of heat. Yet the constable talks proudly of the force as "my family" and with pride he points to the fact that the detachment commander selected him to act as a community liaison officer.

And, even if Dhillon is tight-lipped on the subject, one suspects that he has had his share of problems within the force itself.

If regular recruits had to run hard, Dhillon had to run twice as hard. If regular police officers have to stay pure, Dhillon has to be purer than pure. To this day, rumors constantly surface to the effect that he has quit.

Canadians should be thankful to have young people like Dhillon in the RCMP. Would that all our sons and daughters had his fortitude and work ethic and character. Against this background, the old men at the RCMP and the Canadian Legion cut a pathetic figure with their campaign against the turban.

They say they are not racist. Why then do they carry on so angrily about the turban – while saying nary a word when white women joined the force a few years ago and wore a totally different head dress?

Alongside Canadians in the world wars, Sikhs died in the trenches – with their turbans on. One Sikh from Golden, B.C., Hari Singh, voluntarily joined the Expeditionary Force in 1914 and fought as a Canadian.

So why do our Legionnaires – in the name of honouring the dead – dishonor so insensitively their living comrades?

What a sad commentary on the state of our society it is when people come to value a hat more than the inner worth of the individual.

During his visit to Calgary Const. Dhillon met with several groups of young people from the Sikh community. His message: Be good citizens. Be honest, work hard and care for others. A role model for all Canadians to emulate.

PQ VICTORY GOOD NEWS FOR FEDERALISM. SEPTEMBER 26 1994

Jacques Parizeau and his Parti Québécois, as predicted, won the September 12 election.

Good news? Yes indeed.

Because the separatist victory was totally hollow. Rather than putting the last spike in the coffin of Canada, the triumph more probably was the opening step in the separatists' Last Waltz.

At least, it was if those of us in the rest of Canada play our cards properly.

Go back to the autumn of 1976. Many Canadians on Quebec election night watched with deep consternation the advancing separatist tide. Lévesque seemed unstoppable and the nationalist victory celebrations in the streets and captured on TV left one sick at heart and aching at the prospect of the demise of the nation.

Ironically, the main achievement of PQ power in the following years was to provide a real shot in the arm to federalism. The separatists as victors became -- as have all ruling politicians before and since -- kings without any clothes. As surely as night follows day, Lévesque's people came face to face with the realities of running a government. They made mistakes. They showed that they were no miracle-men. In due course, they were voted out of power.

The year now is 1994 -- some 18 years later. Much has changed. But a lot has NOT changed.

Politicians are viewed with even greater skepticism now than they were then. Political promises are seen as autumn leaves -- a lot of colour before turning to dust.

Jacques Parizeau's new team is unlikely to prove any exception. Give them the reins of power and we will see how long the honeymoon lasts.

That the next year or two will be fraught with serious risks should not be doubted. Parizeau and his Ottawa mouthpieces will do their utmost to wreak havoc and to generate crisis after crisis calculated to raise the blood pressure of Quebecers.

But not only the blood pressure of Quebecers. A main target of the nation-wreckers will be Canadians outside Quebec. Bouchard and Parizeau would like nothing better than to stick thorns in the side of the rest of us, have us trample on Quebec flags, insult the French language. In short, force us to say and do things calculated to provoke in turn an emotional reaction in Quebec.

The ploy is an old one, used time and again by devious politicians. It assumes that people for the most part are gullible. But it has worked.

If Canada falls apart, the guilty party will -- in all probability -- not be Quebecers. With the PC winning a mere 45 per cent of the popular vote in the election, next year's referendum on separation should go nowhere. If the election results showed anything, it is that hard-core support for separation -- something between 20 and 30 per cent -- has not changed in decades.

Many there are who passionately believe in Canada and who want to see this country move into the next century -- not as a collection of tawdry little republics, but rather as a proud nation setting an example of how diverse peoples can thrive together and build a society whose main features are social and economic justice.

The people who scare me are not the Parizeaus of this world, but rather my neighbors right here in Alberta and throughout the West. Too many there are who have already thrown in the sponge and given up on Canada. There are even some who through some process of convoluted reasoning would have us believe, not only that separatism is inevitable, but that our main objective should be to grease the skids and push Quebec out.

``Let them go!'' has become a popular chant.

Yes, let them go. And what will remain will be a broken nation looking ahead to years of pain and bitterness.

The alternative -- and by far the best -- will be to keep our cool and let the PQ stew in the juices of everyday government. Turn the other cheek. Avoid confrontation and provocation. All the while maintaining faith in the survivability of this country.

If we can maintain our calm and avoid emotional explosions before the coming referendum, the separatists will fail.

But this time, it will for the separatists in all probability be a voyage of no return. Parizeau would have us believe that the separatist cause will never die. That a "No" next year will simply lead to another vote -- and another and another. Such bravado is little more than whistling in the wind, in the hope of adding to the exhaustion of people outside of Quebec with the issue.

The reality more likely is that the coming "No" in Quebec will be resounding and that it will, if anything, put paid to the separatist cause for years to come -- if not for all time. In the early '80s, Quebec independence dropped out of sight and out of mind. Only inept political management brought the issue galloping back onto the front burner.

Canada can be saved. But it can also be lost if those of us who want to preserve a nation -- with Quebec -- allow our voices to be drowned out by the shortsighted who say, "Let them go!"

Acknowledgements

A word of thanks...My first thank you is to Mr. Gorbachev, for writing a generous and gracious foreword for this book. I also want to thank the friends and family members who read the manuscript and helped with input, editing, proofreading and encouragement. These include my brother Tom Warden, Professor Robert Wright, Craig Allen, John B. A. Macleod, Lynne Damant, Joy Gillet and the Professors Karla Poeve and Irving Hexham. I am grateful to Guy Boisvert for assistance with the Iran chapter. Many thanks also to Annie Knibb for creating the cover concept. A special thank you to Professor Nick Zekulin for liaising with Mr. Gorbachev's office and for translating the original Russian foreword. Thanks to my brother Tom, my nephew Ryan, my mother Laine, Guy Boisvert and our childhood friend Richard Pearce Jr. for help with the photos.

Lisa Warden

About the Author

Bill Warden served as a career diplomat in Canada's Department of Foreign Affairs during the Cold War years. His postings included Moscow, Havana, Hong Kong, Macau, Nepal, Pakistan and India. He also worked as an International Election Observer in numerous regions worldwide including Latin America, Palestine and Zimbabwe. After leaving the Foreign Service, he joined the University of Calgary, and spent much of his time devoted to supporting various human rights causes. In addition to his professional success, Bill was an avid motorcyclist and licensed pilot. He retired to Victoria, BC, where he passed away in 2011.